ARTWORKS FOR ELEMENTARY TEACHERS
Developing Artistic and Perceptual Awareness

Sixth Edition

Donald Herberholz
Barbara Herberholz

ARTWORKS FOR ELEMENTARY TEACHERS
Developing Artistic
and Perceptual Awareness

Sixth Edition

ARTWORKS FOR ELEMENTARY TEACHERS
Developing Artistic
and Perceptual Awareness

Donald Herberholz
California State University, Sacramento

Barbara Herberholz
California State University, Sacramento

Wm. C. Brown Publishers

Book Team

Editor *Meredith M. Morgan*
Developmental Editor *Dean Robbins*
Production Coordinator *Carla D. Arnold*
Photo Editor *Carrie Burger*

WCB **Wm. C. Brown Publishers**

President *G. Franklin Lewis*
Vice President, Publisher *George Wm. Bergquist*
Vice President, Publisher *Thomas E. Doran*
Vice President, Operations and Production *Beverly Kolz*
National Sales Manager *Virginia S. Moffat*
Advertising Manager *Ann M. Knepper*
Marketing Manager *Kathleen Nietzke*
Production Editorial Manager *Colleen A. Yonda*
Production Editorial Manager *Julie A. Kennedy*
Publishing Services Manager *Karen J. Slaght*
Manager of Visuals and Design *Faye M. Schilling*

Cover design by Sara Sinnard Design

Contents

Color Gallery of Famous Artworks

Introduction

Art in the elementary classroom is comprised of four areas of study. They are: (1) Art production (producing art), (2) Aesthetics (making judgments about art), (3) Art criticism (responding to art), and (4) Art history (understanding its place in history and culture). These four areas of art study are clearly explained in *Quality Art Education, Goals for Schools: An Interpretation,* a booklet produced by the National Art Education Association.[1] Many state curriculum guides for art—for example, California, Arizona, Connecticut, Florida, Georgia, Iowa, Pennsylvania, South Carolina, Tennessee, Ohio, West Virginia, Texas, and others—have defined the content of art in a very similar way. This agreement as to the concept of art is reflected at the local level in many counties, cities, and individual school districts throughout the country.

A special issue of *The Journal of Aesthetic Education* entitled "Discipline-Based Art Education"[2] and Elliot W. Eisner, in *The Role of Discipline-Based Art Education in America's Schools,*[3] both identify and define the same four similar areas of study for art educators.

Excellence in Art Education, published by the National Art Education Association, Ralph A. Smith gives strong support to the four areas of study in art when he says, "The primary purpose of teaching students to manipulate the material of art is to help them acquire a feel for artistic design and to grasp ideas that will serve them well in their future commerce with art—in short, to cultivate in students an educated capacity for the appreciation of aesthetic excellence."[4]

This book is written in response to the changes that have taken place in art education in the past ten years. It deals with how these changes are reflected in the training of elementary classroom teachers. The major shift is from an art production–centered curriculum to one that incorporates art production in alliance with the study of art criticism, aesthetics, and art history.

This book is focused on these four art areas; it is designed for a one-semester course at the university level for students who have a very limited formal background in art. In addition to the course, further study in all four areas will undoubtedly be necessary to develop the teacher's proficiency in teaching art. Instructors using this text can adapt its content to their students' skill level and work from a simple to complex understanding of the contents of each chapter. For example, if students come into the class with a high level of skill in studio production, then more emphasis would be expected to be placed on the other three areas of art study.

As a student using this text in a pre-service or an in-service course, you will have practice not only in producing art but in making aesthetic judgments and learning about art criticism. You will, through references to art history, extend your knowledge of your own cultural heritage. As clarified in the Holmes Report (Tomorrow's Teachers: A Report of The Holmes Group, Lansing, Michigan: The Holmes Group Inc., April 1986), you will be learning about the subject area of art: "Undergraduate instruction must be revised so that prospective teachers study the subjects they are to teach. . . ." Through responding to artworks and working with art media, you will gain the competencies necessary to enable you to teach art successfully in the elementary classroom. As an elementary teacher, you will need these areas of expertise to successfully implement a local art curriculum or to use one of the art texts or art study programs designed for elementary classrooms. These texts and packaged programs for kindergarten through grade six provide complete, sequential lessons in art.

In **Chapter 1** you will learn how artists perceive their world, what visual things they cherish and collect, and what constitutes their art training and education, along with some of their comments on how they express themselves in their artworks.

In **Chapters 2** and **3** you will develop an understanding of the language of art. The spotlight is on each element and principle of art, one at a time. You'll become familiar with the different qualities and properties of each through studying how different artists have used them in their artworks. You will learn how children use each element of art in their artistic growth. You will have the opportunity to apply each element and principle of art and develop your skills in using art media in the "Producing Artworks" exercises. Your experiences in these two chapters will expand your conceptual base for understanding artworks and will help you as a future teacher in using this knowledge in your art classes.

In **Chapter 4** you will gain a deeper understanding of art by going beyond your own personal preferences for artworks by learning to respond to the aesthetic qualities in artworks. You will reflect upon artworks by describing, analyzing, and interpreting their content before arriving at your own personal judgment. You will become knowledgeable about the different styles of art. Knowledge about the meaning and nature of these styles can help you better understand the art you see. You will find in this chapter models for making oral or written presentations of artworks, as well as how to present an artwork to students in an elementary classroom. Important aspects of visiting a museum are pointed out, as are notations dealing with the use of reproductions in a classroom. You will learn strategies for evaluating and improving your own artworks. "Ways to Involvement" lists numerous avenues to pursue in using reproductions in other areas of the curriculum. You'll find here tips, games, and other activities to enliven student interest in artists and artworks.

Included in **Chapter 5** are some things you will need to know about children's developmental stages of artistic growth. This knowledge is essential when you become a classroom teacher, whether you develop your own lesson plans or use sequential programs as presented in elementary art textbooks. Ways of motivating elementary children for their maximum artistic growth, along with examples of different kinds of motivations for primary and upper grades, are given. In addition, you will learn how to evaluate the artworks of elementary students and how to help them analyze their own works and think of ways to improve them.

In **Chapter 6** you are given a narrative timeline of the history of Western art. This should be used as a reference for the chronology of art and artists. It should be supplemented by additional reading in art history books and art reference books and extended to artworks of other cultures. The student goal should be to develop a concept about the place of art in many cultures and how art has given a greater depth of meaning to each individual culture.

In the **Color Gallery** you will find twenty-two examples of fine artworks. You can use them to examine, relate, contrast, and compare as you engage in creating and responding to the world of art.

List of Reviewers

Mary Frances Burkett
Kutztown University

Pamela T. Gill
Ohio State University

Grace Hampton
Pennsylvania State University

Ann Miller
Tyler Junior College

Marvin Moon
Texas Tech University

A. James Wright
Virginia Commonwealth University

ARTWORKS FOR ELEMENTARY TEACHERS
Developing Artistic
and Perceptual Awareness

Artists and the Images They Make   1

Up through the nineteenth century, artists had limited links with artists in other countries and images made by other artists. Some, of course, did travel long distances to other places to study the paintings and sculptures being produced there, but the sophisticated twentieth-century technology was yet to come that would bring cameras, video, films, and reproductions of artworks to people everywhere and enable the artist to be not only aware of what was going on all over the art world but actually to be bombarded and influenced by it in his/her own artwork. These visual influences are important to artists and have an impact on what they make and do.

Through a study of the lives of artists and the images they make, we will have a better understanding of the place of art in the elementary school curriculum. Let's investigate how artists work, what kinds of things inspire them and what the sources are for their ideas, and what their early art training was like. If we take a careful look at this information we can arrive at some of the purposes of art, develop some criteria for valuing art, and learn some of the reasons why artists express their ideas through artworks. This knowledge will (1) give us a better understanding of why artists make art, (2) enhance the quality of our own art production, and (3) give us some ideas upon which to build art programs in elementary schools.

Why does a person become an artist? How does one train to be an artist? Will the study of art history help produce an artist? What can we do as teachers of art that will help our students produce artworks and assist them in responding to artworks produced by themselves and others?

If we analyze statements made by artists about their own art production, the reasons they make art, and what inspired them, we will gain some insight on how to answer these questions as they relate to the education of elementary students.

Meanings and Functions of Artworks

First let's define as a function of art that of serving as an historical visual record of culture, since artists have always made images and symbols to record and give meaning to their own time and place. Throughout our cultural history, artists have used a great variety of materials, themes, styles, and purposes in producing their artworks. As culture changed, art forms changed, because artists responded to those changes by transcribing them into visual images. Artists have related these changes through a never-ending chain of artworks from cave paintings to today's contemporary artworks.

We can consider the nature and meaning of art when we understand some of the different reasons that artists have had for producing artwork. As we look at the history of art, we can discern that art has been created for many different functions and purposes in diverse cultures and times. Artists make art:

1. to tell stories about events in history, myths, religion, and literature
2. to convince, inspire, persuade, or to move people to action in relation to religious or social causes
3. to keep records of how people looked, behaved, dressed, and how places looked
4. to express the way they feel about the land, sea, city, people, still-life subjects, animals, events, etc.
5. to seek and invent new ways to represent their ideas
6. to represent dreams and fantasy
7. to reveal the pure visual impact and organization of colors, shapes, lines, textures
8. to create items for utilitarian uses

How Artists Work

When we study the lives of artists through the things they have said or written, or have been written about them, we can begin to detect certain patterns of thought and work habits. We can ascertain how their thought processes evolved in responding and reacting to their particular period in history and how they went about creating the images they used in their artworks. When we understand some of the meanings and functions of their art as it relates to the artists' intent and working process, we are better able to see how art may function in the lives of young students.

John Michael conducted a survey about how artists work and arrived at certain conclusions that give us some insights on their work habits, concepts that can impact on art instruction.[1] One of the questions that he asked artists in his survey was, "How many pieces of art do you work on at one time?" **The answers given by artists indicated that they usually worked on more than one artwork at a time.** In fact, most artists stated that they have several artworks in progress at one time, and some artists worked on as many as twenty pieces at the same time. Potters, for example, work on many more pieces at one time than do sculptors, who usually work on one piece at a time.

Most of the artists surveyed focused on a theme in their artworks. They selected a subject, color, shape, or technique and worked in depth over a period of time. They frequently made a series of paintings about one subject or object because they did not feel they could express everything they had to say in one painting. The implication of these two conclusions for us as art educators is that multiple experiences with the same medium or theme are preferable to quick, one-time-only exposures to an art medium, technique, or theme.

However, variety in media or theme offers a challenge to the artist. A contemporary painter, David Hockney, describes how switching to another art medium changed his way of thinking. He explained how exploring a new medium (paper pulp) forced him to think differently: "Finally I realized, because I had these buckets full of blue and buckets full of green (paper pulp), if this was paint and I was doing a painting I wouldn't have the nerve to just throw it around like this and pour it on. With these pictures I was prepared to do this and at the end of the day, to tear them all up if we didn't like them."[2] This leads us to believe that changing to a different or new medium can make the artists think differently about the way they work. Elementary students learn about art by exploring different materials.

The contemporary sculptor David Smith stated that when he was having trouble with his sculpture, he always "painted his troubles out." He described how he related

Figure 1.1 David Smith, *Cubi XII*, 1963.
Hirshhorn Museum and Sculpture Garden, Smithsonian Institution, Washington, D.C.
Smith created outdoor sculpture and frequently chose stainless steel for its practical properties and for the manner in which he could polish its surface to take on the color of the sky. Here he stacked and balanced massive geometric cubical forms that lead our eye upward from the base and downward in a tumbling movement.

his artworks to the history of art. In his book ***David Smith,*** he revealed how he thought about this: "In the actual sense we should not stretch to invent but we should feel what has gone before us, and know what has been found; and what has been found in heritage, and what are problems are the things we are to find, the seeing of things from our vantage point, which is a place no artist has stood before, and not that of invention in the narrow sense but passionately found visions, because they inspired answers to the problems of who we are in the time we are placed to speak."[3]

Figure 1.2   Chuck Close, *Photo of Artist in His Studio,* **1982.**
Pulp paper collage on canvas, 96 × 72 in.
Courtesy of the Pace Gallery, New York.
Photo credit: S. K. Yaeger.

Artists sometimes learn more about their works by reading or listening to a review by an art critic. The American artist, Jasper Johns, talks about how the art critic can help other people see in a new way and even influence the artist in his future work.

There is a great deal of intention in painting; it's rather unavoidable. But when a work is let out by the artist and said to be complete, the intention loosens. Then it's subject to all kinds of use and misuse and pun. Occasionally someone will see the work in a way that even changes its significance for the person who made it; the work is no longer 'intention,' but the thing being seen and someone responding to it. They will see it in a way that makes you think, that is a possible way of seeing it. Then you, as the artist, can enjoy it—that's possible—or you can lament it. If you like, you can try to express the intention more clearly in another work.[4]

The artist is stimulated to change or extend an idea by the dialogue of the art critic, fellow artist, and/or the public, and it is a continuing, never-ending dialogue. Art teachers serve this same function as art critic for their students when they evaluate students' work.

Making metaphorical connections of an unusual sort often helps generate new directions for artists. The artist Chuck Close believes strongly in using photographs to work from: "Just as many different kinds of paintings can be made from photographs as from life."[5] But he didn't always use them for creating artworks and explains what sparked their use during an interview by Linda Chase and Robert Feldman. He was asked what his first realistic painting was and replied, "Actually what I was doing was photographing the painting, and I had some film left and photographed myself to see what it might be like to make a painting of the head. I liked the photo and made the painting. . . . I go to a great deal of trouble to get the specific kind of photograph that is going to have the kind of information that's interesting to me: texture, elaborate depth of field, and the distance I shoot them from is important. . . . If the camera is about six feet away from the subject, it turns out about right."[6] Another fortuitous event was revealed by ceramist Robert Arneson during a recent speech on a university campus. He said that many things inspired him, and that one day when he was thinking of what to do with clay, he saw on the floor of his studio a magazine with photographs of roses. This inspired him to make clay roses weighing one hundred pounds. An open-ended approach in an elementary art program will help students make these sorts of connections and help them learn to rely on hunches and playful approaches in seeking solutions to artistic problems.

Art teachers and artists often serve as role models for inspiration. Robert Bechtle, another photo-realist painter, reveals in an interview by Brian O'Odoherty, in *Art in America,*[7] that the inspiration to do new work came to him from a number of sources and that he became interested in figure painting because of his teacher, Richard Diebenkorn. He also liked the American painters Thomas Eakins, Winslow Homer, and Edward Hopper, and admired Vermeer and Degas very much. Artists study the artworks of other artists both past and present, and their work often reflects this historical knowledge. Knowledge about artists and their artworks can serve as valuable inspiration for elementary students.

Most artists make sketches or drawings before they do their final artwork. This was brought out very clearly in statements by many artists in Michael's survey. Some make their sketches or preparatory drawings on grid paper. This same grid drawing is then transferred to a canvas with a larger grid for the finished artwork. The artist Joan Miró, for example, used this grid system in planning his large paintings. A few artists, such as action painter Jackson Pollock, use a more spontaneous approach, but more often artists mull over the idea or experience for a period of time and make sketches before they make the final artwork. Time to reflect is an important factor. The making of sketches and giving thought to the preparation of an artwork should be encouraged in elementary classrooms.

Although some artists may not make preliminary sketches first, they do have a general idea in mind of what they wish to make, and as they progress the work itself gives them direction. The American painter Robert Motherwell, when asked what one of his pictures meant, said, "I realized there were about ten thousand brushstrokes in it and that each brushstroke is a decision."[8] The

Figure 1.3   Jackson Pollock at work in his Long Island Studio, 1950.
Photo: Hans Namuth, N.Y.
Thick drips and drops, swirls, streaks, and globs of paint create an actual raised surface texture in a technique in which the artist threw, trailed, and splashed paint upon the canvas that rested on the floor.

work in progress becomes the inspiration as each change occurs. Or, as Motherwell said, with the application of each new brushstroke, another decision is made. This is often the way younger children paint. The medium may dictate the way the artist works.

Artists think in terms of the medium while they make preparatory sketches because they have had many in-depth experiences with a particular technique. If artists are not familiar with a new material, as in the case of Hockney, they often approach the new material or technique in a free and playful way and keep up an ongoing dialogue with the new medium until they can judge well what they can and cannot do. This reinforces our belief that elementary students need multiple experiences with each art medium in order to gain knowledge of its expressive potential.

Some artists respond to their environment not only with sketches and drawings but by describing things verbally, as well. Vincent van Gogh was extremely articulate with both words and paintbrush. His letters to his brother Theo testify to this, for he frequently described in vivid and lush details his perceptions and feelings about how he was drawing and painting his surroundings and the people that served as inspiraton for his artworks. One of his letters describes his painting *Night Cafe.*

*I have tried to express the idea that the cafe is a place
where one can ruin oneself, run mad, or commit a crime. I
have tried to express the terrible passions of humanity by
means of red and green. The room is blood-red and dark
yellow, with a green billiard table in the middle; there are
four lemon-yellow lamps with a glow of orange and green.
Everywhere there is a clash and contrast of the most alien
reds and greens in the figures of little sleeping hooligans
in the empty dreary room, in violet and blue. The white
coat of the* patron, *on vigil in a corner, turns lemon-yellow,
or pale luminous green.*[9]

Elementary teachers need to be alert to individual approaches and imaginative ways of making art by their students and to foster the artistic development of each child.
Some artists work on the entire painting at the same time;
they outline areas, lay in colors, and balance shapes and
textures as they work. Some artists start in the center of
a drawing or painting and work outward toward the sides
of the drawing or painting surface. The artist Joseph Raphael works in a very different way; a video, ***Joseph Raphael,***[10] shows the viewer how Raphael completes each
area of the painting, starting in one corner of the canvas
and painting diagonally across the surface until the
painting is completed. Henri Rousseau, the French primitive artist, is said to have started at the top of his canvases
and worked downward until he was finished, never
changing anything along the way. The medium itself
sometimes dictates the manner in which an artist works;
fresco murals are painted by starting in the upper left
corner, unless the artist is left-handed.

What Inspires Artists?

Artists have made many statements about what inspired
their work. **They are often motivated by the observation
and memories of their surroundings.** For example, Monet
relied on the changing effects of light in his garden and
water lily pond for the inspiraton for many of his paintings. He, as well as other artists, have the ability to see
the same object or place in many different and unique
ways. This may inspire them to create a series of paintings
of the same object or place because they feel they cannot
express everything they want to in a single painting. Henri
Matisse at age seventy-one lay in bed ill, but he had a
"library of images" in his mind, and he continued using
his memory to create bright, colorful collages. Marc Chagall based many of his fanciful paintings upon memories
of his childhood in a Russian village. He was also inspired
by imaginative Russian folktales. Grandma Moses didn't
begin painting until she was sixty, but her rich storehouse
of childhood memories provided her with plenty of material for her artworks.

Let's examine how things in their immediate surroundings influenced three sculptors. (1) Louise Nevelson
not only collected wood pieces from various sources, but
it is interesting to note that her family owned lumber yards
both in her native Russia and in the United States. We
can be reasonably sure that these early childhood experiences had influences on the art forms she produced in
her adult life. (2) David Smith, in his early work, collected cut pieces of metal from junkyards and welded them
into sculpture. Smith states he was trained as a painter.
To help support himself as an artist, he worked in an automotive assembly plant and welded parts together to make
cars. (3) Another noted sculptor, Alexander Calder, made
stabiles and mobiles out of large pieces of sheet metal. It
is interesting to note that he was trained as a mechanical
engineer at a time when furnace boilers and steel bridges
were riveted together. Many of his stabiles are riveted together since the art of welding came later.

**The works of other artists have always been a source
of inspiration for artists.** Contemporary artists today have
access to a wider range of artworks than were ever available in the past. These are in the form of books with fine
color reproductions, slides, inexpensive posters and large
reproductions, videos, and exhibits in art museums and
galleries. For instance, Henry Moore was inspired by
sculpture from many different cultures and periods, especially the sculpture of ancient civilizations.[11] Picasso,
Braque, Cassatt, and Van Gogh were inspired either by
African masks or Japanese prints or both. These sources
give contemporary artists access to what is happening
today in the world of art as well as access to the art of the
centuries. Years ago, artists had to travel long distances
just to view works of other artists.

**Artists are avid collectors of almost everything and
anything.** They collect objects that excite their artistic
vision. It could be the uniqueness of the object or any one
of its aesthetic qualities. For example, pop artist Andy
Warhol collected a wide range of unusual objects. Fritz
Scholder, a contemporary painter, has collected an extremely wide range of objects that attracted his fancy, even
though he doesn't use them directly as inspiration for the
paintings he creates. Georges Braque surrounded himself
with many different collected objects, which he kept in his
studio for visual inspiration: a rug, a guitar, thistles, fine
art reproductions, bones, African masks, pebbles, etc. A
number of artists have been fascinated with collecting
animal bones; for example, Henry Moore, Barbara Hepworth, and Georgia O'Keeffe were inspired by them.
Rembrandt spent large amounts of money purchasing
exotic items from around the world, later using them as
costumes and props in his paintings. Artists are usually
highly selective in what they choose to view or what might
inspire them or influence their thinking. Marisol said that
her art was influenced by pre-Columbian Mochica pottery
jars, Mexican boxes with pictures painted inside, and by
early American folk art.[12]

Figure 1.4

Henry Moore's sculptures of reclining figures bear a striking similarity to naturally eroded rock forms as seen in Figure 1.4. Wood, shells, and stones, along with ancient Mexican sculpture were a constant and lifelong source of visual inspiration for this contemporary British sculptor. Have you ever collected natural objects and enjoyed them for their visual forms and tactile appeal?

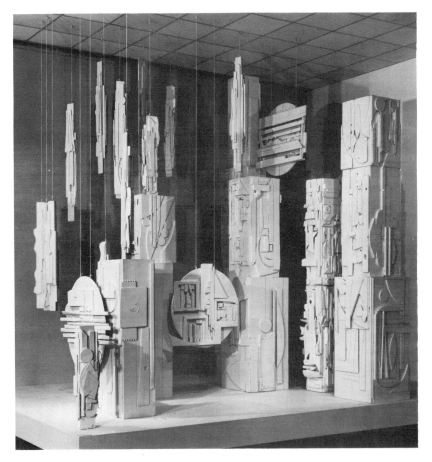

**Figure 1.6   Louise Nevelson, *American-Dawn*, 1962–1967.
Wood, painted white, 548.6 × 426.7 cm.
*Art Institute of Chicago. Grant J. Pick Purchase Fund, 1967.
387.***

The sculptor Louise Nevelson collected "found objects" from the streets of New York because they intrigued her vision, and she later incorporated some of them in her sculptures. She also collected rugs, a Paul Klee, the Mexican Santos, and African sculpture.[13]

These references about artists' inspiration give us some answers as to the sources artists use in making art. If we look at art today, we can readily see that all the purposes we attribute to art historically are still used by artists today when they make art, and similar sources can be used by elementary students.

In summary, the following sources have all served as inspiration for artists:

1. direct observation of their environment
2. their memory of objects, places, or events
3. their feelings and ideas about things
4. their fantasies and dreams
5. the works by other artists and other cultures
6. literary references
7. photographs
8. found materials

The Training of Artists: How They Get to Be That Way

Ben Shahn was a leading American artist who both wrote about art and made art. His writings give us insight into what his ideas were on the training of young artists. He said, "It is the future artist's feeling, insights, and perceptions of the world that we must deal with." Shahn explains in his book, *The Shape of Content,* what he believes should be the education of the artist.

"Attend a university if you possibly can. There is no content of knowledge that is not pertinent to the work you will want to do. But before you attend a university work at something for a while. Do anything. Get a job in a potato field; or work as a grease monkey in an auto repair shop. But if you do work in a field do not fail to observe the look and the feel of the earth and of all things that you handle—yes, even potatoes! Or, in the auto shop, the smell of oil and grease and burning rubber. Paint of course, but if you have to lay aside painting for a time, continue to draw. Listen well to all conversations and be instructed by them and take all seriousness seriously. Never look down upon anything or anyone as not worthy of notice. In college or out of college, read. And form opinions! Read Sophocles and Euripides and Dante and Proust. Read everything that you can find about art except for reviews. Read the Bible; read Hume; read Pogo. Read all kinds of poetry and know many poets and many artists. Go to an art school, or two, or three, or take art courses at night if necessary. And paint and paint and draw and draw. Know all that you can, both curricular and noncurricular—mathematics and physics and economics, logic, and particulary history. Know at least two languages besides your own, but anyway, know French. Look at pictures and more pictures. Look at every kind of visual symbol, every kind of emblem; do not spurn signboards or furniture drawings or this style of art or that style of art. Do not be afraid to like paintings honestly or to dislike them honestly, but if you do dislike them retain an open mind. Do not dismiss any school of art, not the Pre-Raphaelites nor the Hudson River School nor the German Genre painters. Talk and talk and sit at cafés, and listen to everything, to Brahms, to Brubeck, to the Italian hour on the radio. Listen to preachers in small town churches and in big city churches. Listen to politicians in New England town meetings and to rabble-rousers in Alabama. Even draw them. And remember that you are trying to learn to think what you want to think, that you are trying to co-ordinate mind and hand and eye. Go to all sorts of museums and galleries and to the studios of artists. Go to Paris and Madrid and Rome and Ravenna and Padua. Stand alone in Sainte Chapelle, in the Sistine Chapel, in the Church of the Carmine in Florence. Draw and draw and paint and learn to work in many media; try lithography and aquatint and silk-screen. Know all that you can about art, and by all means have opinions. Never be afraid to become embroiled in art or life or politics; never be afraid to learn to draw or paint better than you already do; and never be afraid to undertake any kind of art at all, however exalted or however common, but do it with distinction."[14]

In summary, Shahn's ideas on the education of young artists emphasize:

1. the importance of sensory perception along with constant drawing and painting (sketch books, daily practice)
2. having opinions about things based on knowledge and life's experiences
3. learning to talk about art
4. constantly looking at all kinds of art, observing its aesthetic qualities
5. learning about the history of art

The starting point in the education of artists is their sensory impressions as children. These first impressions are as diverse as the individual styles manifested in their mature artworks. Some artists started to draw and paint images based on their perceptions at a very early age; some had parents who were artists and who provided early instruction—Calder, Davis, and Picasso, to mention a few. Some artists—such as Picasso, Dürer, Davis, and Hockney—had early successes exhibiting their artworks while they were still in their late teens.

A few artists started their art careers when they were much older. Van Gogh and Gauguin were two artists that accomplished this amazing feat. Some artists had extensive training in other professions—the law, medicine, and architecture—before they decided to become artists. A few

Figure 1.7 Ben Shahn, *Handball*, 1939.
Tempera on paper over composition board, 22¾ × 31¼ in.
Collection, Museum of Modern Art, New York. Abby Aldrich
Rockefeller Fund.

were almost self-taught. The training of many artists in the past was that of studying and copying great works of art. As youths, many artists trained as apprentices in studios of professional artists. But one thing all artists have in common, no matter what their age, is an inner drive to create art. Nothing else matters to them except the urge to produce art. It is an all-consuming passion that in most cases drastically changes their lives.

Today in our highly technological world, most artists have formal art training. Oftentimes they start their art careers at home under the guidance of a mother or father who is an artist, or in art classes for children. Public-supported schools provide training for the artist as well as for the doctor, lawyer, engineer, or the elementary teacher. A number of outstanding contemporary artists teach at our major universities.

However, there is no one way that artists have been trained or educated. Most anyone who draws or paints has at some time or other copied from drawings, photographs, or paintings—including the comics—if they are part of one's culture. Even a contemporary artist like Grace Hurtigan set herself a problem to solve by copying the work of the masters. She says that she copied famous artists from history to try to understand where she really came from. She had to find her roots.

To study to be an artist is like studying for any profession: you study the content of the subject. Most artists have stated that they became artists because that is what they always wanted to be and it came from a strong inner feeling. As Louise Nevelson said, when a librarian asked her what she wanted to be when she grew up, "I am going to be an artist. No. I want to be a sculptor, I don't want color to help me." She said this when she was nine years old. She did not become a world famous artist by just wishing to be one. She received training, studied art, and did many other things in her life to enrich her own understanding of herself to accomplish her goal.[15]

Jacob Lawrence speaks of who his favorite artists are and why, when he says, "Perhaps I can explain best [what influences I have experienced] by telling who I like, Orozco, Daumier, Goya. They're forceful. Simple. Human. In your own work, the human subject is the most important thing. Then I like Arthur Dove, I like to study the design, to see how the artist solves his problem, how he brings his subject to the public."[16] Artists today study the works of other artists and know who their favorites are, and this visual information gives them inspiration or a basis for their work. It is interesting that most painters do not start out to be abstract painters; in fact, most artists are still trained today to draw from real objects, natural or of human origin. Their training usually involves a long and intense search to find their subjects and their unique style of expression.

Georgia O'Keeffe thought in terms of shapes and stated that she carried shapes in her mind until she could find the proper colors for them. She also was sensitive to sounds in nature and described different sounds in the letters she wrote to her friends.[17] In a letter to W. Milliken, she answers a question Milliken asked her about the painting *White Flower, New Mexico*. She said she would rather not write about it because she already painted what she knew about white flowers. She went ahead and tried to explain in words what she attempted to do in the painting: "I know I cannot paint a flower. I cannot paint the sun on the desert on a bright summer morning but maybe in terms of paint color I can convey to you my experience of the flower or the experience that makes the flower significant to me at that particular time. Color is one of the great things in the world that makes life worth living to me, and as I have come to think of painting it is my effort to create an equivalent with paint color for the world-life as I see it."[18]

As teachers, we can have our students study artworks, learning about what inspired artists to produce them, and how they related their artworks to their culture. As Kathleen Tompson has said, "If we neglect to exercise our abilities as artists, we are in danger of forgetting what is involved in the process of conceiving, and expressing ideas for use in artworks we expect our students to undertake."[19]

Frederick Spratt further supports the idea that students can learn a great deal about art as they produce it: "The importance of experiencing art production directly is that it enables students to gain insight into many more aspects of art and of the world at large. Such experience develops empathy [which is] crucial to appreciating that communion between individuals and things embodied in some of humankind's most profound works. Furthermore,

students who engage in making art become familiar with the motives that inspired other artists—including the desire to express and share their observations and feelings."[20]

Making artwork means making visual images. We learn to speak the language of art when we draw, paint, or form clay. Each individual's way of knowing and recording can be expressed in a scribble or in a symbol [by child or adult], as a highly realistic representation or as a total abstraction.

Marjorie and Brent Wilson strongly state their belief that children cannot produce artworks without being provided with the necessary information from which to draw—a variety of collected images to which they will respond, much in the manner of adult artists:

"Child art as well as adult art may come from outside— from other art—just as much as or more than from within. What artists and children do is to take existing cultural images and extend them, place them in new contexts, and use them in new ways. Creativity is seldom achieved through the production of the utterly new but rather through taking those things which belong to the culture and using them in individual ways, resulting in images that are often novel and unique."[21]

In studying the lives of artists, the images they make, what inspires them, what they collect, and some of the things they say about their artworks and their working process, we begin to see the diversity of their individual approaches to each of these aspects of their lives. Through examining their production techniques, we can better plan for the studio activities for the students in our care. Through this study, we will be better able to relate this content to our students to assist them in producing and responding to their own artworks.

Questions and Activities

1. View a video about an artist and report to the class on your findings. What four things did you learn about how the artist gets ideas, what he/she collects, what influenced him/her, and why he/she makes art?

2. Keep a diary and/or a scrapbook about artists you read about in newspapers and magazines, see on TV, and learn about on visits to art galleries.

3. Read a newspaper critic's review of an exhibition on display in a local gallery or museum. Then visit the exhibit and compare your observations and reactions with those of the critic.

4. Read about artists in the books listed on p. 155 and make a report on their sources of inspirations and what they were attempting to communicate through their artworks.

5. Read *The Artist* by Edmund Feldman (Englewood Cliffs, N.J.: Prentice-Hall, 1982) and make connections between what he says about the artists' development in society with the chronological history of art in chapter 6.

6. When you draw, paint, or work in three dimensions, what sources do you use for inspiration? Are they similar or different to those of the artists described in this chapter? If you have taken any studio art classes, were you encouraged to use similar sources of inspiration?

7. What objects do you collect? Did you collect anything as a child? What relationship do these things have to any art you might create?

8. Read the epilogue, "Solving the Puzzle of Art," in the book *Invented Worlds* by Ellen Winner (Harvard University Press, 1982) and describe what insight you gained in understanding how, what, and why artists create.

Understanding the Elements of Art: Response and Production

2

Instead of using words as authors do when they write poems or stories, artists use a visual language of "words" called **elements of art** when they create artworks. The elements of art are the basic ingredients, the building blocks of art. They are: **color, line, shape/form, texture, space, and value.**

In this chapter we will put the "spotlight" on one element of art at a time, temporarily placing it "center stage," knowing full well that ordinarily such isolation or separation in artworks is neither possible nor desirable. We will identify and examine each element of art, defining and describing its characteristics and properties to see how artists use it in making art. Then we will turn our attention to applying what we have learned in producing our own artworks.

In **Chapter 3** we will put the center-stage spotlight on the **principles of art,** one by one. We'll endeavor to unravel how an artwork may give us a feeling of informal balance, or how our eyes are led to a focal point by different kinds of lines. We'll come to understand how shapes may be used to create a pattern or how variety and unity must be closely allied.

The first step, then, in understanding and responding to artworks as well as producing artworks is to applaud each "performer" (each element and principle of art) individually as each one "takes a bow." Just as the actors, lighting technicians, and stagehands each have an important part in making a dramatic production a "hit," so do each of the elements and principles of art have an important part in making an artwork a "masterpiece." Our thoughtful analysis and reflection, as well as our hands-on involvement with each art element and art principle, will start us on our way to becoming enthusiastic and interested viewers of artworks as well as confident, eager producers of artworks.

Understanding Artworks

Learning about COLOR

Painters, poets, writers, actors, and scientists of all sorts respond and react to the wonderful world of color; indeed, think for a moment of living in a black, white, and gray world. Color appeals to our sense of beauty whether we recognize and respond to it in natural objects or in works of human origin. We can't help but be absorbed in watching the changing moods of a beautiful sunset. We delight in the incredible range of colors in the petals of flowers, on the bodies of tropical fish, or on the wings of a butterfly—or in the wonderful colors of a fine Impressionist painting.

People use and have used color for many purposes, one of the earliest being that of **personal decoration.** For centuries, individuals have decorated their bodies for special occasions or tribal ceremonies. This practice continues today in the use of cosmetics, clown faces, and in theaters where actors and dancers have specific ways to reveal character through facial design and color. All of us probably know which colors look best on us when we select a dress or shirt.

In **our surroundings,** color plays an important part also. We have color preferences in the way we furnish our homes. We may be quite fussy about the color we choose when we buy a car. And most chefs and home cooks know to plan to have a pleasing variety of color in the foods they arrange on a dinner plate. We would probably not find a dinner visually appetizing that consisted of halibut, mashed potatoes, cottage cheese, white bread, and vanilla ice cream!

Besides being decorative, color has long been associated with a **universal or cultural symbolism.** Certain colors are associated with each holiday: red for Valentine's, orange and black for Halloween. We think of light colors for spring and warm reds, oranges, and browns for fall. Red, white, and blue are patriotic colors for Americans. We tend to associate blue as standing for truth (true-blue), green for hope and everlasting life, black with sorrow and death, and the color of purple with royalty. Perhaps the latter symbolism began in Egypt many centuries ago when the sun-god Ra was assigned that color because of its rarity and the difficulty people had in obtaining it. Ever since then, kings have been symbolized by purple. In our culture, we often think of white in association with purity and weddings, but brides in India wear red and in Israel, yellow. Especially in artworks made hundreds of years ago, we find particular colors that stand for certain ideas and have special meanings.

While **emotions** are often linked symbolically to colors (we speak of being "green with envy," "good as gold," and "feeling blue"), a number of individuals have expressed **unique and personal reactions** to different colors. Mary O'Neill, in her book *Hailstones and Halibut Bones,* wrote poems that connected colors not only to feelings but to the **senses** as well. She associates green with the smell of a country breeze and blue with the sound of the wind over water. In her poem about gray, she says it is sleepiness and bad news. White is called the sound of a foot walking lightly as well as the part we can't remember in a dream. The Russian artist Wassily Kandinsky, who worked in the early part of this century, felt that each color had a **corresponding musical** note. He searched for a visual system in which he could express his conviction of an "inner mystical structure of the world." His splendid and often abstract canvases often exploded with color as he divorced himself from the necessity of using any subject matter at all. With Vincent van Gogh, color took on its own symbolic function since he used colors not locally true from the point of view of realism, but colors that spoke strongly of the emotions of his intense personality. Yellow for him was the color of love, warmth, and friendship, and we see it frequently, especially in his sunflower paintings. It is especially dominant in the painting he made of his own bedroom in the little house in Arles.

Color often serves a **functional purpose,** too—that of **categorization** and **identification.** When a number of related objects are "color-keyed," it simplifies sorting them out and grouping them by certain colors. Football players wear uniforms showing team colors. The colors of different pages of a catalog may denote different categories of items. Long ago, kings assigned **heraldic** colors to knights for their brave deeds, and thereafter the colorful coats of armor and shields served to identify the knights, since their faces were covered by visors.

Artists and scientists both make sharp **observations of colors in nature,** each for different purposes. Artists and designers are inspired by the colors that they see, letting them suggest blends and combinations to be matched and used to represent the things they see or to enhance and decorate a given surface. For instance, sharp observation shows us how nature uses color **to conceal, mislead, hide, attract, and warn other creatures.** Flowers use their vivid colors to attract insects to help in pollination. The Gila monster warns of its venom with its colored, beady scales. The chameleon changes its color from green to brown to gray, according to its surroundings. Male birds that must seek food among flowers and leaves have more vivid colors than their duller colored mates which remain concealed on nests made of dried grasses. Tigers and zebras, with their highly contrasting patterns of stripes, appear almost invisible against a shadowy background. Indeed, armies have hired persons trained in art to study nature's camouflages and help them design concealing devices for machines and soldiers in wartime.

When artists paint pictures, they may choose to use color in one of several ways. A **representational** use of color shows the actual or real colors of the object that is depicted. This is sometimes referred to as the **local color.** Or they may choose to use colors **decoratively** to ornament or enhance a composition. Then again, they may choose to use color **arbitrarily** if they wish to express a strong emotional feeling. And sometimes they use color **symbolically** to express an idea.

People have always been in awe of the glowing, pure colors seen in the enormous arch of a rainbow. Hindus in India tell stories of the god Indra, who threw thunderbolts during storms and used a rainbow to shoot his lightning arrows. Polynesians believed a rainbow was a ladder for heroes to climb to reach heaven. Some North American tribes thought that the rainbow was the beautiful bride of their rain-god. Pit River Indians of California believed that the rainbow was a "rain-clear sign" sent by Old-Man-Above, who shaped the rainbow like the coyote's tail and colored it with the blue of the bluebird, the red of the rising sun, the yellow of the coyote's fur, and the green of grass. The Old Testament tells of the rainbow being a covenant made by God with Noah after the Flood.

The beautiful colors of the **rainbow** can, of course, be explained scientifically. The rainbow is a curtain of large raindrops in front of us, with the sunshine behind us. It appears in the west in the morning and in the east late in the afternoon. When the sun strikes the rain, each drop acts like a tiny prism, separating white light into colors. The red arc is on the outside and the purple inside. A second bow is sometimes above the first. It is pale, and the colors are reversed.

Rainbows and color wheels both have orderly arrangements of colors. The **color wheel** (see Colorplate 1, at front of the **Color Gallery**) is a useful tool for learning the mechanics of color and for helping us select different combinations of colors or **color schemes.** It was invented by Isaac Newton around 1666. The **hues** (another name for colors) appear on the color wheel in the same order as they do on the rainbow. Think first of an equilateral triangle placed on top of the circle, and then think of placing one of the **three primary colors**—red, yellow, and blue—on each corner. These colors are called primary because they are basic and cannot be made by mixing any other colors together. If we mix any two of the primary colors together, we make another color. If we do this three times with a different pair of primary colors each time, we will have made the **three secondary colors**—orange, green, and purple (violet). (Red and blue make purple; yellow and blue make green; red and yellow make orange.) Each of these secondary colors should be positioned on the color wheel midway between the pair of primary colors that were used to make them. If we now mix one of the secondary colors with the primary color that is next to it, we will make an **intermediate color.** There are six of these: yellow-orange, red-orange, red-purple, yellow-green, blue-green, and blue-purple. This can be carried one step farther by changing the proportions of the two colors you are mixing and making another complete set of colors. You would then not only have yellow-orange but orange-yellow, the first being more yellow than orange and the second more orange than yellow.

Analogous colors are several colors that are adjacent to each other on the color wheel. They are often called a family of colors in that they all tend to resemble each other a little bit. They share one color in common and can mix with each other without becoming dull or gray. A set of analogous colors is red, red-orange, orange, and yellow-orange; all of these colors have some red in them.

A pair of colors that are opposite each other on the color wheel are called **complementary colors.** If we place these two colors at their full **intensity** (full concentration) close together in a design, they will quickly attract your attention because they contrast strongly, often almost seeming to vibrate. If we mix a little of one color of paint with its complement, we will find that its intensity is **dulled,** or grayed. The more of a color's complement that we mix with it, the duller it becomes. If a pair of complementary colors are mixed in equal amounts, a mousey or gray-brown color results. Artists find it very useful to be able to mix a great variety of colors by using this dulling property of complementary colors. For instance, if a landscape has a great many different green tones in it—fields, trees, foliage—we can mix a great number of dull greens by adding differing amounts of red to the pure green. And, of course, we can make lighter tones or darker ones by the addition of either white or black to the blended color.

An interesting phenomenon occurs when our eyes become saturated by staring for a few seconds at one color. Place a small square of red paper in the center of a large piece of white paper. Stare at it for thirty seconds and then remove the red square and look at the white paper. You will see a "ghost" green square, its complement. Try this with other colors. What colors do you think you would see on a white surface after staring at the American flag?

When we plan to produce a particular visual effect, whether we are making a painting, decorating a room, selecting clothing, or choosing a color for our car, we often think of colors as **warm or cool.** This is due to associating them with either warm or cool places or things in our environment. Water, lakes, ice, and snow are cool and so we think of green, blue, and purple as cool colors. Conversely, fire and heat are associated with warm colors—red, yellow, and orange.

A color's **value** has to do with its lightness or darkness. We add white to a color to create a **tint.** We add a bit of black to a color to create a **shade.** We can mix a **graded scale** of the tints and shades of one color. If we make a design or a composition with the tints, shades, and different intensities of one color, we call our artwork **monochromatic** (mono—*one,* and chroma—*color*).

While we don't find black, white, and gray on the color wheel, we usually need them in creating artworks. They, along with tan and brown, are called **neutrals** and can be mixed with and used harmoniously with any color or set of colors on the color wheel.

Children Use Color

Children of three and four years of age find visual pleasure in the colors they see around them. They sometimes select a particular color and have it as their "favorite." When they first begin drawing symbolic representations of people, trees, houses, and such, they usually do not relate the color they are using to the actual color that the object is. We may see green faces and purple hair on a figure. Adults at this time can point out particular colors in the environment in the course of normal conversations with children rather than correcting the choices that children have made in their drawings. (I like your red sweater, Elaine. Jim has made a fine painting of a dog that is chocolaty brown. Thank you for the pretty bouquet of pink and yellow roses.) Children can take "color discovery walks," identifying colors and making lists when they return of everything they saw that was a particular color.

To increase children's perceptual and cognitive awareness of color, the teacher can ask them to **describe the colors they see in an artwork,** whether it is their own or one by a great artist. For instance, we could ask the children to point out all the places where Franz Marc used green or blue in the painting *Yellow Cow.* They could decide which color they see first when they look at the painting, and which color is used the most. They could find a dark blue and a light blue. When they also notice the areas of green, yellow, red, and violet colors, they would then be told that the artist mostly used the primary and secondary colors for his composition. He was careful to balance the colors. Children need to have a number of occasions to observe artworks and describe the colors they see. Before long, children are confidently identifying the colors they perceive and beginning to use more realistic and/or expressive colors in their symbolic representations of things that are important to them in their artwork.

When they arrive at the realism stage, at eight or nine years, children are rather insistent about using representational colors. They can be helped by directing their attention to and discussing the variety of colors they see in landscapes, posed models, and still lifes. They can profit from a familiarity with the color wheel and by learning the nuances of mixing light and dark hues, dulled colors, and blends of analogous colors to match the colors they see in trees, houses, streets, animals, and such. They may choose, however, to make an expressive rather than a realistic use of color and choose colors that communicate a particular emotion or dramatic or fantasy event. Once again, a study of several artworks in which artists used expressive colors can help them gain the concept that different modes of expression call for personalized color choices. In describing Picasso's *Tragedy,* we might ask the children to find where the artist used unrealistic colors. We then might ask the children to imagine how the sad feeling of the picture would be changed had Picasso used realistic colors.

Producing Artworks

Daubs of Color: Impressionism

The student will create a small tempera painting in the manner of the Impressionist artists that painted their canvases with tiny daubs of color placed closely together in order to show how shimmering light was reflected on the surfaces of the things they saw. They depended on the viewer's eyes to mix the colors rather than combining and blending the colors on their palettes in the traditional manner.

1. Find a color photograph of a landscape. Then use L-frames to help you search out and identify a pleasing detail of the landscape. Then use a pencil and lightly sketch in the major shapes and parts of the composition you have selected on a small piece of white paper, about 6″ × 9″.

2. Use a small, round bristle brush or a Q-tip and enlarge the detail you have framed by dipping the tip in thick tempera and **daubing** it on the paper. Do not stroke or blend the colors with your brush or Q-tip. Let several colors pile up on top of each other and be close to each other. Let each color dry before you apply another color on top of it.

A pair of L-frames gives students a choice of many options in selecting a portion or detail from a photograph.

3. Cover the paper in the manner described. If you seek to portray a light green, apply green and then white and perhaps some yellow or blue. If you wish to show a dull color, daub in a pair of complementary colors; if you wish to show a dark color, daub in purple or blue.

Wild Colors: Fauvism

The student will create a painting of a person using "wild colors" in the rather flat manner of the Fauves, a group of artists associated with Matisse around 1905–07, who were dubbed "Wild Beasts" for their bold, startling, and unrealistic use of colors. The student will use direct observation of a posed model as the basis for the artwork.

1. Make a contour drawing (see p. 25) of a friend's face. Divide it with lines into different parts. Feel free to exaggerate and distort the shapes of the features. You may wish to draw the face with a thick, black marking pen.

2. Use tempera or acrylic paints, choosing bright and unrealistic colors in a flat manner to paint the face. Be sure to paint the background, too.

A Composite Painting: A Group Project

Each student will make an enlarged drawing of a small square cut from a reproduction of a famous artwork. Then the student will look closely at the colors in the small square and blend paint to match them to paint the larger square. When all the enlarged squares are completed and adhered to a background, a composite painting showing the famous artwork will be completed.

Students chose bold and unlikely colors in painting this Fauve-like portrait.

Elementary school students each enlarged a square from a Picasso reproduction and then assembled this composite group project.

1. Find a reproduction of a painting, either a museum postcard or a small print that you are free to cut. Mark it off in approximately the same number of squares as there are students in the class. On the reverse side, number each square in a sequential order. Then cut them apart on the paper trimmer and attach each to a small piece of paper with clear tape. Be sure each square is numbered properly and marked as to which side is the top.

2. Give each student a five-inch square piece of heavy white drawing paper and one of the small squares from the cut-up artwork of a great master.

3. Use a ruler and draw a line both vertically and horizontally across the five-inch square of white paper. Then lightly draw lines across the small detail of the reproduction, vertically and horizontally. You have now divided the small detail of the reproduction and the larger piece of white paper in fourths. Use a pencil and enlarge the small square on the white paper. Match what you see, part by part.

4. Use liquid tempera (or tempera cakes, acrylics, or watercolors) and practice matching the color blends and brushstrokes that you see in the great master's work. You will need to decide if a color is a greenish blue with some white added, or if it might be a dulled green that can be matched by mixing some red with it. Paint your square carefully, trying to obtain the same values and intensities of colors that were used by the great master.

5. When everyone finishes, paste the large squares in numerical order on a large poster board or piece of paper that has been ruled off in the matching number of five-inch squares.

6. Students can now identify the painting and make an evaluation as to how successful they all were in mixing and blending the colors they saw before them.

Tints and Shades

The student will use direct observation of nature in painting a simplified composition of flowers and leaves, using one color and mixing a number of tints and shades of one color; the student will then paint the same composition again but will use tints derived from a number of different colors.

1. Make a contour drawing (see p. 25) of several flowers and leaves or a leafy twig. Be sure to let some of the lines and shapes extend off the edges of the paper to create negative spaces and to make your composition more balanced and visually interesting.

2. Mix each color you use with either black or white and then paint the entire design with a variety of tints and shades. Be sure to paint the negative spaces, also.

3. Duplicate your contour drawing, but when you paint it the second time, use only tints of a number of different colors.

Understanding Artworks

Learning about LINE

Think back about ten to fifteen thousand years ago to a time when the Ice Age was ending and when huge glaciers were receding. This was the Stone Age and from it came our earliest known artworks. This was the time when people lived in caves and depended upon large animals for their food and clothing, animals that they could hunt and kill with primitive weapons or that might kill them if they were unsuccessful.

If you had lived then, perhaps you would have looked at the ceilings and walls of your domicile one day and in the undulating bulges and rounded forms of their surfaces seen what might have suggested to you the powerful forms of bison, horses, and other animals with which you were familiar. Do you think you might have been tempted to try tracing your finger around the edges of what you imagined that you saw?

Perhaps you would have had the desire, as well as the ingenuity, to fashion a tool of some sort from bones and plant fibers or animal fur. You would have dipped it into a coloring agent you had made by mixing animal fat with charcoal or powders you made by grinding rocks. You might have discovered that if you held your hand on the surface of the cave and blew around it with dry, powdery pigment through a hollow bone or reed, you would have created the outline of your hand. That was your "signature" and, incidentally, the first stencil. You might even marvel so much at your accomplishment that you would repeat it and perfect your line drawings on the walls of the cave in an effort to have some control over the enormous and often frightening creatures upon whom your very existence depended. By making such a good likeness of these creatures with your lines, the other men and women in the tribe probably regarded you quite highly and thought you had special powers.

Figure 2.1   Rembrandt, Van Rijn, 1606–1669. *Self-Portrait.* **c. 1637.**
National Gallery of Art, Washington, D.C. Rosenwald Collection.
The artist has used a variety of lines in this expressive sketch. Contour lines define the forms; others suggest texture, while others are combined in hatching effects to create volume. The drawing tool and surface of the paper contribute to linear quality.

Ever since these early times, artists have used lines in many ways and have made many different kinds of this important element of art. And certainly today we have many more sophisticated drawing implements than the early cave artists did.

Line may be defined as the mark left by a dot or point moving continuously through space or over a surface. It starts someplace and stops someplace and leaves a path as it is drawn across the paper or other surface.

Probably the most common use for the element of line is to show the edges, that is, the **contours** of an object. The line marks the place where the object stops and the air or space around it begins. When we make a contour line drawing, we draw both the inner as well as the outer contours of the person or thing, or else we would only be drawing a flat shape with no details. This is usually thought of as a silhouette. In a line drawing, contour lines inside the object give it a three-dimensional quality. Strong, black outlines and hard edges add clarity and interest and create a sharp definition of the shapes in an artwork. They also make things stand out, as well as adding a decorative

Figure 2.2 Edvard Munch, 1863–1944. *The Scream.* **1895.**
National Gallery of Art, Washington, D.C. Rosenwald
Collection.
Curving and straight lines contrast to create repeated patterns
that intensify and clarify the mood and give emotional impact
to the subject matter in this powerful and intense print. Strong
diagonal line leads the eye to the central figure and creates a
dynamic tension between it and the two figures in the
background.

accent. Many painters do not use contour lines at all. They
show the contour of an object by separate colors or textures. Turn to the **Color Gallery** and identify three artworks in which the artist used lines to show edges; now
locate three artworks in which the edges of shapes are separated by different colors rather than outlines.

The **drawing tool** with which a line is made relates to
its character. The thin, neat sharpness of a pen-and-ink
line looks very different from the fuzzy, blurry one made
with a crayon. The fluid, undulating line made with a soft
sable brush is very different from a crisp, constant pencil
line. Of considerable importance also is the **drawing surface** upon which a line is made. An absorbent, coarse paper
will respond to the same drawing tool in a different way
than would paper that has a hard, smooth surface.

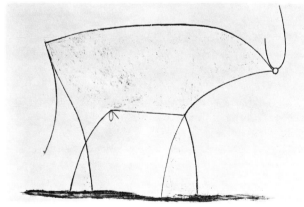

Figure 2.3 Pablo Picasso, *The Bulls.* **B-31998 The Bull;**
B-31999 The Bull; B-32001 The Bull, 1945.
National Gallery of Art, Washington, D.C. Ailsa Mellon
Bruce Fund.
Picasso uses a favorite theme of his, that of a bull, to create a
series of drawings that begin with a representational image
and end with a simplified, abstract linear design.

Figure 2.4   Utagawa Hiroshige I., *Yokkaichi (The Hurricane)*
(Tokaido Gojusan Tsugi).
Cleveland museum of Art, Gift of Mrs. T. Wingate Todd, from
the collection of Dr. T. Wingate Todd, 48-307.
Movement and action are seen in the masterful use of line in
this woodblock print. Thick lines mark the posts on the dock.
Delicate lines give a feeling of gesture in the wind-blown
grasses and leafy tree branches. Lines of the hat strings lead
our eye to the running figure. Can you find horizontal and
diagonal lines that direct your eyes to the focal point?

Line has a number of characteristics. It has **direction:** horizontal, vertical, and diagonal. **Vertical lines** suggest such qualities as strength, stability, and dignity, and remind us of lofty or quiet things. They lead our eyes upward. Think of tall pine trees in a forest or a row of columns in Greek or Roman architecture. **Horizontal lines** give us a restful feeling and make us think of calm, peaceful things. Think of floating on your back on the smooth surface of a lake. **Diagonal lines,** on the other hand, tend to create tension, movement, and even uneasy feelings. They suggest motion and lead our eyes in a slanting upward, downward, or forward direction. Think of waves tossing on a stormy sea, or a skier on a steep slope. These lines draw our eyes up, across, or down. Compare your reaction to the direction of the lines in Orozco's *Zapatistas* and to Picasso's *The Tragedy* in the **Color Gallery.** Now compare how Homer and Eakins have used horizontal and diagonal lines in their artworks in the **Color Gallery.**

Our eyes are led along the path of curving, angular, or diagonal lines, or by lines that meander and intertwine.

For examples of this, turn to the **Color Gallery.** How are Picasso's *Girl Before a Mirror,* Kandinsky's *Painting No. 198,* and Franz Marc's *Yellow Cow* alike in the use of line? How are they different?

Lines that have been repeated in a rhythmic or random manner may also lead our eyes in a certain direction. We call lines that capture a fleeting movement or the posture of a subject, **gesture lines.** These lines are usually scribbled, free-flowing, and made with a quick and continuous movement of the hand. An **implied line** also can "take our eyes for a walk" in a composition. This means that a series of lines not linked with each other suggest a directional path or contour that our eyes tend to connect. Because we expect a line to be continuous, our eyes follow it even beyond the format of the picture.

Line has other characteristics as well. Lines have **length and width;** they may be short or long, thick or thin. They may be **dark or light in value,** either **blurred and uneven** or **sharp and clear-edged.** They may change from thick to thin and be called a **gradated line.** They may be **continuous** or **broken.**

Figure 2.5   Vincent van Gogh, *Grove of Cypresses.* **1889, reed pen and ink over pencil on paper, 62.5 × 46.4 cm.**
Gift of Robert Allerton © The Art Institute of Chicago. All Rights Reserved.
Vincent's characteristic swirling, curving strokes are repeated again and again to create restless trees in this landscape. The artist was skilled in achieving the utmost effect from a flexible pen.

Figure 2.6   Henri de Toulouse-Lautrec, *In the Circus Fernando: The Ring-Master.* **1888, oil on canvas, 100.3 × 161.3 cm.**
Joseph Winterbotham Collection, 1925. 523 © The Art Institute of Chicago. All Rights Reserved.
Lautrec takes a bird's-eye view and guides our eyes throughout this dynamic composition by the use of directional lines, making optimal use of curving diagonals and contours.

Figure 2.7   George Rouault, *Christ Mocked by Soldiers.* **Oil on canvas, 36¼ × 28½″.**
Collection, The Museum of Modern Art, New York. Given anonymously.
Bold black outlines are used to enclose shapes that are filled with thick paint that has been applied with strong, thick brushstrokes. Colors appear jewel-like in their stained-glass type of enclosures.

Artists have various intentions when they utilize the element of line. Line may be used **realistically,** or the artist may intentionally use it in an **expressive** way to show objects that are distorted and exaggerated. We say that a line is **decorative** when it is used to embellish surfaces. In this capacity, it is often **repeated** in an orderly arrangement to create a **linear pattern.** An **abstract** use of line is one that focuses on the line quality itself rather than the object it is depicting.

Line is most generally used by artists in making drawings and etchings. Line drawings may exist as ends in themselves and be regarded as artworks, or they may be created as preparatory plans for paintings, pieces of sculpture, crafts, or architecture. Making a line drawing is a process of coordinating the eye, the hand, and the mind, a process that requires practice. Instruction in making

**Figure 2.8 Hans Memling, *The Presentation in the Temple;*
Master of the PRADO Adoration of the Magi; [Date: c. 1470–
1480; Wood 0.598–0.483 (23½ × 19 in.)]**
*Samuel Kress Collection. National Gallery of Art,
Washington, D.C.*
Vertical lines in the architectural elements and in the robes
and clothing of the figures lend dignity, solemnity, and stability
to this composition.

contour lines can help students learn to see lines in the
natural environment and to develop the necessary skills to
make drawings that are personally and individually expressive.

Children Use Line

When very young children embark upon their first adven-
tures with art, they begin by making lines. Somewhere
around two years of age, they begin enjoying the kinesthetic pleasure of moving their hand and arm around while
it holds a crayon or pen. We say that the **scribbling stage**
has begun. Soon they realize that they can control the lines
they are making, and they proceed to make quite a variety
of repeated movements. These are generally referred to
as **circular and longitudinal scribbles.** A fascinating metaphorical connection was made by Rudolf Arnheim,* who
noticed that these circular patterns of scribbles are similar to the manner in which particles of matter in outer
space are organized into wheel-like shapes of spiral neb-
ulae.

*Rudolf Arnheim, Art and Visual Perception; A Psychology of the
Creative Eye, 2d ed. (Berkeley: University of California Press, 1974).

At about three or four years of age, the young scribblers discover that when the arm is moved around in this
circular motion and then stopped, they have made circular shapes. They discover that they can make repeated
lines, some short and some long, and that putting these
circles and lines together stirs their imagination into seeing
in front of them something they recognize and call
"mommy," "daddy," or "me." Soon they are making all
sorts of linear symbols and calling them "houses," "my
dog," "the school bus," etc. When they **name** their scribbles, we know that they have now established a connection
between the lines they are making and the surrounding
world. They are now set to explore the world through the
use of line, making marks that will show their degree of
perception, their intense involvement with an experience,
and their emotional responses to what they have seen,
thought, and felt.

During the **symbolic or schematic stage** that follows,
they will develop their line- and shape-making skills, as
well as their muscular coordination in handling drawing
tools, and, if encouraged and motivated appropriately, will
maintain a flexible, fluent, and original approach to the
creation of images of things that are important to them.

At about eight years, children begin to be more critical of their artwork and usually become dissatisfied with
the rather simple linear symbols they have been using.
They are ready for direct instruction in how to draw more
realistically. It is the teacher's role at this time to provide
experiences that will develop their perceptual skills and
that will help them learn media techniques that will enable
them to create artworks that are acceptable to their ma-
turing critical eyes.

Children can be encouraged to identify, describe, and
evaluate how they themselves have used line in their artwork, as well as discover how artists have done so. For
instance, they could be asked to compare the ways that
Rouault's lines in *Christ Mocked* differ from Rembrandt's in his *Self-Portrait.* They could compare van
Gogh's *Grove of Cypresses* and Yokkaichi's *Hurricane* to
discover similarities and differences as well as how the use
of the drawing implement had some degree of control on
the line quality. They could describe the emotional feelings portrayed in these two artworks through the use of
line. In other artworks, they could search out places where
line was used to create a variety of textures and patterns,
and in still other artworks, ways in which the use of line
expresses a feeling of strength and dignity, gesture and
movement, or is used in a decorative manner.

Producing Artworks

Drawing Contour Lines

Contour drawing is an art skill that helps you "take the
leap" from drawing the symbols associated with early
childhood to the more realistic drawing associated with

adulthood. This is often referred to as utilizing the resources of the right hemisphere of the brain instead of the left.*

Learning to see edges with intense visual concentration helps eliminate the "I can't draw" feeling. Contour drawing is an excellent way to establish contact with our visual powers of observation. It is the fastest way to establish one's belief in one's ability to draw. It is a way to help students start drawing and to affirm in a positive way that they really can draw what they see right in front of them. The success of this technique may simply be that due to our total concentration we arrive at a state of heightened perception. When this occurs, time seems to stand still, and after awhile the drawing is accomplished with very little effort. Great artists seem to have taken this leap naturally, with little or no outside help. Many of them have not realized that "seeing like an artist" is not something that everyone can do with no instruction. The great artist Matisse was once asked if he saw a tomato the way everyone else did. He replied that if he were going to eat it, yes; if he were going to draw it, he "saw it like an artist."

Betty Edwards describes an unusual technique that helps students understand this phenomenon and convince them that they really can draw what they see in front of them. A line drawing by an artist—for example, one by Picasso or Matisse—is placed on the table in front of the student, but it is placed upside down! The student is less able to see the rather complex arrangement of in-and-out lines, curving and angular lines, intersecting lines such as fingers, arms, hair, and such. The student is asked not to name the parts of the picture and to eliminate words from his/her thought pattern, intently focusing on one line at a time, copying it, and connecting it with another line. Gradually, the drawing is accomplished and, when turned right side up, surprisingly enough bears a striking resemblance to the original drawing by Picasso or Matisse. While we can't turn landscapes, objects, and people upside down to draw them, the intense perceptual experience of observing contours in a manner in which we are not accustomed to seeing them (upside down) can be transferred to other situations when the student is drawing something else—a flower, cowboy boot, or an eggbeater.

It is thought that our left brain tends to label and categorize things through the use of words. Claude Monet, the great Impressionist painter, said that in order to see we have to forget the name of the thing we are observing. As young children, we tend to think mostly in pictures, not in words, anyway; however, by eight or nine years, children seem to stop visualizing things freely and start putting word labels on them instead. Too often the school's stress on verbal and digital skills rules out visualizing

things to the extent that students no longer see anything with clarity and sensitivity, and only recognize things by their labels.

To demonstrate how artists have perceived contours, place a large sheet of clear acetate over a large print by a great master. For instance, you might choose a portrait by van Gogh, Gauguin, or Leonardo. Use a waterbase black marking pen and slowly draw a continuous line around the outside edges of the figure or the face; then draw the inside contour lines. Now remove the acetate and place it on a white surface and you will see a contour drawing. (The pen marks may be removed with a damp paper towel and the acetate used again.)

Edwards states that it is the left half of the brain that talks to us and tells us that we can't draw, insists on a hurried symbolic representation, and gives names to things. The right side, on the other hand, is nonverbal and is fascinated with the way a contour line, or edge of something, curves in here, out a little farther down, meets another edge at another place, and so on. Whether it is right or left or our whole brain that is involved, the following drawing technique works with adults and older children that feel that they can't draw.

Simply stated, **contour drawing is using a continuous line to draw the outer as well as inner edges of an object while you are intensely looking at the object.** You'll need some white paper, masking tape, and a soft lead pencil or a fine-tipped nylon pen. (The use of a pen is preferable in that the student is discouraged from stopping to erase.) Here are a few suggestions to help you make contour drawings.

1. Find several objects for practicing this technique— a leafy twig, a flower, a doll, your car keys, a pair of pliers, a rubber glove, a turkey feather, your shoe, etc.

2. Tape a piece of white paper on the table in front of you so it won't move. Your concentration will be intensely focused on what you are observing. You don't need to be distracted by using your hand to keep the paper from moving.

3. To break the old habit of keeping your eyes on the paper rather than on the object you are drawing, your first few drawings will be **blind contour drawings.** To prepare to do this, poke the point of a pencil through the middle of a 4½-by-6-inch piece of paper. Hold the pencil with your hand under the paper so that you won't be able to see your hand or the pencil point as they move on the drawing paper. This protective shield will force you to keep your eyes on the object you are drawing and not on your paper. Plan on making your drawing at least as large as the actual object.

*Betty Edwards, Drawing on the Right Side of the Brain (Los Angeles: J. P. Tarcher); Kimon Nicolades, The Natural Way to Draw (Boston: Houghton Mifflin Co., 1975).

Student Drawing 1.

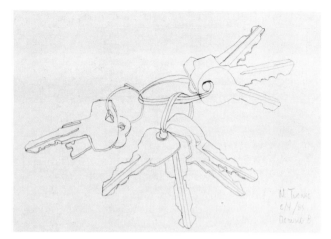

Student Drawing 2.

4. Sit comfortably and relax. Listen to soft relaxing instrumental music (no words!) if you wish. Plan to spend about ten minutes or so with each of your first contour drawings.

5. Place the object you are going to draw in front of you. Pick a point on the object and a corresponding point on your paper. Convince yourself that your pencil and eye are simultaneously following the outer contours of the object. Better still, convince yourself that your pencil is actually **touching** the object and moving along its edges rather than touching and moving on the surface of the paper.

6. Draw **slowly!** The line you make will be **continuous** and will follow every little in-and-out curve, bump, wrinkle, indentation, or angle that you see. To break any old habit you may have of drawing in a rapid, sketchy manner, pretend that a very sleepy little ant is crawling along the edge of the object and that your pencil is right behind it, pushing it along. You will not lift your pencil while you are drawing a particular contour line. When you reach a stopping

point and need to reposition your pencil to draw another contour line, stop drawing, take a peek under the protective shield, lift your pencil, find a new starting point, and continue drawing another contour. But don't start drawing again until your eyes are **on the object.**

7. Draw **inside contour lines,** also. Keep adding as many linear details as you can find. Remember that a contour is where the edge of one thing stops and something else begins. Inner contours add realism and give your artwork three-dimensional form.

8. After you have made several blind contour drawings, remove the protective shield and begin making **modified contour drawings.** While you do this, your eyes should focus on the object about 90 percent of the time, and your eyes on the paper the remaining 10 percent of the time. Try to look at the paper only enough to keep your lines meeting in the appropriate places. A slowly drawn, sensitive line is the result of careful observation.

9. It is recommended that you find some place where you can practice drawing without interruption for about twenty minutes a day. Try making a contour drawing of a landscape, a person's face (your own in a mirror or a friend's), a mounted bird, a butterfly. You can use contour drawing skills working from photographs as well as with real objects.

Lines that are Curving and Straight: Drawing with Glue

The student will draw by squeezing a bottle of glue onto black paper, leaving a trail of curving and straight lines. When the glue dries, the lines show up as black because of the transparency of dried glue. Chalks are then applied to the black paper to add color.

Student work: Painting bold, black lines with tempera.

Student work: Drawing with glue.

1. Make a contour drawing with a pencil on a piece of 12 × 18-inch black construction paper. Use pictures and scale models of dinosaurs, or use mounted butterflies, photos of birds or flowers, etc., as your source of visual information. Carefully observe the outer and inner edges of your subject matter. Look for curving lines and those that are straight, angular, and wavy. Make your object large and include some background. Use lines to enclose shapes and to make repeated patterns. Have some of the lines extend off the edges of the paper.

2. Go over your pencil lines by squeezing a trail of white glue from the bottle. You can make thick and thin lines, gradated lines, broken lines, and small dots. Let the glue dry. It will take several hours or overnight.

3. Use chalk to color the shapes your lines created on the black paper. Blend colors together with the fingertips. Limit your color selection and endeavor to create a contrast between the subject and background.

4. Spray the drawing with fixative when finished to keep chalk from rubbing off.

Thick Black Lines: Painting with Tempera

The student will use a photo as a visual resource and paint thick, black lines to enclose shapes that will then be painted with mixtures of color in the manner of the artist Georges Rouault.

1. Use L-frames and a photograph that interests you: a butterfly, an insect, an animal, a face, etc. Look at the basic lines and shapes that you see and simplify them as you make a large drawing of the object with a piece of chalk on a piece of white drawing paper. Enclose the various shapes and parts of the object you have drawn with strong contour lines. Divide the background area with horizontal, vertical, or diagonal lines that go to the edges of the paper. Think of stained glass and how strips of lead enclose each separate piece of glass.

2. Use some black tempera and a flat or round stiff-bristle brush and paint over your chalk marks, making bold, black lines. Let the paint dry.

3. Choose two colors, or one color and white (or black). Try using two primary colors together, or two colors that are next to each other on the color wheel, or a pair of complementary colors. Brush the first color inside one of the enclosed areas and add the second color to it. Brush until the surface of the paper inside the enclosed space is covered. Try not to brush until all the colors are smoothly mixed. Let your brushstrokes show in the manner that the artist Rouault did. (This manner of applying thick, opaque paint is referred to as "impasto," in that textural features of the paint and brushwork show on the surface of the painting.) Choose two more

colors and continue painting inside each of the enclosed areas until the entire surface of your paper is covered.

4. Let your painting dry. Press it with an iron on the reverse side to flatten it before mounting or matting it.

Repeated Lines: Relief Prints

The student will make a relief print by making indented lines in a soft sheet of Scratch-foam.

1. Choose a newspaper photograph and use L-frames to help you select the part you want to use as visual information for your print.

2. Cut a half sheet of Scratch-foam. Prepare a preliminary line drawing the same size as your Scratch-foam sheet. Plan areas where you will repeat long or broken lines, crosshatched lines, or dots to create a pattern. Plan where you will have thick and thin lines and where you will have white areas. Plan where you will have a center of interest. Your composition will be more interesting if you make some of the lines extend off the sides of the composition. Remember: everything that is **up** will print black; everything that is pressed **down** will print white.

3. Place your prepared sketch on top of the Scratch-foam sheet and go over the lines firmly with a pencil. This will imprint the lines on the surface of the Scratch-foam. Remove the paper and go over the lines again to be sure they are imprinted deeply enough. If they are not, they will fill with ink and not show on the print.

4. Put about a teaspoonful of water-soluble printing ink on a small tray and roll a brayer lightly over it in two directions so as to obtain an even coating of ink on the brayer. The brayer should roll over the surface of the tray, not slide.

5. Place the sheet of Scratch-foam on a piece of newspaper and roll ink onto it from the brayer, going in both directions.

6. Place the Scratch-foam in the center of a sheet of white ditto paper or a colored sheet of Fadeless, Astrobright, or Brighthue paper. (Colored construction paper has a rough, porous surface and does not make a sharp print.) Turn the paper and the Scratch-foam over and rub the backside of the paper. Remove the paper from the Scratch-foam and let the print dry.

Student work: Making lines in relief prints.

7. If you wish to make a number of prints, you will need to re-ink the Scratch-foam for each printing. Try using colored and white printing inks instead of black, for a variety of effects.

Decorative Lines: Paper Batik

The student will use a resist technique known as **batik** to create a linear design. Batik is an ancient process of decorating fabrics. Traditionally, melted wax is applied to fabric to cause it to resist the colored dyes that are applied later in the unprotected areas. In this simplified version of batik, Dippity Dye paper is used instead of fabric.

Drawn Batik

1. Use as a visual resource photographs of tropical fish, birds, flowers, etc., or adapt a motif from symbols used by Aztecs, Mayas, Japanese family crests, or Southwestern Indians and create a linear

design with a pencil on a piece of white butcher paper, 12″ × 18″. Then place a piece of Dippity Dye paper of the same size on it and trace over your lines with a thick, black **water-soluble** marking pen. You will be able to see your lines through the Dippity Dye paper. (Permanent markers will **not** work with this process.)

2. To melt wax safely, do not use an open flame, an exposed heating element, or boiling water. Instead, melt a small amount of candle wax or paraffin in a deep-fat fryer or electric skillet. You may wish to line the skillet with foil and place in it a small, low can of wax. Dip a natural-bristle brush (synthetic bristles may melt in the hot wax) of medium size in the melted wax and carefully brush over all of your black lines. Let the wax extend on both sides of the lines. This creates a decorative white border on the sides of the lines in the finished product. **Be sure to protect all the black lines with wax** or they will dissolve later when the color washes are applied to the paper.

3. Make a food color solution by mixing about one-fourth cup of water with about one-fourth teaspoon of the kind of highly concentrated food colors found in cake decorating stores. Use large brushes or the inexpensive sponge brushes found in paint and hardware stores. Brush these colors over the different parts of your design.

4. Let the Dippity Dye paper dry. Apply more wax over the dyed areas of the paper. This will assure an even surface on the finished product after it is ironed.

5. Place Dippity Dye paper (and the butcher paper beneath it) between newspapers and iron it. Lift the Dippity Dye paper off the butcher paper while it is hot.

6. Display your paper batik with a white backing paper or hang it in a window, as the final product is translucent.

Plain Batik

1. You may choose to make an allover repeat pattern of lines and dots. Or you may choose to create a design based on a natural object. Draw your plan on white butcher paper and place the Dippity Dye paper on top of it.

2. Use stiff natural-bristle brushes (synthetic ones may melt in the hot wax) and/or **tjantings.** Tjantings are the traditional tools used for batik. They have a wooden handle with a tiny funnel at one end. When dipped in hot wax and then trailed over the surface of the Dippity Dye paper, they create a flowing,

Student brushes food color wash over wax lines.

fluid line that has graceful gradations. Tjantings are available in art supply stores and catalogs.

3. Begin your batik by applying the wax with a brush or tjanting where you wish to have white lines in the finished product.

4. Choose a light color (yellow is recommended) of food color wash as described above and brush it onto the white paper. Let it dry.

5. Apply more wax lines with a brush or tjanting in the yellow areas. The areas where you apply the second waxing will be seen as yellow in the finished product. Then choose a second and darker color of food color wash to apply over the yellow paper. Let it dry.

6. Apply more wax and then a third (the darkest color) of food color wash. Let it dry.

7. Apply wax to the unwaxed areas to assure having an even finish in the final product. Then iron the paper between newspapers, lifting it off the butcher paper while it is hot. Display as described on pages 28 and 29 in *Drawn Batik.*

Understanding Artworks

Learning about SHAPE and FORM

Do you remember as a child standing motionless between a strong light and a blank sheet of paper while someone carefully drew the shadow that was cast by your profile? The **shape** was a **silhouette.** It was a fairly good likeness of you after it was cut from black paper and mounted. It could even be identified as yours when all the silhouettes of your classmates were finished, even though it had no distinguishing details within its shape. We are often able to recognize an object by its shape alone. Etienne de Silhouette, who lived in the eighteenth century and served as the French controller-general, introduced economic reforms that made him the object of ridicule and hostility from the nobles, who thereafter used his name to apply to a "mere outline profile drawing."

When a line moves around and comes back and meets itself, it makes a shape. You can draw the shape of an apple with a line, or you can use a paintbrush and paint an apple with no outlines at all. In an artwork, a **shape** is a two-dimensional area. Its length and width are defined in some way, either by an outline or boundary around it, or by being a different color or texture from the space around it.

Whether we are describing an artwork or creating one, there are some important considerations to be taken into account about the element of shape. Shapes have **size;** they may be large or small. Artists may create shapes that have sharp, clearly defined **hard edges** or **soft, blurry contours** that blend into other shapes surrounding them. If they contain no interior details and are the same color or value, they are called **flat** shapes. In composing an artwork, artists know that shapes may be repeated to create a regular or irregular **pattern.** If they place shapes close together in an artwork, they create a feeling of **unity** and compactness. When shapes **overlap** each other, they tend to give us a feeling of depth; the one in front is seen as being closer to the viewer. If an artist places similar shapes throughout a composition, our eyes tend to **follow the path** from shape to shape.

Artists frequently use **realistic shapes** in a two-dimensional artwork to represent three-dimensional objects (or forms) that they see in the natural world. Sometimes artists simplify or change the shapes they see, **abstracting** the important parts and planes and letting them serve an **expressive** purpose, or letting the shapes serve as symbols, ideas, or concepts. They are more interested in the form of the object than they are in the subject matter itself. Look at Picasso's *Girl Before a Mirror* in the **Color Gallery** and observe how the artist simplified shapes for heads, breasts, and abdomens as he shows a young girl confronting the image of herself as she will be as an old woman. Look at the variety of open and closed shapes in

Figure 2.9   Marsden Hartley, *Mount Kaiahdin, Maine.* **Date: dated 1942; Hardboard; 0.760 × 1.019 (30 × 40⅛ in.)** *National Gallery of Art, Washington, D.C.; Gift of Mrs. Mellon Byers.*
Soft, blurry edges define the basic shapes in this landscape adding to the mood and feeling of the scene.

Kandinsky's *Painting No. 198* in the **Color Gallery.** Kandinsky often created shapes in his artworks that have little or no relation to things in the natural world at all. He was more interested in the shapes and colors than he was in depicting natural objects, and in using those shapes and colors to express particular feelings and emotional qualities. He has stated that objects got in the way of his paintings. We refer to this sort of shape as being **nonobjective.** Can you think how you might draw an ominous shape, a restful shape, or an exultant one?

The kinds of shapes that artists choose to use are determined by the message or visual statement that they wish to make. In the **Color Gallery,** we see Raphael's *Alba Madonna* and Marisol's *Women and Dog,* both artworks featuring women and children. The artwork from the High Renaissance, painted in a round format called **tondo,** has a religious theme and uses highly realistic shapes to depict specific people—Mary, Jesus, and John the Baptist. On the other hand, Marisol seeks to make a very different kind of visual statement, so she has chosen abstracted forms for the bodies of her people and has shown us a group of individuals, along with a dog on a leash, anxiously watching for traffic as they go on yet another shopping trip.

When you wish to make a realistic drawing of something, the technique of **blocking in the shapes** can help you perceive the configuration of the object. First look at the total, overall shape of an object or a creature, a photograph of perhaps a squirrel or a hen, or a real one. Then look for the major smaller shapes that make up the total shape of the creature. The hen's body is somewhat like a large egg, an oval shape. The tail-feathers tend to form a

Figure 2.10   Marsden Hartley, *The Aero.* **Date: c 1914; Canvas; without frame: 1.003 × 0.812 (39½ × 32 in.) with frame 1.067 × 0.877 (42 × 34½ in.)**
National Gallery of Art, Washington, D.C.; Andrew W. Mellon Fund.
Large and small, curving and straight, the clearly defined shapes in this non-objective composition overlap in a shallow field to present a quite different mood from Hartley's peaceful Maine landscape.

Figure 2.11   Henri Matisse, *Beasts of the Sea.* **Date: dated 1950; Paper on canvas (collage); 2.955 × 1.540 (116⅜ × 60⅝ in.)**
National Gallery of Art, Washington, D.C.; Ailsa Mellon Bruce Fund.
Pieces of cut paper which the artist "drew with his scissors" and then pasted onto the canvas in a floating, flowing rhythmical arrangement show a great variety of shapes. The artist combined flat organic and geometric shapes that symbolize marine life in this carefully balanced composition. The two columns represent ocean depths with creatures from the ocean floor—coral, shellfish, eels, and snails—at the base, and fish shapes and spiky little black stylized predators near the top. Which shape shows an abstract seahorse?

triangular shape; the neck is a short, tapered rectangle with a round head attached. These individual shapes could all be lightly blocked in with a pencil or charcoal and then the details of feathers, beaks, eyes, and feet added to complete the sketch. Try this technique with a squirrel, a cluster of trees, the human figure, or any object. Being able to perceive the small shapes that make up the big shape and then blocking them in on your paper can enhance your drawing skills. The shapes you see depend, of course, on your **point of view,** that is, the angle from which you see an object. Although the top of a table may be in the shape of a rectangle, the shape you draw will depend upon where you are sitting while drawing it.

Form in art has to do with objects that have three dimensions—length, width, and depth. Generally, we speak of form in relation to sculpture, architecture, and the various craft areas, such as ceramics. Such artworks take up space and enclose space.

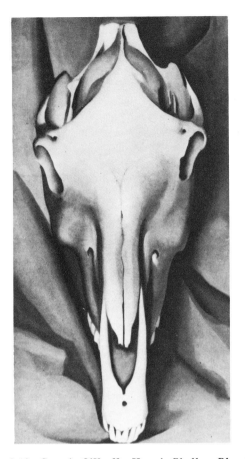

Figure 2.12   Georgia O'Keeffe, *Horse's Skull on Blue,* **1930. Oil on canvas, 30″ × 16″.**
The University Art Collections, Arizona State University, Tempe. Gift of Oliver B. James.
O'Keefe collected objects that she treasured and later used as subjects for her paintings—bleached bones, smooth stones, antlers, and shells. Rather than seeing death in a clean severe form of this horse's skull, she was fascinated with the positive shapes and negative spaces and painted it in a realistic manner.

Figure 2.13   Horse's skull.
Collection of the authors.

We also refer to form in two-dimensional artworks when an artist depicts solid objects on a flat surface. The French artist Paul Cézanne in the latter part of the nineteenth century rebelled against the emphasis on the surface quality of light striking objects that was the impassioned work of the Impressionists, and insisted instead that everything in nature could be seen as having basic forms: cylinders, cones, spheres, and cubes. His pioneering work in this field led to Picasso's and Braque's explorations with Cubism; hence Cézanne is called the "father of modern art."

When artists make sculptural forms, they work in either the **additive or subtractive** process. In the first, the form is built up by adding bits and pieces of clay, soft wax, or other pliable material. Oftentimes the final product is

cast in metal when it is finished. In subtractive works, the artist carves or takes away wood or stone from a large mass to form a figure or animal.

Both shapes and forms may be classified as being either **geometric or free-form. Geometric shapes** are two-dimensional and remind us of mathematics—circles, squares, triangles, and the variations and combinations, such as ovals, crescents, semicircles, rectangles, hexagons, and such. **Geometric forms** are three-dimensional and are reminiscent of cubes, cylinders, spheres, dodecahedrons, and such. Geometric shapes and forms are often used for decoration and make up more highly organized and structured artworks. They often seem less emotional than free forms and give the viewer the feeling of perfection and intellectualism.

Free-form shapes and forms are irregular, uneven, and unmeasured, and they remind us of those objects that we observe in nature. Many artists delight in the beauty of the natural forms of smooth, weathered driftwood, bleached bones, well-worn river rocks, and delicate seashells. They are stimulated to incorporate the characteristics of these natural forms in their own artworks. The

Figure 2.14 El Greco, *St. Martin and the Beggar*. (Dominikas Theotokapoulas) Date: 1597/1599; Canvas; 1935 × 1.030 (76⅛ × 40½ in.)
National Gallery of Art, Washington, D.C.; Widener Collection.
Elongated shapes of the horse, rider, and standing figure contribute to the intensely religious feeling of this artwork done in the Mannerist tradition.

British sculptor Henry Moore's studio was filled with a lifetime collection of such forms, and his massive works show evidences of the inspiration that they provided him. His *Reclining Figure* in the **Color Gallery** is an example of subtractive sculpture, having been carved from elmwood. Its curving forms and carefully designed positive

shapes and negative areas remind us of stones, or bring to mind rolling hills or mountain ranges.

Both Moore and O'Keeffe—one creating three-dimensional artworks and the other, two-dimensional—were very cognizant of another important facet of working with shapes and forms, that of relating them to the **negative spaces** within and around the **positive shapes.** The positive shapes and forms in a composition are the objects themselves, and the negative spaces around them are vitally important in contributing to the unity, variety, and balance of an artwork.

Children Use Shape and Form

When children are about four or five years old, they begin depicting symbols that stand for faces, figures, and objects in their environment. They rely heavily on geometric shapes rather than on realistic or free-form shapes. They often make a round shape and add an oval or triangle for a body, and perhaps two long rectangles for legs and two more for arms. A hand is often a circle with lines or loops symbolizing fingers. Houses are seen as squares and rectangles topped with a triangular roof and a square chimney, balanced precariously, perpendicular to the roofline. A tree is often seen in the very young child's artwork as a long rectangle topped with a circle. This is often referred to as a "lollipop tree," one the child may tend to repeat in a stereotyped manner if not motivated, as he matures, to remember his own specific experiences with trees and be assisted in making more detailed sensory observations.

The geometric shapes that very young children use in depicting symbols for figures and objects will not be adequate for their own critical eyes when they reach the age of eight or nine years and want the things they are drawing to "look right." At this time, children need motivational experiences, including discussions to help them remember, and opportunities to act out their experiences with trees, such as climbing a tree's branches, playing in a swing or tree house, observing a ladder against a tree in an orchard, picking fruit, seeing a bird or squirrel's nest, observing a tree bending and swaying in the wind, and catching a kite in its branches. They need to be directed in observing a tree's seasonal changes in color, in feeling its rough bark, and in seeing the shape of its trunk, branches, and mass of foliage, as well as the shape of the individual leaves.

An emphasis on careful observation of the different shapes of things seen in the environment can help children make the transition from drawing geometric symbols in their early childhood years to drawing more realistic free-form shapes as they reach the stage of realism. These they will find more satisfying and acceptable to their own increasingly critical eyes.

Producing Artworks

The Shapes of Fruits and Vegetables

The student will differentiate with cut-paper shapes the distinguishing and basic characteristics of the shapes of fruits and vegetables, making multiple cuts of several different ones to be arranged in an overlapping and pleasing arrangement.

1. Collect an assortment of fresh fruit and vegetables or photographs of them. Compare and constrast the different shapes. How would you describe the shape of a radish, a carrot, celery, pineapples, and green beans? How are the sizes alike or different? How is a green bean like a peapod? How are the shapes of pears and eggplants different? Compare an apple with a slice of watermelon. Describe the shape of broccoli. Discuss how the grocer arranges the different bins in the produce section of the market. Are some vegetables and fruit stacked, overlapping, in rows, in baskets?

2. Use an assortment of colored paper and cut out the shape of one vegetable or fruit. Then make multiple cuts of the shape by cutting three or four pieces of paper at once so you will have a number of items for your arrangement of fruit and vegetables. Think of how produce is arranged in the market.

3. Place your fruit and vegetable shapes on a piece of white or colored paper and let the shapes overlap and be clustered in a pleasing arrangement. Do the same with several other different fruits and vegetables. Make your composition fit your paper. Paste them down and then use a black marking pen to outline the separate shapes and make them distinct.

Combining Shapes for a Tagboard Print

The student will cut geometric and free-form shapes for a composition that will be pasted to a background and form the design for a relief print.

1. Make sketches or collect several photographs of Victorian houses, trucks, birds, landscapes, etc. Observe your selection closely to see all the different shapes that make up the whole.

2. Use tagboard and cut out the shapes you see. You may choose to simplify, distort, exaggerate, repeat, delete, and change the shapes to suit your purposes and intent.

3. Arrange the shapes on a piece of tagboard, about 6″ × 9″, letting some of them overlap. Paste them down securely. This is called your **printing plate.** Be sure the glue is dry before you print.

Student work: Tagboard print. Geometric shapes were cut out and glued to background before student made print.

4. Use black water-soluble printing ink and place a spoonful on a printing tray. Roll a printing **brayer** over it back and forth to cover the brayer evenly. Place your printing plate on a piece of newspaper. Then roll the brayer over your printing plate. The cut shapes will have a white "shadow" around them. This will accent the different shapes when you make your print.

5. Place your printing plate on a piece of white ditto paper, Fadeless, Astrobright, or Brighthue paper. These colored papers are less absorbent than colored construction paper and will produce a sharper printed image when using water-soluble printing ink.

6. Turn the paper plate and paper over and rub the backside of the paper with your fingers to insure an even printing. Then remove the paper from your printing plate and let it dry. You may make several prints by re-inking the plate each time.

Creating a Three-Dimensional Form: Modeling the Figure

The student can model a seated, kneeling, or reclining figure in the manner of the sculptor Henry Moore by beginning with a cylinder of clay.

1. Use a canvas mat to work on. This enables you to rotate your artwork as you progress to observe it from all its sides. It also helps keep the surface of the table clean. Use a piece of clay about the size of an orange. Form it into a cylinder that is about six or seven inches long and about one-and-a-half inches thick.

2. Use a tongue depressor and make a vertical cut at one end of the cylinder to form the legs of the figure. Squeeze the other end of the cylinder to form a neck and head.

3. Take another small piece of clay and roll a coil to make the arms. Cut it in half. Score the shoulders and the ends of the cylinders that will be attached for arms and then apply a little bit of slip. **Slip** is a creamy thin mixture of clay and water. Attach the arms to the body and use the end of the tongue depressor and your fingers to make a smoothly joined area.

4. You have created the basic figure and are now ready to bend the knees, elbows, waist, and neck into a seated, kneeling, or reclining position. Be sure to give consideration to the negative spaces.

5. Smooth the surface of the form or give it a textural quality. The emphasis in producing this artwork is on the form and not on details of the face or clothing.

Constructing Forms with Clay Slabs: Castles

The student will combine a variety of clay slabs to create an imaginary miniature castle (or other type of building).

1. Collect photographs of different kinds of castles and analyze them to distinguish and identify the different parts that make up the form. Find battlements, parapet walks, the bailey, buttresses, turrets, towers, drawbridges, etc. Then use your imagination to create a miniature castle (or a cathedral, temple, Indian pueblo, Victorian house, etc.).

2. Roll clay out on your canvas or vinyl mat with a rolling pin. Make a base for your construction, no larger than six inches in any direction. It may be geometric or free-form. It need not be level.

3. Use a potter's needle or a plastic knife and cut out slabs from rolled-out pieces of clay to make the walls, towers, and such. Try not to have any slabs

thinner than one-fourth inch. Score any parts to be joined, being sure to apply slip to the two surfaces. You may need to roll out a tiny coil of clay and apply it to the places where two pieces of clay have formed a right angle to insure that no cracks will appear when the piece is dry.

4. You may add roofs, but be sure to cut out windows or doors to allow air to escape when the finished castle is fired in the kiln. To make a cone-shaped roof, cut out a pie-shaped section from a circle of clay and form it into a cone.

5. Create textures by imprinting objects in the soft surface of the clay or by adding bits and pieces of clay or by dragging a tool over the surface.

6. Remember to keep looking at the form you are creating from all sides to insure a balanced and unified design.

7. When the clay castle dries, it is called **greenware.** Then fire it in a kiln. This is called the **bisque** stage. You may apply **ceramic glaze** to your castle and fire it again. Or you may choose to rinse your castle in water, apply white or colored tempera, and then wash the tempera off under running water. This creates a **stained** effect with the tempera remaining in the low areas and the color of the bisque in the higher areas. You may then brush on a clear coating of Joli glaze. Or you may choose to paint your castle with **acrylic paints.**

Creating a Three-Dimensional Form: Making Box Sculpture

The student will design a piece of additive sculpture by collecting small cardboard boxes, adhering them and decorating them in the manner of the artist Marisol (see *Women and Dog* in the **Color Gallery**). She imaginatively assembled a variety of materials—including wood, fabric, and plaster—to create boxy sculptures that made visual comments on contemporary life. Or make an abstract sculpture in the manner of sculptor David Smith (p. 4).

1. Collect a number of boxes of various sizes. You may work on a small scale with film boxes, cereal boxes, and such, or you may choose to work on a large scale and use corrugated cardboard cartons.

2. Stack and assemble them to create a figure or group of figures or an abstract arrangement. Attach them with masking tape.

3. Cover them with paper-toweling strips dipped in wheat paste mixture or liquid starch.

4. Let your sculpture dry. Then paint it and glue on bits of fabric, photographs, and patterned paper to complete your box sculpture.

Understanding Artworks

Learning about TEXTURE

We have all observed how curious very young children are. They learn through their senses, and they especially have a strong urge to explore and discover things in their world through their sense of touch. Adults often move those objects out of reach that might be breakable or that might cause injury to children, or admonish them, "Don't touch!"

But not only the very young find the impulse to touch natural objects irresistible. How many of us love to stroke the soft fur of a kitten or puppy? The silky, lustrous quality of satin against our skin feels better than the scratchy roughness of burlap. On the other hand, we learn through experience about the texture of sandpaper or cactus and usually prefer not to touch them. Through previous association, people sometimes find the texture of a toad or snakeskin repugnant.

The **tactile** quality of things appeals to our sense of touch, and this surface quality, whether we are describing natural objects or artworks, is referred to as **texture.** We use such words as rough, smooth, hard, soft, slick, bumpy, fluffy, etc., to refer to it.

Our senses respond to texture in artworks as well as in nature. The smooth surface of a piece of ceramics, the rich and wooly fibers used by weavers, or the polished sheen of a pewter bowl appeal to our tactile senses. Works of sculpture in museums are often so inviting to our sense of touch that they must have signs posted and even guards on duty to insure that museum visitors keep "hands off." Our senses are attracted to a smooth marble surface, the warm finish of polished wood, or the burnished surface of a bronze statue. But even though we aren't allowed to touch these surfaces, we know how they would feel because we remember having touched similar objects.

We like **variety** in texture, too, and we plan our clothing as well as our interior furnishings to have different surfaces. An architect will choose several textured building materials in designing a structure—perhaps glass, stone, and wood—to achieve a pleasing effect and create unity. Having too great a variety of textures creates a chaotic effect. We enjoy variety in the textures of the foods we eat; steak and potatoes in toothpastelike tubes were abandoned when astronauts complained about the sameness of texture.

Artists are aware of this tactile appeal and use texture to express a particular **emotion** or feeling, or to **enhance** their artwork in some way. They may want to use soft, fluffy textures to create a feeling of warmth, comfort, and welcome, knowing that hard, slick surfaces seem cool and less inviting. They may also choose to depict the character of a person by the use of texture, showing the rugged, wrinkled face of a sea captain or, as Renoir did, the porcelain-smooth skin of beautiful young girls and women.

Figure 2.15   George Catlin, *The White Cloud, Head Chief of the Iowas.* **Date: c 1845; Canvas; 0.705 × 0.578 (27¾ × 22¾ stretcher size).**
National Gallery of Art, Washington, D.C.; Paul Mellon Collection.
The spiky, sharp eagle quills in the headdress and the grizzly bear claws strung around White Cloud's neck accentuate the soft texture of the white, furry wolfskin that hangs from the chiefs shoulders. Catlin devoted his life to making realistic images of members of various tribes of Indians.

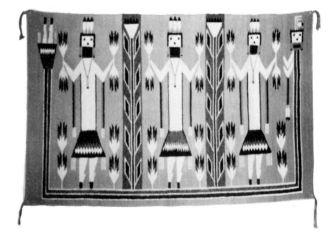

Figure 2.16   American Indian Rug.
The actual wooly texture of the fibers used to weave this decorative artwork contribute to it's appeal.

Figure 2.17 John Frederick Peto, *The Old Violin.* [Date: c 1890; Canvas; 0.772 × 0.581 (30⅜ × 22⅞ in.)] *National Gallery of Art, Washington, D.C.; Gift of Avalon Foundation.*
A passion for portraying objects exactly as the artist saw them resulted in a form of visual realism called *trompe l'oeil.* The eye is tricked into thinking actual objects are being viewed rather than paint on a canvas. The textural qualities of wood, both painted and varnished, metallic hinges and a key, and torn sheet music attract and fascinate our eyes.

In responding to artworks, as well as in creating artworks, we refer to two kinds of texture:

1. **Actual texture** is the real surface of something, one that could be felt with our eyes closed. We most often associate it with three-dimensional art—sculpture, architecture, and crafts. The appeal of Navajo weaving is not only in its symmetrical, stylized arrangement of shapes; its actual rough, woolen texture appeals to our sense of touch. A painting itself may also have actual texture if the artist applied the paint in a thick manner. Sometimes artists use palette knives as well as brushes and build up several layers of paint to create a real textural quality. This is referred to as the **impasto** technique. Van Gogh's thick, swirling brushstrokes were sometimes created by squeezing the paint directly from the tube onto his canvas.

Figure 2.18 Vincent van Gogh, *La Mousmé,* **1888.** Oil on canvas, 28⅞" × 22¾". *Chester Dale Collection, 1942. National Gallery of Art, Washington, D.C.*
The texture created by the artist's brushstrokes contribute to the strong appeal of the works of van Gogh. Often intent on getting a large amount of paint on his canvas, he would squeeze colors directly from the tube, sometimes using a palette knife or even his fingers to spread the paint and achieve the rich, textural impasto.

Occasionally this intense artist even painted with his fingers! Jackson Pollock created an actual textured surface on his artworks by dripping and flinging paint upon the canvas while it rested on the floor. It is, of course, easier to see this sort of actual texture when looking at an original painting rather than a reproduction. Other kinds of actual texture used in two-dimensional artworks may be found in collages, which may incorporate real pieces of burlap, string, and such.

2. **Visual texture (or simulated texture)** is created by the artist in two-dimensional artworks to give the **illusion** of real texture. A finely detailed texture in an artwork appears to be closer to us; blurred, indistinct textures appear to be farther away. Our eye is attracted to texture, so an artist may use an appealing texture or a richly textured area to focus our attention on a particular area in an artwork. Texture provides **visual interest** for our eyes and gives more life to a painting, drawing, or print. While such texture appeals to our tactile sense, we don't need to touch the surfaces represented to know how they feel, as we have

touched the real equivalents in nature. George Catlin worked closely from direct observation to achieve the fluffy texture of the fur of a white wolf around White Cloud's shoulders, as well as the spiky eagle-quill headdress on his portrait on the Head Chief of the Iowas. We tend to admire the technical skill of artists who are able to create a variety of textures in an extremely realistic manner.

A French term, **trompe l'oeil,** meaning to "deceive the eye," is used to describe the illusionistic skill in paintings that depicts the textures and colors of objects so realistically that one is "tricked" into thinking that the actual objects—perhaps a fly, bit of yarn, nails, pieces of wood, and such—are actually on the surface of the painting. Two nineteenth-century painters often associated with still lifes in the trompe l'oeil manner are William Harnett and John Frederick Peto.

We often use the terms "texture" and "pattern" together in describing an artwork since they are related but not the same thing. A pattern is usually made by repeating a line or shape many times and spacing it evenly over an area. The effect may give the illusion of texture; however, a pattern of repeated lines and shapes may exist as a pattern alone and not refer to a surface texture at all.

Children Use Texture

Children explore texture in a variety of ways. They may cut and paste a variety of papers and fabrics, yarn, and such to make an abstract collage design. Bits of textured materials may be used as "idea starters" for young children, since the concept appeals to their sense of touch. In this activity, children choose a scrap of textured material and ponder upon what it suggests to them or of what it reminds them. For instance, a scrap of sandpaper may remind them of the beach or a sandbox, and after they paste it onto a piece of paper, they can use crayons, pens, pencils, or oil pastels to make the rest of their picture. A bit of foil might be the beginning of a drawing about spaceships; a scrap of flat sponge, feather, or a bit of ribbon can trigger all sorts of inventive ideas and increase fluent responses simply due to the tactile imagery that they evoke.

Another avenue for children to pursue with texture is that of making a variety of crayon rubbings of different textures found in and around home and school. The found textures can then be cut and pasted into pictures and designs by the students.

Older children enjoy creating simulated textures in their drawings and paintings, and with instruction can develop a certain amount of skill in showing the visual surface qualities of their subjects in their artworks.

Producing Artworks

Creating Actual Texture in Relief Sculpture

The student will create a variety of **textures** on a clay slab to create a relief sculpture of a flat building, a figure, or an animal, either by **imprinting** it with a variety of objects repeatedly, by **dragging** an implement across it, or by **adding** bits and pieces of clay on top of it.

1. Decide on a theme for your textured slab project. You may wish to use visual reference materials such as sketches you have made of Victorian houses, or you may find pictures of them in reference books. You may wish to create a "Frontier Town" for a group project, with each student making a different storefront to make up an entire street. Or you may wish to make a figure or animal. Keep each clay slab about six or eight inches high. Make a paper pattern of the shape of your object.

2. Roll out a **slab** of wedged clay on a piece of canvas or on the fabric side of a piece of vinyl. Use a rolling pin, placing the chunk of clay between two thin sticks of wood to insure that the slab will be of an even thickness. The sticks of wood should be about ⅜ of an inch thick.

3. Place your paper pattern on the clay slab and cut it out with a needle cutter or a plastic knife. Remove excess clay.

4. Create a variety of textures on your house, storefront, figure, or animal by imprinting with different gadgets and tools. Try dragging a tool across the clay. Try adding tiny bits and pieces of clay to the surface. Be sure to brush some slip over the surface first. (Slip is made by mixing water with clay until it is creamy and thick.)

5. When you are finished, let your textured slab dry. The dried piece is called **greenware.** After it is fired in a **kiln,** it is called **bisque.** You may glaze it and fire it again. Or you may paint it with acrylics or tempera. Or you may dip it quickly in and out of water and apply thinned tempera, white or a color. Hold it under water and brush off excess paint, leaving a stained, "antique" effect. When it is dry, brush on Joli glaze.

Actual and Simulated Textures

The student will create a collage that includes **actual and simulated textures** by using several differently textured fabrics and papers, and oil pastels.

1. Collect a variety of textured materials, both fabric and paper, such as velvet, felt, corrugated paper, sandpaper, glossy paper, corduroy, velour, ribbon, sponges, etc.

2. Select a theme for your artwork, such as one of the following: Fishing in the river; Walking in the rain; Robots on parade; Dancers on the stage; Birds in a tree, etc. Decide upon several different textured materials and cut from them some of the objects you will include in your composition. These will serve as **actual textures** in your artwork. Try placing them on a piece of 9-by-12-inch background paper, white or colored, thinking of how you will relate them to the environment and other objects in the composition. Set them aside.

3. Place your background paper on several sheets of a newspaper. This will enable you to work more easily with oil pastels, since it provides a cushioned surface rather than the hard surface of the table. Use the oil pastels to create **simulated textures** for the other items in your composition. You may create a rough, scratchy texture or a smooth texture to represent the texture in nature. You may want to use a sharp tool and scratch some of the areas where you have applied a thick layer of oil pastels. Several colors of oil pastels may be blended by rubbing them with your fingertip. You may add black, white, or another color on top of a color.

4. When you have finished with the oil pastels, paste or glue in place the objects you made in Step 2.

Creating Actual Texture: Weaving

The student will use a variety of yarns of different textures to weave a small tapestry on a flat cardboard loom. Small chipboard looms (6½″ × 13″) with slits already cut across the top and bottom may be purchased from art supply catalogs. Or you may make your own loom by cutting a small rectangle from chipboard, mat board, or corrugated cardboard and then making short slits, about ¼ inch apart across the top and bottom. The appropriate needles and a variety of weaving yarns are also available from art supply catalogs.

1. To **warp** the loom, wrap the warping fiber around and around the loom through the slits at the top and bottom. Use pearl cotton, string, or other nonstretch fiber for warps. Tie the beginning of the warp to the end of the warp on the backside of the loom.

2. Select a variety of yarns that have different textures for your **wefts** (nubby, rough, smooth, shiny, fuzzy, etc.). Limit your selection of colors to achieve unity.

Try a monochromatic color scheme. Or try using two or three neutral colors and one or two brighter colors.

3. Cut a piece of yarn about a yard long and thread your needle. Needles should be blunt-pointed and have a large eye to enable the yarn to pass through. Begin weaving across the warp strings, going over and under in alternate rows. This process is called **tabby weaving.** To speed up the process, you may wish to use a **pickup stick** to lift the warps. To do this, use a flat stick such as a ruler and weave it across the warp fibers, going over and under each string. Then turn it on its side and it will lift alternate warps, enabling you to send your needle across the loom more rapidly. However, you will have to weave manually back across the loom, as the pickup stick only allows you to use it in one direction.

4. Pack your rows of wefts tightly and neatly together with a plastic comb, fork, or your fingers.

5. You may weave the weft in curves rather than making straight rows across the loom. You may weave only partway across, leaving a slit or interlocking the wefts. You may choose to include some natural found objects—bark, lichen, twigs, and such—in your weaving.

6. When you are finished, cut the warps in the middle on the backside of the loom and tie the first warp string to the one next to it, and so on across the top of the loom. Tie knots in the same manner at the bottom of your woven piece. On the backside of the tapestry, weave in the loose ends of the wefts with your needle, or you may use glue to secure them in place.

7. Cut lengths of yarn for fringes across the bottom. Double each one over, thread the loop into your needle, insert it through the bottom of the tapestry, and make a lark's head knot. Repeat across the bottom edge to add a decorative effect to your tapestry.

Understanding Artworks

Learning about SPACE

Raise your arms above your head. Stretch them out in front of you. Take two steps forward. You have moved in **three-dimensional space**—not "outer space" frequented by spaceships, astronauts, and little green people, but the kind that we deal with in looking at artworks and the kind that sometimes presents head-scratching problems for us in

Figure 2.19   Edward Hicks, *The Cornell Farm*. Dated 1848; Canvas; 0.933 × 1.244 (36¾ × 49 in.)
National Gallery of Art, Washington, D.C.; Gift of Edgar William and Bernice Chrysler Garbisch.
The Quaker preacher who painted this pastoral scene in 1848 had no formal art training, yet he knew how to create the illusion of great spatial depth by the use of diminishing sizes, elevated placement of objects, and lighter tones and fewer details in the background.

Figure 2.20   Frédéric Bazille, *Negro Girl with Peonies*. Date: dated 1870; Oil on canvas; 0.603 × 0.755 (23¾ × 29¾ in.)
National Gallery of Art, Washington, D.C.; Collection of Mr. and Mrs. Paul Mellon.
The light shining from the right on the girl's face and body gives her three-dimensional form and creates a highly realistic illusion of depth.

creating art, especially two-dimensional art. Natural objects—as well as those forms created by sculptors, architects, and craftspersons—all exist in space. They are defined by the space around and within them. Three-dimensional space is the emptiness or areas around, above, below, and between objects, as well as inside hollow objects.

Architecture is concerned with enclosing **actual space** in a functional and unified manner. Landscape architects and people involved in city planning design spaces where people will live, work, and play. They are skilled in making practical and beautiful use of environmental spaces, and this involves how they will combine forms, colors, and textures. **Sculpture** is also an art form that takes up actual space. It is freestanding and the viewer must move through the space and around it to view all its sides. **Relief sculpture** is somewhat different in that it projects outward from a flat surface and is viewed from only one point of view, the front side.

One kind of actual space that we deal with in responding to artworks and in creating our own is the **flat surface of the picture plane.** This is the space that is determined by the length and width of the canvas or paper upon which the artwork is created. Artists plan carefully to achieve a feeling of balance and unity throughout a composition, leaving no spaces that do not function in harmony with the rest of the artwork. Piet Mondrian, one of

whose compositions appears in the **Color Gallery,** had a keen desire to order space in his stark compositions. His later works are devoid of any aspect of volume or three-dimensional form. He extracted the essence on several themes, moving from relatively naturalistic drawing through vividly unnaturalistic and expressive color to a linear simplification that shows a two-dimensional space divided in perfect relationships of squares and rectangles painted with black, white, and the primary colors. He lived in Holland where the horizon is as flat and sharp as if drawn with a ruler, and the space in his work is similarly flat, sharp, and in perfect balance.

In learning about space, it is important that we understand the difference between, and the close relationship of, **positive shapes** and **negative spaces** in the two-dimensional space contained within the format of the picture plane. The figures or objects themselves are the positive shapes, while the empty spaces between and around them are called the negative spaces. In painting, we frequently refer to this as **figure-ground.** An artist creating a two-dimensional composition strives to intermingle and relate the positive shapes and negative spaces so as to achieve harmony. If we would place a piece of tracing paper over a composition such as Rubens's *Lion* and draw around all the negative spaces, we could readily see how, when we have finished, we have inadvertently drawn the positive shape of the animal.

Figure 2.21 Fernand Léger, *Starfish*, 1942.
Oil on canvas, 58 × 50 in.
Solomon R. Guggenheim Museum, New York. Fractional Gift of Evelyn Sharp to the Solomon R. Guggenheim Museum, 1977.
Photo: Robert E. Mates.
The artist maintains a shallow spatial depth by using overlapping shapes. The dark starfish is closest to us; figures in lighter tones peek from behind it. Sharply defined shapes fill the actual two-dimensional space of the picture plane in this abstract composition. Leger utilized the surface in such a manner to give the viewer a feeling of balance and harmony.

This knowledge about the relationship of positive shapes and negative spaces can help us draw an object that otherwise might seem perplexing and complicated. Hold a viewfinder very steadily in front of you. Keep one eye closed and focus on a section of a bare-branched tree. You will see branches and the trunk creating negative spaces between each other as they extend off the four sides of the viewfinder. Use a pencil and concentrate on drawing these negative spaces on a 9″ × 12″ piece of paper, drawing them exactly as you see them through your viewfinder. When you finish, you will have drawn the section of the tree. The positive and negative spaces fit together like the pieces of a jigsaw puzzle. Being able to concentrate your attention on negative spaces, rather than on drawing the more complicated positive shapes of what you are observing, can help you solve some drawing dilemmas.

Many sculptors include negative spaces within their artworks, planning carefully to strike a pleasing balance between positive and negative areas and create a variety of interesting open areas. The British sculptor Henry Moore (**Color Gallery**) in 1929 pierced his first opening through a solid mass in a piece of sculpture and began exploring the many ways negative spaces could be emphasized as a more integral part of three-dimensional artwork.

How to create the **illusion of actual space** and give a feeling of depth to a two-dimensional artwork has long been a challenge that has perplexed and fascinated artists. Objects in space have three dimensions—height, width, and depth—yet the flat surface of a piece of paper, a wall or ceiling, a wood panel, or a canvas has only two dimensions—height and width. During the Renaissance, artists began studying nature much more closely to determine just how this illusion could be accomplished more accurately and realistically. The German artist Albrecht Dürer contrived a gridded frame through which he could look at an object directly in front of him and then copy, and even foreshorten, what he was seeing on his drawing paper that had a similar grid. Other artists puzzled over the use of converging lines and vanishing points. Others found that shading a face or arm from light to dark would make it look rounded rather than flat. These early artists attempted and succeeded in using the picture plane or surface to make a painting that made viewers feel that they were looking through a window to the real world.

Let's try this window-to-the-world idea. Look out a window and locate which things are nearest to you. If you were making a painting of this scene, these objects would be said to be in the **foreground.** The part that is farthest away is the **background,** and the space in between is the **middle ground.** If you wanted to draw or paint this window scene, you would be creating the illusion of space on your paper. You would find it helpful to know about the ways that artists have discovered and employed to show the illusion of space that are listed below. Sometimes they choose to use only a few of these techniques. Sometimes they use all of them, depending on whether they wish to create a very realistic and representational view; whether they wish to express some emotion or feeling about what they see by exaggerating, omitting, or distorting the images; or whether they are more interested in the shapes, lines, and colors of what they see than they are in the actual depiction of what is in front of them.

1. **Overlapping** occurs when one opaque object covers part of a second object. The one in front seems closer to us. If there are only a few overlapped shapes in a composition, and if that is the only way the artist used to show depth, we say the composition has **shallow or flat space.**

2. **Size** plays a large part in depicting three-dimensional space on a flat surface. Picture two ballplayers on a field. One is several feet away from you. The other one is far away; you could raise your

**Figure 2.22   Maurice Utrillo, *Rue à Sannois*, circa 1911.
Oil on canvas, 21½ × 29¼ in.**
*Collection, Virginia Museum of Fine Arts. Collection of Mr.
and Mrs. Paul Mellon.*
Streets are frequently painted by Utrillo, always defining
three-dimensional depth with sharp use of one- or two-point
perspective. Here, the sides of the street converge at a
vanishing point on the eye level line. Buildings are smaller and
higher from the bottom of the picture as they recede into
space.

hand and block from your view his entire figure. In
a two-dimensional artwork, large objects in the
composition appear to be closer to us than small
objects. A very small object appears to be farther
away in the distance. This is often referred to as
diminishing sizes. If our eyes are led far back in the
picture plane, we say the composition has **deep
space.**

3. **Placement** of figures and objects also plays an
   important part in the illusion of creating space on a
   flat surface. Figures and objects that are placed on
   the ground and lowest in the picture plane appear

to be closer to the viewer than those placed higher
up. Those that are farthest away are highest from
the bottom of the picture, and they are found near
or on the eye-level line or horizon line. Now picture
what happens to this rule when we regard the sky,
which is, of course, above the horizon line. The
largest clouds (or balloons, helicopters, or birds) are
those that are closest to us, and they are at the top
of the picture. The most distant clouds (or other
objects) are smaller and are seen lower and toward
the horizon. Next time you drive down a highway,
notice the size and placement of the clouds that you
see through your windshield. Turn to the **Color**

Gallery and notice how the boats on the horizon line lead your eye back into the distance in Winslow Homer's *Breezing Up.* Shield these small boats with your hand and you will immediately see how the picture changes and no longer suggests deep space.

Try placing a sheet of clear acetate over an artwork such as Georges Seurat's *Sunday Afternoon on the Island of La Grande Jatte* in the **Color Gallery.** Use a water-soluble black marker to trace around the largest figure and then several smaller figures that are elevated from the bottom of the composition. Remove the acetate and observe size and placement of figures. Clean acetate with a damp paper towel. Try tracing over photographs of figures, trees, and such to see how smaller objects are higher up to show distance.

4. **Details, colors, and textures** of the figures and objects closest to the viewer are clearest and brightest, have the sharpest edges and the most visible details of texture. On the other hand, objects farther away lack textural detail, have hazy or blurred outlines, and indistinct patterns. Lighter, less brightly colored objects seem farther away. Can you remember being out in a hilly region and observing several layers of mountain ranges and noticing that the closest one to you was the darkest and that each succeeding one became a lighter blue? This is often called **atmospheric or aerial perspective.** "Sfumato" (meaning smoke) is defined as the effect created by a slight blurring of the edges of figures and objects in a painting to create a hazy effect. Notice the dramatic grandeur of aerial perspective that the artist Albert Bierstadt has achieved in his rendering of an American landscape in *The Rocky Mountains,* in the **Color Gallery.**

5. **Directional light** gives **modeled form** to three-dimensional objects. When a light shines on a figure or object, the side closest to the light is shown as lighter; the side away from the light is darker. Think of a white circle on a red background. It is flat. Now think of a white sphere. What makes it appear to have three-dimensional form? It is a gradual change from light to dark. This gradation of light to dark gives the illusion of depth and form. This was introduced during the Italian Renaissance by such masters as Leonardo and Raphael. (Turn to the **Color Gallery** for two examples: *Ginevra de'Benci* and *The Alba Madonna.*)

6. **Converging lines** lead our eye back into the deep space of the picture. The ways these lines seem to converge and where they seem to meet are somewhat rule-governed if an artist seeks to make a realistic or representational picture. But, as in all rules for creating artworks, we can distort,

exaggerate, omit, or change the rule to create a desired expressive effect. At any rate, perspective with converging lines simply means that you, the artist, establish an **eye-level line.** This is usually an imaginary horizontal line that you project in front of you, somewhat like a horizon line. As you start to draw, you notice all the vertical lines, such as the upright sides of a building, fence posts, legs of a table, etc. You will be drawing them straight up and down on the paper, parallel with the right and left sides of the paper. You will draw the corner of the building, the leg of the table, or the fence post that is closest to you first. But all the lines that are horizontally parallel to each other that move away from you in space will seem to converge and meet at a place on the eye-level line called a **vanishing point.** Different sets of parallel lines meet at different vanishing points. These vanishing points are often off the paper—that is, the eye-level line is extended beyond the sides of the paper. Notice how the artist Thomas Eakins has indicated precise perspective in his painting, *Max Schmitt in a Single Scull,* in the **Color Gallery.** He worked out his images mathematically, often using a brick and small models of boats in his studio to help him achieve precise perspective.

Try placing a sheet of tracing paper over a reproduction such as Utrillo's *Rue à Sannois,* or over a photograph of a street scene. With a ruler and pencil, trace over the converging lines, then remove the tracing paper and see how horizontal lines that are parallel to each other meet at a vanishing point on the eye-level line.

A special kind of perspective called **foreshortening** is seen in Edouard Manet's *The Dead Toreador* in the **Color Gallery.** While the term perspective refers to entire scenes, foreshortening applies to a single object within a scene. We see the figure of a bullfighter lying on the floor, below our eye level, and the artist has represented its long axis by contracting its lines so as to produce an illusion of projection or extension in space.

Artists in ancient Egypt weren't usually concerned with aspects of visual realism as presented by perspective. Medieval art took a somewhat similar position and placed theological over physical truth. One-point perspective was common in mid-fifteenth century artworks but was gradually replaced by two- and three-point perspectives. Systems of perspective were developed during the Renaissance both in Italy and in northern Europe, and artists since then have been free to use perspective in ways of their own choosing. Some twentieth-century painters argue that perspective is a deception and deny its use on a two-dimensional canvas.

In addition to knowing these perspective rules, we oftentimes use a **"sighting"** technique to help us draw objects in space. To do this, we hold a pencil in front of us, at arm's length, and with one eye closed, we measure the comparative lengths and widths of objects. We also use sighting to determine the angles of lines, using the vertical and horizontal directions of the pencil to determine the angle at which lines are converging. We then draw the angles we see on our paper, using the vertical and horizontal sides of the paper to guide us.

Children Use Space

Young children go through several stages in their explorations of space. Scribblers soon begin to identify heads in the tangled web of their circular scribbles and, with exaltation, add two eyes and a mouth and tell us, "This is me!" This usually occurs sometime during the third or fourth year of their life. Then one day they discover that they can add two long lines to a circular shape and make what for them is a satisfying figure, one which has often been referred to as the "head-feet" or "tadpole figure." At this time, they are content to fill the paper with variations of head- and hairpin-type people, letting them randomly float around on the picture plane with little or no relationship in space or even to one another. They like to give names to things they are depicting: "There is Mommy. There is my dog. There is my house," and so on.

Sometime during their fourth or fifth year, children begin to connect objects in space in their drawings, and they begin to tell and show us what they know about spatial relationships in their artworks with such themes as taking the dog for a walk or how a clown sits on a swing. More organization of objects and more relationships and connections of objects in space begin to occur.

When children are about six years old, they make a significant spatial discovery: they put several objects on a line that symbolizes the ground. This line is often referred to as the **baseline,** and it will be used repeatedly as children deal with the problem of telling about their experiences with things in the environment. The baseline represents the child's ability to relate objects to one another in space: placing them on a line that symbolizes the ground.

For the six-year-old, the sky is typically seen as a line or band across the top of the picture plane, with the space between the baseline and the sky thought of as "air." At this time in their development, they are drawing what they logically know about space, rather than what they are visually aware of perceiving.

Since the baseline concept of the six- and seven-year-old is based more on nonvisual and expressive uses of space rather than on realistic representations, it is important that their thinking be kept flexible and fluent. At this time, the adult can help to sharpen and strengthen their awareness of how objects exist in the three-dimensional world. If children are limited in their depictions of space to a rigid straight line drawn across the bottom of the paper to represent the ground and another line drawn across the top for the sky, they will be quite restricted in solving a number of spatial problems in their artwork. To encourage and stimulate their growth in regard to the nonvisual and expressive uses of space, the following themes or topics are suggested as motivations:

1. "We are climbing a mountain (or going skiing)." This calls for the baseline to be **bent** in a curve or placed on a diagonal. (Did you ever climb a mountain? Was the trail flat or steep? Did you get tired and out of breath as you climbed higher and higher? How tall were the trees? Did you see any rocks, rabbits, or squirrels? Was there a waterfall? How were you dressed? etc.)

2. "Horses at the racetrack; picking fruit in an orchard." This topic needs **several baselines** in order to have the space to place different objects on each one. (Did you ever pick apples or cherries in an orchard? Do you remember how the trees grew in long, straight rows? You could walk up and down between the rows of trees. Did you climb a ladder to pick the fruit, or could you reach it standing on the ground?)

3. "Under the sea; inside a mine; ants under the ground." An **elevated** baseline is required in order to show the subject matter that is below the surface, it being more important than what is actually on the surface. (If you could be a deep-sea diver and explore underneath the ocean, what do you think you would see? Probably a lot of different kinds of fish, shell creatures and plants. You could leave your boat on the surface of the water and descend downward and see all kinds of sea life. What shapes would they be? How would you be dressed?)

4. "We are playing checkers on the table. We are having a picnic at the beach." The child will frequently **mix plane and elevation;** that is, the top of the table and checkerboard (or picnic table) will be drawn as if we are looking down on them, while other objects will be drawn on eye level. (Taking a picnic to the beach is a lot of fun. We can spread a cloth on the sand or put it on a table and then put our food on it and sit around it to eat. What kind of food would you take on your picnic? Would you take your family and a friend or two? Would you set up near the water and maybe take along an umbrella to protect you from the hot sun? Would you play ball after you ate?) In some similar conceptualizations of space, the child mixes plane and elevation in such a manner that if the sides of the paper were folded upright, it would be quite

realistic three-dimensionally. For instance, the child may solve the spatial dilemma when drawing a topic such as "floating down the river on rafts," or "a parade on Main street," by mixing the plane and elevation and showing the river or street lying flat in the middle of the composition, with the objects on each side drawn perpendicular to it. If the sides of the paper are **folded up,** the buildings and trees on the sides of the river or street appear as they do in the natural world. (Did you ever go with your family on a raft and float down the river on a hot summer day? You wore a life jacket and your bathing suit, and you probably used a paddle to make the raft move. As you floated down the river, what did you see when you looked to the left of the raft? Houses, docks, trees? What was on the right side?)

When children reach the age of eight or nine years, they generally arrive at the **stage of realism.** They usually have a strong desire to make things look more representational. They tend to abandon the symbolic way of depicting space, as detailed in the aforementioned baseline deviations. They are looking for more realistic ways of solving the problems of depicting three-dimensional space on a flat surface. They can be assisted in their spatial explorations by instruction that incorporates the use of direct observation of people, animals, objects, and landscapes. They can begin to use viewfinders and L-frames to assist them in selecting and focusing on what they see. They can discover how sighting can help them measure the relative sizes of objects, as well as helping them perceive angles in the natural world and how they are related to the sides of the paper. In addition, instruction in the basic tenets of perspective and shading will help them achieve their goals of drawing in a more realistic way than when they were content with symbolic representations.

Producing Artworks

Three Figures in Space—Diminishing Size and Placement

The student will make an artwork that gives the illusion of depth and distance by placing three figures of diminishing sizes on different elevations of the picture plane.

1. Cut three figures of different sizes from colored paper. Choose one of the following for your theme or choose a similar type of figure: scarecrows, dancers, sailors, cowboys, robots, mermaids, mountain climbers, surfers, skiers, kings, queens, clowns, knights, farmers, etc. You can cut the different parts for the figures out separately and then paste each figure together. Make the largest

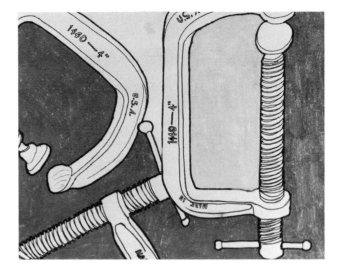

Negative spaces are accented when filled in with strong colors.

figure about five or six inches tall; make the medium-sized figure several inches shorter, and make the smallest figure about an inch high.

2. Arrange them on a piece of paper. Place the largest figure low on the paper. This is the foreground. Place the medium-sized figure a little farther up. This is the middle ground. Place the smallest figure farther up on the paper, in the background.

3. You may cut out the environmental details that you will need from other pieces of colored paper, or you may use oil pastels or crayons to complete your picture. If you do the latter, wait to paste your figures in place until you have finished using the oil pastels or crayons.

Accenting the Negative Spaces

The student will create and color the negative spaces by making three or more contour drawings of the same object, making the shapes overlap, touch each other, and extend off the edges of the paper.

1. Choose an object with a relatively simple shape, such as a pair of pliers, a scissors, a seashell, a large feather, etc. Use a 9-by-12-inch piece of colored paper, and with a black marking pen make a contour drawing of the object somewhat near the center of the paper.

2. Turn your paper around and make a second contour drawing of the same object, making the second drawing touch or overlap the first. Make part of it extend off the edge of the paper. You may use a different point of view and make each drawing a

different size. Repeat this another time or two, making sure that your drawing each time touches another drawing and extends off the paper. You are creating negative spaces.

3. Select three colors of oil pastels and color in the negative spaces, bearing down heavily to make the colors bright and velvety. Do NOT color in the positive shapes. They will be seen in the final product as the color of the paper itself.

Floating Boxes: Two-Point Perspective

The student will follow step-by-step guidelines for two-point perspective to draw a series of boxes that are viewed above, on, and below the eye-level line.

Look at photographs of streets and buildings. Or take a few pictures with your own camera. Select several and place a piece of tracing paper over each one, then use a pencil and ruler to draw the vertical lines and the converging lines that you see. This will help you understand how horizontal lines that are parallel to each other in nature appear to converge at the same point on the eye-level line when you draw them. Lines in nature that are vertical are vertical when we draw them. They should be drawn parallel to the sides of the paper. When you make a perspective drawing, the eye-level line is a horizontal line straight ahead of your eyes. If you are drawing objects that are below your eye level, you will see the tops of the objects. If you are drawing objects that are above your eye level, you will see the bottoms of the objects. Use a ruler or any straightedge and a pencil for this exercise. You will be drawing nine lines to complete each box. You will see three sides of the finished box.

1. Fold a piece of 12-by-18-inch white drawing paper horizontally, a little below the middle. The fold-line is the eye-level line. At either end of the line, mark "VP."

2. Somewhere above the eye-level line, draw a 1½ inch line vertically. This is the closest corner of a floating box that you will be drawing. It will be above the eye-level line.

3. Use your ruler and pencil and connect the bottom and top ends of this short line to the vanishing point on the left side of the paper.

4. Connect the top and bottom ends of this short line to the vanishing point on the right side of the paper.

5. Draw a vertical line on each side of the first vertical line. These two lines will be somewhere in between the long lines you drew toward the vanishing points. They will mark the two corners of your box that are the farthest away.

6. At the base of the vertical line that you just drew on the right, draw a line with your ruler connecting it with the vanishing point on the left.

7. At the base of the vertical line that you just drew on the left, draw a line with your ruler connecting it with the vanishing point on the right. This line will intersect the last line that you drew. You have completed drawing a box. Erase the lines that go beyond the box.

8. Draw some more floating boxes in the space above your eye-level line. Make one box overlap another. Draw a long, narrow box piercing a large box. Try adding windows, doors, wings, and words, using guidelines that are made by drawing the nearest vertical first and extending lines from its top and bottom to the vanishing points.

9. If you turn your paper upside down, your floating boxes will seem to be on the ground. You can draw boxes below eye level in a similar manner as just described.

10. To draw boxes on the eye-level line, make a vertical line that intersects the eye-level line. This is the corner of the box that is nearest you. Then draw lines from its top and bottom to the vanishing points. Then draw the two verticals to determine its dimensions. You won't see either the top or bottom of this box, just the two sides.

11. Now, using your knowledge of two-point perspective, observe a building and try making a drawing of it.

Drawing Negative Spaces

The student will look through a viewfinder and concentrate on drawing the negative spaces, one by one, rather than on drawing the more complicated positive shapes of the selected subject. The positive shapes and the negative spaces in a picture fit together like the pieces of a jigsaw puzzle, and by drawing the more easily perceived negative spaces, the student will inadvertently draw the object itself.

1. A viewfinder is like a small camera. Look through it and adjust it until the subject you see is so framed that parts of it are touching three or four sides of the viewfinder. This creates negative spaces for you to draw. Your drawing paper should be in proportion to the small rectangle cut in your viewfinder—8½″ × 11″.

2. For your subject matter, use a bicycle, an eggbeater, a piece of machinery, a potted plant, a portion of the trunk and branches of a tree, or some other object that has clearly defined parts. Sit near it and look through your viewfinder, keeping one

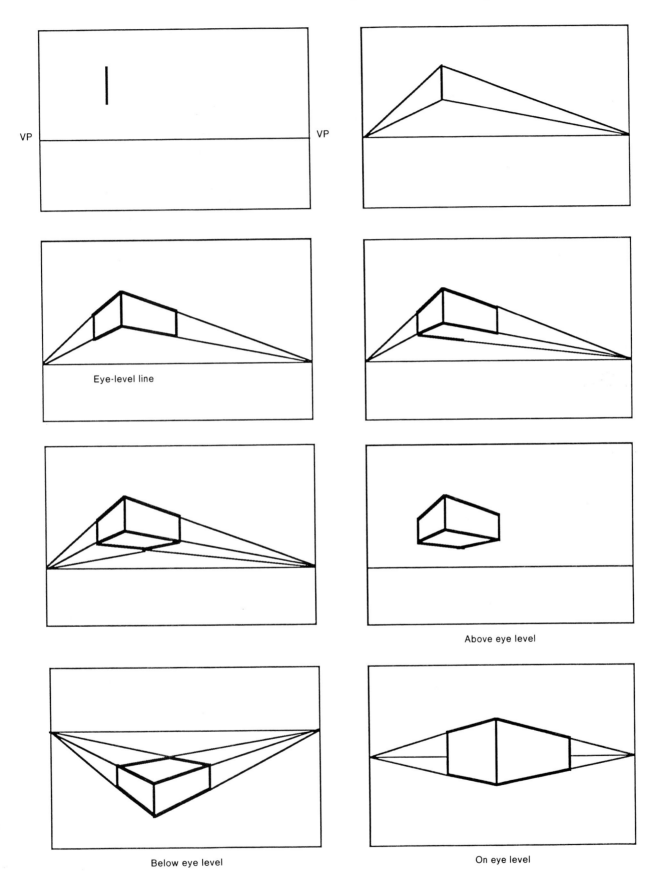

VP

VP

Eye-level line

Above eye level

Below eye level

On eye level

Floating boxes: Diagram for 2-point perspective.

Using the viewfinder. Hold viewfinder and frame portion of what you see through the opening.

Figure 2.23   Albrecht Dürer, *Melancholiah 1.*
Philadelphia Museum of Art.
Purchased: Lisa Norris Elkins Fund.
In this etching, Durer creates a variety of dark, medium, and light values by the skillful repetition of fine lines. Straight line hatching shows the flat planes of geometric forms; curving lines give the illusion of rounded forms.

eye closed. Hold the viewfinder steady and always at the same distance from your eye so that the negative areas do not shift and change.

3. Look through the viewfinder, concentrating on seeing each negative shape. Try not to see the object itself. Then make a contour drawing of each negative shape on your paper, making the lines touch the top of your paper in the same place that the line touches the top of the viewfinder. Draw all the negative spaces. When you draw all of them, you will have drawn the object.

4. Use a black marking pen or a brush and india ink and fill in the negative spaces, leaving the object itself white.

Understanding Artworks

Learning about VALUE

When we use the term value, we are referring to the element of lightness and darkness in an artwork. A color's value may show a range of **tints and shades,** that is, white has been mixed with a pure hue to make a **gradated scale** of tints, and black has been mixed with the same pure hue for a scale of shades. An artwork that uses only variations of one color has a **monochromatic** color scheme. Turn to the **Color Gallery** and notice the range of light and dark blues in *The Tragedy* by Pablo Picasso. Within an artwork that utilizes a number of colors, an artist may use a great variety of tints and shades of one hue. This is seen in Marc Chagall's *Green Violinist* in the **Color Gallery.** Notice the many tints and shades of purple in the man's coat.

But value is not always dependent on the lightness and darkness of a color. Many artworks that have no color at all depend on value to communicate their message. These include pen and ink, charcoal, and pencil drawings; etchings; block prints; and black-and-white photographs. A piece of sculpture may be all one color or black, white, or gray, and by its three-dimensional form catch the light in such a way as to present the viewer with quite a range of darks and lights. Directional light changes the carved-wood surface of Henry Moore's *Reclining Figure,* in the **Color Gallery,** so that we see accents of light areas contrasted with darker ones.

Artists use value in their artworks in several ways. In drawings, paintings, and prints, they can create the **illusion of the form of a natural object** by using changes in value. We refer to this technique as **shading or modeling.** It was first introduced and developed during the Renaissance, the arrangement of light and shadow being called

Figure 2.24   Rembrandt van Rijn, *Self-Portrait.* **Dated 1659;
Oil on canvas; 0.84 × 0.66 (33¼ × 26 in.)**
*National Gallery of Art, Washington, D.C.; Andrew W.
Mellon Collection.*
Deep sorrow and the troubling events in his life are reflected
in this expressive portrait that the artist made of himself a few
years before his death. Rembrandt understood the dramatic
effect of contrasting dark against light values in an artwork.
He was extremely skilled in blending colors to create shading
and show form.

chiaroscuro, an Italian word derived from "chiaro,"
meaning bright, and "oscuro," meaning dark. Works of
art before that time tended to be rather flat since they
lacked light and dark modeling to show three-dimensional
forms. Many works of art since then have continued to use
differences in value to show modeled form, but many artists show little change in value within shape, depicting
forms as flat areas of color.

The angular surfaces of buildings or boxes call for the
artist to make **sharp changes in value** from one side of the
structure to the next. This helps us to see the buildings or
boxes as being three-dimensional. On the other hand, the
curving, rounded surface of any cylindrical or spherical
form is handled differently. Think of an apple sitting on a
table. The side that is closest to the light source is the
lightest because that is where the rays of light hit it most

directly. The other side of the apple is the darkest, the
change being very gradual as it goes from light to dark.
Therefore, if we wish to depict the curving, rounded surface of any cylindrical or spherical form, we need to show
a **gradual change** in value.

Darker values of a color are seen as being closer to
us, while lighter tones are viewed as being farther away.
Notice how Albert Bierstadt in *The Rocky Mountains,* in
the **Color Gallery,** has used this device to create **near and
far.** Also note the emphasis he created with light tones
against dark in the middle ground where a waterfall
plummets into a lake.

There are four shading techniques to help us create
different values to show the illusion of three-dimensional
form on a flat surface:

1. **Hatching** is done by making a series of fine parallel
   lines of the same or different lengths. Hatching is
   best accomplished with pens or pencils since they
   make sharp, clean lines. The closer the lines are,
   the denser and darker the value will appear. When
   they are spaced farther apart, the effect is a lighter
   value. Hatching can also be accomplished in several
   printmaking techniques, such as woodcuts and
   etchings.

2. **Cross-hatching** is done by making two or more
   intersecting sets of parallel lines. The farther apart
   that both hatched and crosshatched lines are, the
   lighter the value; the closer together they are, the
   darker the value. It sometimes helps to squint your
   eyes to help you see the darks and lights and the
   differences and changes in value, and thus perceive
   the three-dimensional illusion of the form. To be
   effective in creating the illusion of form, both the
   hatched and crosshatched lines should follow the
   contours—that is, the curves of cylindrical or
   spherical objects. To show the flat surface of a
   building or box, the lines should run parallel to one
   edge of the surface.

3. **Stippling** is done by making many repeated dots
   with the tip of the drawing instrument. If the dots
   are very close together, even touching each other,
   they present a dark value; more widely spaced, a
   lighter value.

4. **Blending** consists of a gradual, smooth change from
   dark to light value. Lead pencils ranging in the
   degree of softness may be used and the blending
   accomplished with the fingertips or a small piece of
   tissue. Charcoal is frequently used in black-and-
   white studies to accomplish blended values. Chalk
   and pastels are easily rubbed and blended, also.
   And of course oil paints, watercolors, acrylics, and
   even crayons and oil pastels present blending
   possibilities.

Figure 2.26   Edward Hopper, *House by the Railroad,* **1925.**
Oil on canvas, 24″ × 29″.
Collection, Museum of Modern Art, New York. Given
anonymously.
Sharp edges in value define the architectural elements in this
old house as well as giving it expression and a lonely, even
mysterious, feeling of isolation. Shading is accomplished in flat
areas, with the cast shadow forming a triangular shape that
further demarcates the building's structure.

Figure 2.25   Emil Nolde, *The Prophet,* **1912.**
Woodcut: 126 × 88⅕ in.
National Gallery of Art. Washington: Rosenwald Collection.
In this woodcut, the artist shows a dramatic and harsh
contrast between the light and dark spaces. Mystery and mood
are intensely contained in this jagged and angular close-up
portrait.

Another use for the element of value, in addition to
showing the three-dimensional qualities of modeled forms,
has to do with the way that strong darks and lights can
elicit **expressive** responses by their strong **dramatic** qualities. The variety of contrasting dark and light areas often
grabs our attention and provokes intense feelings. Artists
can create **emphasis** by using the direction of light to show
a strong contrast of light and dark shadows. Notice the
effect that the seventeenth-century Dutch artist Jan Vermeer has created in *The Girl with a Red Hat* in the **Color
Gallery.** While most of the face, figure, and background
are in dark tones, the light enters from the right and creates a strong and compelling emphasis. Character is revealed in Rembrandt's portraits, whether they were of
himself or others, the effect he created usually relying

heavily on a light source from one direction that emphasized the person's character. Notice how the dark background accents the highlighted sadness of features in his
own *Self-Portrait*. Emil Nolde uses contrasting flat dark
and light areas in *The Prophet* to make a strong dramatic
statement.

Children Use Value

When children reach the realism stage, along about eight
or nine years of age, they begin to pay more attention to
wanting things to "look right"—that is, they want to represent people and objects in a more realistic manner. Direct
instruction in shading techniques, as well as in directed
observation of angular and rounded objects and how to
represent their dark and light areas, can assist them in
their art production. They can also observe how artists,
both painters and graphic artists, have succeeded in
showing three-dimensional form by the four shading techniques. Good examples of hatching/stippling techniques
can be found in newspaper and magazine illustration and
political cartoons. Reproductions of paintings and original
works of art seen in museums can help the child see how
blended paint can create the illusion of form on a flat surface.

Figure 2.27   Georgio De Chirico, *The Delights of the Poet,* 1913.
Oil, 27⅜ × 34 in.
Collection of Mr. and Mrs. Leonard C. Yaseen.
Strange and dreamlike, this haunting composition of a broad landscape with a bright light sharply defining the shadows makes a highly dramatic use of dark, medium, and light values.

Producing Artworks

Lights and Darks: A Monochromatic Design

The student will paint a monochromatic design that has concentric bands of one color that become either increasingly lighter or darker as they encircle the shape of an alphabet letter in the center of the paper.

1. Make a **value scale** of one color. Cut a 2-by-12-inch strip from a piece of white drawing paper and mark it by inches along its length. Start with white tempera and paint the first inch-wide strip across one end. Then mix a tiny bit of one color with white. Brush this **tint** next to the white on the long strip. Then add a bit more color to the white and paint another inch-wide strip next to the last one. Continue until you reach the middle of the strip, where you will paint a strip of the pure hue. Then add a tiny bit of black to the pure color to make a **shade** and paint it next to the pure hue. Continue adding a little bit more black to the blend until you have reached the end of the strip, where you will paint a section of pure black.

Value Scale

Use a pen or soft lead pencil for hatching, cross=hatching and stippling. Use a soft lead pencil for blending.

Light—————————————— to —————————————— Dark

[rectangle]

Hatching

[rectangle]

Cross-hatching

[rectangle]

Stippling

[rectangle]

Blending

Value scale.

2. Draw a letter of the alphabet with pencil or chalk in the center of a piece of white drawing paper, 12″ × 12″. Make the letter about six inches high and about an inch or so thick. Draw five or six concentric bands encircling the letter. They may vary in width, and as they reach the sides of the paper, they may form an incomplete or broken encirclement.

3. Pour a small amount of one color of tempera in an egg carton. Also, pour some white and some black paint in separate cups of the egg carton. Use the lid for a palette. Use a small or medium-sized flat-bristle brush. You will be using tints and shades of the color. Be sure to wipe your brush clean on a paper towel or damp sponge before you mix a new tone.

4. You may either paint the letter the pure color you have chosen or you may mix a tint or shade of the color. Then begin painting the bands around it, lightening or darkening each concentric band to make a gradated arrangement of colors around the alphabet letter. Fill the paper with paint.

Showing 3-D Form with Gradated Values

After completing four value scales, the student will use a variety of hatched, crosshatched, stippled, and blended values to shade a small contour drawing of a leafy twig or several overlapping feathers.

To make **value scales,** use a ruler and a soft lead pencil to draw four rectangles, 1″ × 6″ each. In the first rectangle, use hatching to show a gradation from light to dark. In the second rectangle, use cross-hatching to show such a gradation; in the third, use stippling, and in the fourth, use blending. Hold your pencil on its side rather than in the writing position when blending so you won't be making lines. Rub the surface with your fingertip or a bit of tissue to help you make a smooth blend from dark to light.

1. Place a large sheet of black paper close to you on the tabletop. Then place two or three overlapping turkey feathers (these may be ordered from art supply catalogs) or a leafy twig on the black paper. Close one eye and hold a viewfinder in front of you in such a way that part of the feathers or leaves extend off the four sides, thus creating negative spaces. Make a modified contour drawing, as explained on p. 25, on a piece of white paper, 5″ × 7″ in size. The parts of the leaves or feathers that touch the top of your viewfinder as you look through it will be the things that you draw on the top of the rectangle on your drawing paper; the things that touch the sides and bottom will be those that you draw on the sides and bottom of your paper. (Drawing the contours of the negative spaces rather than the shape of the object itself sometimes helps us draw the object.) Complete your composition by drawing inner and outer contour lines on the feathers or leaves.

2. You are now ready to shade your drawing using your new skills in creating gradated values. Endeavor to show the curving forms of the feathers or leaves by making a gradual change from light to dark. Use all four techniques—hatching, cross-hatching, blending, and stippling in your feather or leaf drawing. Squint your eyes at the feathers or leaves to see the darkest areas. Refer to your value scales to help you decide where to show the darkest parts, the lightest (or white areas), and the in-between values. You may need to use an eraser to keep the white areas clean. Plan on shading in the negative spaces rather than leaving them white.

Creating Value with Hatching

The student will form a figure such as a scarecrow by making small patches of different densities of hatches, placing them close together to create different gradations of dark and light values. No outlines will be used.

Student work: Showing 3-D form with hatching, cross-hatching, and stippling.

1. Use a ballpoint pen and make a variety of practice patches. Make some patches in which the lines are far apart; others where they are close together. Make crosshatched patches with several layers of lines going in several directions. Squint at them. Which patch is the darkest? lightest? Cut them out and arrange them in a progression from the lightest to darkest value.

2. Look at real scarecrows or remember ones you have seen. Or find photographs of them. Then imagine being a scarecrow, arms outstretched. Try standing in this position. Would you stand straight or be slightly tipped to one side? How would it feel to stand this way in the sun, wind, and rain day after day? Would you be lonely? Would birds be afraid of you? Or would you welcome a few friendly crows on your outstretched arms? Would you be wearing shabby clothes? What would be on your head? Would there be tall cornstalks near you? Perhaps a fence? a moon? sun? barn?

3. Now very lightly draw a tall vertical axis and a crossbar for outstretched arms on a piece of 8½-by-11-inch or 9-by-12-inch white paper. Begin making small patches of hatches and crosshatches of various densities to build the form for your figure. Vary the patches in size, shape, and value. They may overlap. Let the hatched patches suggest details of a tattered garment—hat, scarf, hair, eyes, etc. As hatching is added, the scarecrow grows. Do not use any outlines.

4. Make another hatched drawing. This time create a rocky landscape, a cluster of flowers, a group of trees, a mermaid, a magician, a witch, a sports figure, a dancer, etc.

Questions and Activities

1. To provide you with visual information for producing artworks, make a photo file by collecting photographs from magazines, calendars, and such. Look for specific categories: buildings, trees, flowers and plants, birds, fish, animals, insects, people at work, people at play, faces, machines, transportation, landscapes, seascapes, clouds and skies. Trim the photos and attach to tagboard or railroad board cut to 8½″ × 11″. Keep your collection in an expandable legal folder or in a notebook.

2. Select a theme or a particular subject matter and use it with several different techniques or media. Reflect on how the technique or medium affected your interpretation of the subject matter you used. Make a list of what art elements were used and the effects of each on the outcome.

3. Explain how emulating the style of an artist helps you understand the artist's technique and increases your own understanding of how you use specific aspects in your own work.

4. Investigate how the elements of art are used in teaching art to children by reviewing the lessons in the grade-level text and accompanying Teacher's Manual for one of these two student textbooks: *Art in Action* and *Discover Art* (see Resources, pp. 157–159). Select one element and follow its sequencing in grades one through six. Note how many different approaches and media are suggested and how the student skills become more sophisticated with each lesson.

5. Select a fine-art example from each of the elements of art described in the text. First emulate the style of the artist, then make an artwork of your own using the same style but with subject matter of your own choice. For instance, draw a house or bird using pen and ink in the manner that van Gogh used in making his drawing of cypresses, p. 23.

6. Make a small poster about color. Clip photographs from magazines, travel folders, calendars, and such that illustrate warm colors, cool colors, primary colors, analogous colors, complementary colors, neutrals, etc. Also include postcard reproductions of famous artworks that demonstrate some aspect of color.

7. Make small posters about each of the other art elements using photographs from the natural world and from the world of art. Label and use to teach students about line, shape/form, texture, value, and space.

Understanding the Principles of Art: Response and Production 3

If you have ever made a casserole or a cake, you measured, chopped, mixed, sauted, or baked according to some directions. First you read the list of the ingredients and then read more carefully as to how much of each one, whether you had to slice or sift, in what order to combine them, and how long it would take to bake the dish or dessert before it was ready to consume.

When we make an artwork, our "ingredients" are the *elements of art: color, line, shape and form, texture, value, and space.* Some individuals organize and make a careful plan for their artworks; others, such as naive or primitive artists and young children, tend to work more on an intuitive basis, achieving an aesthetic result almost unconsciously. Similarly, some cooks take "a pinch of this and a cup or so of that," while others read the recipe and measure each item very carefully!

Whichever way we work, intuitively or consciously, when we put an artwork together—whether it is a painting, a piece of sculpture, a building, or a magazine advertisement—we are planning, using, and controlling the **principles of art.** We can improve our own ventures in creating artworks by learning to recognize each principle. We can gain a richer understanding of the artworks of the great masters if we analyze how they handled the principles of art and achieved harmony in their artworks.

The principles of art are basic guidelines that are essential in producing certain effects upon someone who is looking at, and responding to, artwork. Whether we wish to understand an artwork or improve on our own art production, it is most helpful to be able to analyze it and use appropriate language in describing how the principles work. The principles of art are: **balance, emphasis, proportion, movement, rhythm, repetition and pattern, and variety and unity.**

Understanding Artworks

Learning about BALANCE

Balance, as seen in artworks, is more a **visual feeling of weight** rather than an actual quality of being heavy or light. Our eyes seem to seek things that "feel balanced." Have you ever walked into a room where a picture was hanging crooked and felt a compelling urge to walk over and set it straight? Have you ever made an arrangement of flowers and then stepped back to check your work and thought, "Somehow it doesn't feel balanced yet," and then added a few more zinnias to the left side? An artwork that gives us a feeling of imbalance creates an uneasy response. Something is "wrong." We might even be distracted from seeing the subject matter of a painting or the finely detailed textures that the artist has created. What causes this feeling of balance or imbalance?

We speak of two kinds of balance in artworks. The first is called **formal (or symmetrical)**, and the second is called **informal (or asymmetrical)**. In the first, there is either a real or an imaginary median line in the center of the composition. The parts and details, the shapes, colors, and lines on one side are an exact duplicate or mirror image of the other side. Think of a butterfly with its wings flattened as an example of formal balance. Our own bodies seen from the front show formal balance. Formal balance is the simplest kind of balance, and it usually produces less visual interest in a composition than does informal balance. Many pieces of traditional architecture appropriately show formal balance. Can you find any examples of formal balance in buildings in your community, perhaps public buildings such as courthouses, office buildings, museums, churches, and capitol buildings? Do they

Figure 3.1   Philadelphia Museum of Art.
A clear example of formal balance in architecture, this form of symmetry lends itself well to a feeling of dignity, stability, and enduring values.

Figure 3.2   Papercut.
Formal balance on a vertical axis is evident in this delicately cut design from Mexico. Paper is folded in half and then cut to create perfect symmetry before being mounted on bark paper.

elicit in you a feeling that the work or worship that goes on there is dignified, stable, and enduring? It is more difficult to find paintings and sculptures that show formal balance, perhaps because artists that make these artworks want to hold our attention longer by presenting our eyes with less predictable parts in their compositions. The monotony of perfect balance can be offset or relieved by a variation called **approximate symmetry.** Here, the artist arranges the objects on either side of the central axis in an almost formal manner with just enough variation to hold our attention.

We sometimes see another kind of formal balance in addition to approximate symmetry. This occurs when the lines, shapes, and colors radiate outward from a central point and form a circular design. This is called **radial balance,** and it is often used for decorative purposes in architecture, textile design, jewelry, stained glass, and other crafts. Radial design occurs in nature as well as in artworks. Nature has many examples of radial symmetry—the petals of a flower, the cross section of an orange. Can you think of others? If you were ever fascinated with the ever-changing designs seen in a kaleidoscope, marveled at the six-pointed symmetry of an enlarged photograph of a snowflake, or stood in awe as light streamed in through a stained-glass rose window in a cathedral, you will understand the basic concept of radial balance. The city of Paris was planned as a radial design. In Oriental art and religion, the **mandala** is a round design that symbolizes the universe. Some barns in Pennsylvania have large hex signs painted on them to bring good luck to the owners. They too are radial configurations.

Informal balance, on the other hand, gives us a comfortable visual feeling of weight even though both sides of the artwork are dissimilar. In this type of balance, the elements work to offset each other to make a harmonious whole. When artists use informal balance, they strive to achieve a comfortable, even casual, feeling by the way they arrange the elements. Though informal balance may seem to take less planning on the part of the artist, it can be very complicated and difficult to achieve. Can you describe how Picasso has achieved a comfortable feeling of balance in *Girl Before a Mirror* in the **Color Gallery?** Though the composition is divided in half by the post of the mirror frame, both halves are different and are connected by the arm reaching toward the reflection in the

Figure 3.3 Dome.
Frank Lloyd Wright combined metal and glass in the radial design of the dome for the Guggenheim Museum in New York.

Figure 3.5 Berthe Morisot, *The Artist's Sister at a Window.* Date 1869; Canvas; 0.548 × 0.463 (21⅝ × 18¼ in.) *National Gallery of Art, Washington, D.C. Ailsa Mellon Bruce Collection.*
A clear example of asymmetrical balance, this painting places a dark shape on the left with a similar one on the right and gives our eyes a feeling of comfortable weight. Try "erasing" any one shape in the composition to see how the informal balances change.

Figure 3.4 Henri Rousseau, *The Football Players, 1908.* Solomon R. Guggenheim Museum, New York/Photo: Robert E. Mates.
Rollicking ball players seem to dance politely and gracefully between nearly identical rows of trees in this carefully arranged composition. Would you call its balance formal, approximately formal, or informal?

mirror. What differences in size, shape, pattern, and line can you find on either side? What does the way the artist has achieved balance contribute to the mood of the artwork?

Let's think about how artists are able to arrange the elements of art in an informal way and still elicit a comfortable feeling of balance in the viewer. First, we know that a very bright color draws our eyes to it more so than does a low-intensity color. So an artist may achieve a feeling of balance by using a **small area of bright color to balance a larger area of a duller color.** We also need to remember that **warm colors appear heavier to our eyes than cool colors,** and so an artist would probably choose to use a lesser amount of red and orange than blue and green.

Second, a strong contrast in value between an object and its background has more visual weight than does an object that is closer in value to its background. A **dark**

value of a color seems heavier than a light value of a color, so if we were making a composition, we would probably tend to use less of a shade than a tint to achieve balance.

Third, our eyes are attracted to the more interesting textures in a composition, those that are rough or bumpy rather than those that are smooth and even; so we can balance a **small, rough-textured area with a large, smooth one.**

Fourth, shapes need to be so positioned in the two-dimensional space that large ones near the center or the dominant area of a composition are balanced by smaller objects placed farther away. **A large shape seems heavier than a small one,** so several small shapes may be needed to balance a large one. Notice in Seurat's *Sunday Afternoon on the Island of La Grande Jatte* in the **Color Gallery** how the two large figures on the far right provide balance for the groups of smaller figures on the left. Can you find other ways that the artist has shown informal balance in this pointillist artwork? In a similar manner, shapes that are **more complicated** may catch our eye first and appear heavier than those with simpler contours. Knowing this, we would probably choose to balance a large, simple shape with a small, complex one.

Turn to the **Color Gallery** and select several artworks to use with this chart. Analyze them to see how each artist achieved balance through one or more of the elements of art.

	Color	Line	Shape/ Form	Texture	Space	Value
Balance						

Producing Artworks

Formal Balance: Fold and Blot Designs

The student will use a fold-and-blot technique with paint and paper to create a formally balanced design based on visual observation of things in nature.

1. Fold a piece of white drawing paper in half. Unfold it. Use watercolors or tempera paint and apply some paint to the paper on one side of the fold. Quickly fold the paper along the crease, blotting the painted area onto the opposite side of the paper. Think of things you have seen that show formal balance and continue applying paint, folding and blotting. You may wish to paint a face or mask, butterfly, insect or spider, frog, reflections of trees in a lake, a full frontal figure, alligator, etc.

2. When the paint is dry, you may wish to use a black marking pen or a small brush and black ink to add flourishes and linear details.

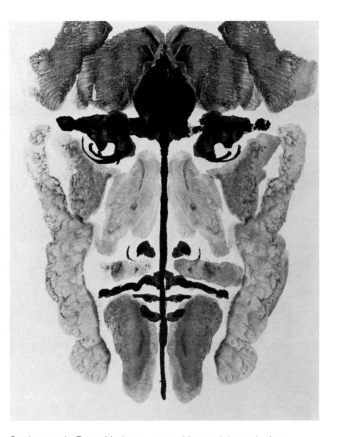

Student work: Formal balance created by applying paint in a controlled manner before folding and blotting.

Informal Balance: A Cut-Paper Mural

A group of students will work together to design and complete a cut-paper mural in which the figures, animals, and objects are arranged in a harmonious, unified, asymmetrical manner. Themes for cut-paper murals may be taken from literary sources, social studies, and sciences, as well as other areas of the curriculum.

1. Suggested theme is **"The Circus."** Books, videos, filmstrips, and posters about the circus should be used as motivational materials and for visual information about costumes, action poses, etc. A list of items to include is placed on the chalkboard, from which students will choose the items they wish to make from cut paper: clowns, thin person, fat person, trapeze artists, strong person, fire-eater, person shot from cannon, animals in cages, highwire act, bear act, tattooed person, contortionist, sword swallower, lion tamer with flaming hoop, balloon seller, popcorn and cotton candy seller, elephant act, seals balancing balls, circus wagon, ringmaster, band, etc. The scale should be decided upon; usually, agreeing that most objects will be about the size of one's hand establishes a good proportional relationship.

Figure 3.6 After studying the historical context, the symbolic content, and the way in which the American folk artist Edward Hicks achieved balance and dealt with space in his early nineteenth century painting of "The Peaceable Kingdom," students made their own version of the theme in cut and torn paper.

2. Students select from a variety of small, cut-up pieces of paper of various colors and surfaces. From these they will cut and assemble the different parts for their figures and animals. From folded paper, a symmetrical shape may be cut. From several thicknesses of paper, multiple cuts may be made for repeated shapes that may be needed. Students should endeavor to show the action, color, and excitement of the circus. Each student should also make one or more small head-and-shoulders of cut paper to be placed row on row for the audience.

3. A large piece of colored banner or butcher paper is prepared for the background. Upon it a large shape for the circus tent and the rings should be adhered with paste. The background paper should be placed flat on a tabletop for assembling the individual items.

4. As students finish their figures and animals, they may place them temporarily on the background until all of the items that the students are making are completed. Then by shifting, moving, and overlapping the objects, the students will arrive at a comfortable feeling of informal balance in the arrangement (e.g., a group of small dogs on one side could balance a large elephant on the other side). Give consideration to having one or more centers of interest, overlapping objects, and repeating shapes to create a feeling of movement, rhythm, and unity. Remember to place objects so that the viewer's eye is led around the composition.

Place all the head-and-shoulders closely together to represent the audience. Paste items securely in place and hang the mural on the wall.

Understanding Artworks

Learning about EMPHASIS

What catches your eye first when you look at Judith Leyster's *Self-Portrait?* Is your attention drawn to the pleasant oval face framed by the stiff white collar and coif that were popular in seventeenth-century Holland? Then do you see the delicate curve of her hand holding the brush that points to the canvas where we see the image she is painting of a happy musician? Perhaps the artist may have planned to emphasize her face in this manner and also make it a focal point by the rather dramatic lighting coming from the right side. Sometimes artists emphasize a subject or object in a definite and forceful way; sometimes they stress a focal point in a less direct manner. Which approach do you think Leyster used in this artwork?

Emphasis is the principle of art that directs and centers our attention on one significant part of an artwork. This **focal point** or **center of attention** is the one object or area that is **dominant** over the other objects and areas. There may be more than one emphasis, the secondary areas being subordinate to the main center of interest. Artists usually try to avoid having too many focal points in creating an artwork, as this tends to be very confusing. On the other hand, it isn't always necessary for an artwork to have a center of attention; for instance, fabrics, with their patterned motifs, present a repetitive, allover design that moves our eyes over the surface with no special place designated as the focal point.

Our eyes are normally drawn immediately to the center of a picture, so anything placed **near the center** will most likely be noticed first. However, most artists don't place their focal point in the exact middle of their artwork. This could tend to make for a boring composition, involving the static and less interesting qualities of formal balance. So most artworks create emphasis by **placing to the right or left of center** the object or area they wish to use as a focal point. Not only is the dark oval shape near the center in Monet's *Rouen Cathedral,* in the **Color Gallery,** but the triangular shape of the spire also directs our eyes to it. Cézanne, in *Le Château Noir,* in the **Color Gallery,** has not only placed the building in the center of his composition, but he has made it the lightest area and aimed the branches of several trees in its direction.

Figure 3.7   Frederic Remington, *The Apache.*
Rockwell Gallery, Corning, New York.
What do you see first in this scene from America's wild west?
The Indian sits astride his horse, resting his rifle on the
diagonal line of rock, a slanted line that moves toward the
covered wagon in the distance. The reins of the bridle are
draped over his arm, creating lines that move our eyes upward
to the Indian's face. He points his rifle directly at a covered
wagon. Even the lines of the cactus point to the unsuspecting
pioneers.

Figure 3.8   Hughie Lee-Smith, *Boy with a Tire.*
Detroit Institute of Arts, Michigan. Gift of Dr. S. B. Milton,
Dr. James A. Owen, Dr. B. F. Seabrooks, and Dr. A. E.
Thomas, Jr.
With his hand on a tire, the tall, isolated figure stares intently
at us and rivets our attention. The light area of concrete where
he stands is framed and defined by the fence on the left and
the dark shadow on the right. Notice how the sharp, pointed
shape of the shadow of a utility pole on the right points to the
secondary focal point, the unoccupied shabby building in the
background.

There are several other ways that artists use to create
emphasis. The **subject matter of the artwork itself** sometimes draws our attention automatically. We are naturally
drawn to works of art that have **figures and faces** in them
since we are human beings ourselves and we respond to
the images of other human beings. Infants learn very early
to focus their attention on the faces of the people around
them. The face is often the center of attention in an artwork since we are already accustomed to looking at someone's face during a conversation, and so we respond in the
same manner when we look at a portrait. The eyes especially rivet our attention, often claimed to be "mirrors of
the soul." The portraits by Vermeer and Leonardo in the
Color Gallery gaze directly at us. They hold our attention
in a compelling way, almost as if the personages they represent were looking at us from the centuries ago when they
were painted.

When faces are presented in an **unusual** way, our attention is especially drawn to them, since we are accustomed to a more natural visage. For instance, the human
face, even in a mask form, is normally seen as being symmetrical; therefore, when we see a Cubist portrait that
shows both frontal and side views of the face all at once,
such as Picasso's painting *Girl Before A Mirror* in the

Color Gallery, or when we look at one of the face-masks
of the Iroquois Indians with its twisted, lopsided features,
we almost do a double take. When we look at Marisol's
Women and Dog in the **Color Gallery,** we can't help but
be intrigued with the triple-faced images on two of the
figures. If the subject matter of an artwork is itself **surprising** and presents an **unusual combination** of factors, or
if it contains **shocking material,** such as blood and gore,
our attention is caught. Notice how the blood beneath the
bullfighter's shoulder in Manet's *The Dead Toreador,* in
the **Color Gallery,** directs our attention to his face and
thence to the rest of his prostrate form.

Another way that artists create emphasis is through
lighting. Just as theatrical directors throw a spotlight on
the stage to direct our attention, some artworks also use
this same device. In the seventeenth century, the Dutch
artist Vermeer was one of a number of artists who caught
our attention by having light from outside the composition
directed at their models. Notice how in his *Girl with a
Red Hat,* in the **Color Gallery,** he has emphasized the face
and hand of his subject with this sort of lighting effect.

Another way that artists use to direct our attention
to a focal point is through the use of **pointers.** Did you ever
notice someone standing on a street and looking up to the
sky? Did you then direct your gaze upward to see what

Figure 3.9   Philip Evergood, *Sunny Side of the Street.*
The Corcoran Gallery of Art. Museum Purchase, Anna E.
Clark Fund, 1951.
Converging lines of one-point perspective meet in the distance
to focus our attention on the busy activities of this city street.
Within the triangular shape they create, the white lines for
children's games on the concrete, the blind man's white cane,
the white figure on the right, and the white hockey sticks
provide focal points that create a lively, active scene.

Figure 3.10   Judith Leyster, *Self-portrait.* **Date: c 1635;**
Canvas; 0.723 × 0.653 (29⅜ × 25⅝ in.)
Gift of Mr. and Mrs. Robert Woods Bliss. National Gallery
of Art, Washington, D.C.
Her pleasant face, off to the left, gazes at us through the
centuries. Framed by her coif and bit of dark hair, we almost
wait for her to speak to us. The horizontal line of her
assuredly placed arm takes our eye to the diagonal of her
paintbrush and upward to the secondary emphasis, the figure
on the canvas that she is painting.

had caught his/her attention? The same thing occurs if
the eyes of a person in a picture are looking in a certain
direction; we feel compelled to look there also. When you
wish to direct someone's attention to something, do you
ever point your finger? Sometimes the subjects themselves are pointing at something or holding an object, perhaps a hockey stick or a sword, that directs our attention
to the center of interest. Sometimes the arrangement of
these pointers is very subtle; at other times, it is quite obvious, with the direction of the lines "framing" the focal
point.

The **converging lines** of perspective, as seen on a
winding road or city street, often encourage our eyes to
"take a walk" to a primary or secondary focal point. The
converging lines of radial configurations also may direct
our attention to the center of a circular arrangement.

If an object is all alone in a composition, placed apart
from other shapes, our eyes are drawn to the object that
is **isolated or set apart.**

Artists also create emphasis by using **contrast**—contrast of shape, color, line, value, or texture. Think how one
large rock stands out from a lot of pebbles. Think how one
person with black hair stands out in a room of red-haired
people. There are innumerable ways to create such contrast in an artwork.

Long used by artists as a basis for pictorial compositions, the **triangle**—with its base at the bottom of the
canvas and its apex directing us to the focal point—gives
emphasis to an important face or figure that becomes the
center of attention.

Figure 3.11 Mary Cassatt, *The Boating Party*. [Date: 1893/ 1894; Canvas; 0.902 × 1.171 (35½ × 46⅛ in.)]
National Gallery of Art, Washington, D.C.; Chester Dale Collection.
The artist carefully created a focal point in this painting by using the massive curving lines of the boat to sweep our eyes upward to the woman and the child she is holding. The triangular bit of sail on the left is tied to the boat by a rope that points to her sleeve. The oar in the gentleman's hand also directs our eye to them. The dark, clearly defined shapes of the water and the man tend to contrast and frame the lighter colored shapes of the woman and child.

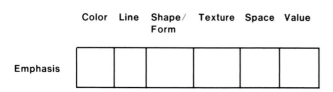

	Color	Line	Shape/ Form	Texture	Space	Value
Emphasis						

Turn to the **Color Gallery** and select several artworks to use with this chart. Analyze them to see how each artist achieved emphasis through one or more of the elements of art.

Producing Artworks

Creating a Center of Interest: A Watercolor Landscape

The student will create a pleasing composition either by (1) using L-frames and a colored photograph of a landscape, (2) using a viewfinder and an actual landscape, or (3) projecting a slide of a landscape on a screen and using a viewfinder, selecting a portion that clearly has a focal point. The student will make a contour drawing of the main lines in the selected portion and then apply watercolor washes.

1. Use L-frames and move them over the surface of a landscape photograph until you focus upon a small portion of the scene. (Or use a viewfinder to frame a portion of an actual landscape or one seen on a projected colored slide.) You may choose either a vertical or horizontal format. Frame your composition in such a way that there is a definite focal point, the place that is the center of attention and is dominant over the other parts of the composition.

2. Use a small-tipped black pen and a piece of 9-by-12-inch white watercolor paper or heavy white drawing paper and make a contour drawing of the part you have selected. (If you have a drawing board, you may want to soak the paper first and tape it down with gummed tape around all four sides. Let it dry to stretch it tightly before painting on it.)

3. First put a few drops of water on each color in the watercolor tray to soften the pigments. Look for the dark and light areas in the section of the photograph or scene so that you can paint light and dark areas on your paper. Apply watercolor washes on your contour drawing in a loose, free manner. Paint the large background areas first. When the paper dries, details such as fence posts, windows, tree branches, etc., may be added with a smaller brush. Use soft sable brushes, round and flat. When working with watercolors, it is best to work for a fresh, clean, spontaneous effect, leaving some white paper showing to create contrast and sparkle. Be sure to include the following watercolor techniques:

Wet on wet: The edges of objects done in this wet-on-wet technique will look soft and blurred. It is recommended for backgrounds, skies, and water. First cover an area of your paper with clean water, back and front, to make it stick to the tabletop. Place a little water in the lid of your watercolor box and add pigment to it to make a wash. A lighter color requires more water; darker washes need more pigment. Then apply the wash with your brush onto the wet paper with smooth strokes. You may flow another color in while it is wet, but try not to scrub and overwork the colors. To make a gradated wash, going from dark to light, keep adding more water as you work downward on the paper. While it is still wet, you may blot the paper with a sponge or a wad of paper towel for a special effect. While the paper is still wet, you may sprinkle it with a bit of salt to create tiny, dark specks of color.

Wet on dry: The edges of objects done in this technique will look clear and precise. Washes are applied on dry paper with a wet brush. Mix your washes in the lid of your watercolor box and apply them to the paper. It is

Student work: Watercolor landscape created by applying washes over contour pen drawing.

recommended that you apply light colors first and let them dry before placing darker layers on top. Do not scrub and brush back and forth or the colors become muddy and overworked.

Showing Emphasis: A Washaway Painting

The student will use tempera and india ink to design a composition, using a theme of his/her choice that places the subject matter either to the right or left of center, that uses pointers to direct the viewer's attention to the dominant object, or that uses contrast to make one object stand out from the rest. After washing off a final application of ink, the overall effect will be that of having created a focal point.

1. With a pencil make a simple line drawing on watercolor paper of your subject, using a photo (or actual model or object) as a visual resource. Simplify, distort, exaggerate, omit, enhance, combine. Try to make enclosed shapes.

2. Draw over your pencil lines with a black marking pen.

3. Mix tints and blends from a variety of different colors of tempera and apply them to your composition. In mixing tints, be sure to add the color to the white paint rather than adding white to the color. Just before you apply the paint to one of the shapes in the drawing, mix in a few drops of white glue. Try not to paint over the black pen lines. You may let a layer of paint dry and then apply a second layer of color in some areas if you wish. Any areas of white paper left exposed will be black in your finished composition.

Figure 3.12 Elisabeth Vigée-Lebrun, *Portrait of a Lady.* Dated 1789; Wood; 1.07 × 0.83 (42⅛ × 32¾ in.) *National Gallery of Art, Washington, D.C. Samuel H. Kress Collection.*
Realistic proportions in both figure and face were used by this 17th-century artist to show the subject to best advantage.

4. Apply india ink with a brush over the entire surface. Let it dry thoroughly.

5. Place the paper on a cookie sheet or other flat surface and hold it under running water. Rub gently to remove the black ink.

6. Let the paper dry. Press it with a warm iron on the backside before matting or mounting.

Learning about PROPORTION

Proportion has to do with **relationships.** It can be concerned with the relationship of one part to the whole or of one part to another part. Have you ever used the term "out of proportion" or commented on the lines of a car as having "good proportions?" Proportion in an artwork may take into account the sizes and amounts of colors, shapes, textures, and lines.

Figure 3.13   Jacques-Louis David, *The Oath of the Horatii.*
The Louvre, Paris.
This austere history painting is a masterpiece of the
Neoclassicist (renewed classicism) movement, and the artist
has been called the "father of propaganda art." It tells a story
of self-sacrifice for a higher good. David looked for early and
less sophisticated examples in Roman art and architecture and
shows his preference for "noble simplicity and quiet grandeur"
through the depiction of realistic and accurate relationships
and proportions in both figures and architecture.

In the days of ancient Greece, when people were
striving for the perfect body, the perfect mind, and perfect
artworks, they began seeking an ideal for harmony and
beauty that could be applied to their architecture and
sculpture. They wanted a rule that would establish a
mathematical ratio of comparisons of sizes that could be
used to insure the uniformly perfect results that they desired. Pythagoras, in the sixth century B.C., found that he
could apply mathematical equations to both geometric
shapes and music. Then in the third century B.C., Euclid
found that he could divide a line in two parts so that the
smaller line is to the larger as the larger is to the sum of
the two, a ratio of 1 to 1.6. This ratio is called the **Golden
Section,** and when the ancient Greeks used it, they felt

they had found the perfect proportion for sculpture and
architecture. Centuries later, artists in the Renaissance
rediscovered this proportion and began consciously using
it as the basis for their compositions. In the succeeding
years, some artists continued to use it, some consciously
and others unconsciously, because it "looked right." But
of course the Golden Section's ratio is not the only arrangement of parts that presents us with harmonious relationships. Most artists do not believe that there is only
one rule for "correct" proportions.

We speak of **realistic proportions** when we see in an
artwork the same relationships of parts that we see in a
person, a place, or a thing. One of the best devices to help
us perceive realistic proportions is called "sighting." This

Figure 3.14 Amedeo Modigliani, 1884–1920, *Head of a Woman*. 1910/11
National Gallery of Art, Washington, D.C.; Chester Dale Collection.
Inspired by African masks and sculptures, this artist boldly distorted the shapes and proportions on this sculptured head.

Figure 3.15 African Mask.
The Metropolitan Museum of Art, The Michael C. Rockefeller Memorial Collection, Bequest of Nelson A. Rockefeller, 1979.
This example of tribal art, with its unrealistic and distorted placement of the features and decorative linear patterns, is an emphatic presence.

is a technique that can be easily learned and that can be vitally helpful when we draw. By holding a pencil at arm's length with one eye closed, we can measure the relative proportions of whatever it is before us that we wish to draw. Try observing a chair from a distance of ten or twelve feet. Hold a pencil vertically as described and use your thumb to measure the overall height of the chair. Now measure the height of one of the chair's legs. You can use these relative measurements when you draw the chair.

But of course, artists don't always choose to use such realistic proportions. When they **exaggerate, distort, or deviate** from what we expect as normal proportions, the effect can be powerfully **expressive,** or it can be quite **decorative.** Moods and feelings are more readily shown through elongated faces, and grace and movement through extremely curving or spiraling forms.

The art of young children often has emotional proportions that have to do with the intensity of the emotional or physical experience the child has undergone. For example, a child will draw a huge foot to demonstrate how it felt when he/she stubbed a toe. A child may draw a sister or brother disproportionally large if that sibling is bossy and dominant over her. This is similar to the manner in which the ancient Egyptians painted the pharoah much larger than the less important servants. Later, when children reach the stage of realism, which occurs about the age of eight or nine, they want things to "look right," and they need to be assisted in observing and in using realistic proportions.

Whether we choose to use realistic proportions or whether we want to achieve a special effect by exaggerating and distorting, we need to know what the normal

	Color	Line	Shape/ Form	Texture	Space	Value
Proportion						

Turn to the **Color Gallery** and select several artworks to use with this chart. Analyze them to see how each artist dealt with proportion through one or more of the elements of art.

Producing Artworks

Proportions of the Figure: Crayon Rubbings

The student will cut sixteen rectangular pieces of paper that approximate the relationships of the different body parts; then by arranging them on a paper, the student will create a figure-in-action and make a crayon rubbing.

1. Cut from a piece of lightweight tagboard or a piece of construction paper an oval about one inch high and place it on a piece of lightweight white paper (ditto or typing paper). Then cut a strip that is about twice as wide as the head. From this cut the torso in two parts: the upper torso is about 1½ heads high and the lower torso is about 1 head high. (If you wish to make a profile figure, cut the torso in half vertically.) Place the two pieces beneath the oval shape of the head. Try letting the torso bend to one side at the waist to achieve a feeling of gesture and movement.

2. Now let your own arms drop to your side and feel where your elbow touches your body. The upper arms are about the same length as the upper torso. So cut another strip, quite a bit narrower than the strip you cut for the torso, and cut two pieces from it that are the same length as the upper torso. Place them on the shoulder. Cut two pieces for the lower arms that are the same length as the upper arms and place them at the elbow joint. You can overlap these different pieces.

3. The thighs are also about 1½ heads high but are thicker than the upper arms, so cut another strip of paper and make the upper legs. The calves are thinner but are about the same length as the thighs. A narrower strip will serve for the hands and feet. Try measuring your hand in relation to your head and you will find it is the same length as the face from chin to hairline. Your foot is a head high. Cut a small piece for the neck of your figure, and you will have a sixteen-piece figure that can be bent at the joints and made to perform almost any action.

Figure 3.16 Donald Herberholz, *Pregnant Woman.* Collection of the authors.
How would the feeling and mood of this piece of bronze sculpture be altered had the artist made the head in more realistic proportions? Why do you think he chose to do it this way?

proportions of the human figure are since so much of the art in the world deals with depicting the human form and so much of what students do is related to the human figure.

The proportion of the average adult is about 7½ heads high. Children, of course, and especially infants, have larger heads in relationship to their bodies than adults. A child is about 5 or 6 heads tall, and an infant is 3 heads long. In drawing the human figure, we can establish the height of a figure's head and have a unit of measurement to complete the rest of the figure.

Student work: Crayon rubbing of a figure in action utilizes cut shapes for different parts of the body.

4. When you are satisfied with the proportions of your figure and with its action pose, use a tiny amount of paste or glue and attach the sixteen-piece figure to the white paper background. (Large blobs of paste or glue will show through later on the crayon rubbing and be a distracting element.) Then place the paper on a thick pad of newspapers, and place another piece of lightweight paper on top of it. (Avoid making a crayon rubbing on the hard surface of a tabletop.) Use the side of a thick black crayon with the paper removed and make a crayon rubbing. (To remove the paper from crayons quickly, soak them for awhile in warm water.) Hold the crayon on its side and make a number of short, firm strokes to bring out the sharply cut edges of the figure. Make its silhouette stand out from the background.

5. Practice with several more pieces of paper until you are able to make a crisp rubbing that has a strong contrast of dark and light. You might like to try moving the paper over a bit and making a second

and then a third rubbing on the same paper. This gives the feeling of motion. You might like to try brushing a watercolor wash or a food-coloring solution over the figure or the background. You might also want to use a larger paper and combine your figure with those of several of your friends. For such a group project, place a length of white butcher paper on a table and have students bring their cut-paper figures to it and make a composite rubbing of figures in action.

6. To make a clothed and detailed figure, place a sheet of lightweight paper over your crayon rubbing and hold them both on a window so you can see through the top paper. Then draw your figure, adding clothing, facial details, and environment. You may use crayons, felt pens, oil pastels, pencils, etc.

Proportions of the Face: Crayon Rubbings

The student will experience the actual proportions of the face and then make a crayon rubbing of a portrait.

As preparation, stand very still in front of a mirror and close one eye. Draw around the contour of your head on the mirror with a marking pen or crayon, starting at the top of the head. Then make a line across the center where you see your eyes on the mirror. Now step back. The eyeline is in the middle of your head. Step back to the mirror and position your head back in the oval shape that you drew. Mark the tip of your nose and then make a line between your lips. You will have divided the bottom half of your face approximately in thirds.

To further experience the relationship and placement of the facial features, place your thumb on the bridge of your nose and stretch your third finger up to the very top of your head. Hold your hand in this caliper-like position and measure from the bridge of your nose to your chin. Once again, you will perceive that your eyes are halfway down from the top of your head. You might try measuring a photograph of a face in a magazine or in a realistic portrait by a great master.

Other facial proportions that are important are these: Use your fingers as calipers again and measure the width of one eye. Then measure the distance between your eyes. You'll find it to be the same width as the eye. Place your finger directly below the center of one eye and move it downward. You'll find the corner of your mouth directly below the center of your eye. Now place a thumb and forefinger on the top and bottom of your nose and move it to one side. You'll find your ears are about the length of your nose and are level with it. Your neck is not as wide as your head, and it extends downward from the side of your ears that is closer to your head.

Student work: Crayon rubbing of a portrait shows student's understanding of realistic sizes and placement of facial features.

1. To make a crayon rubbing of the front view of a realistic portrait, fold a 9-by-12-inch piece of tag or construction paper in half and draw a half-oval shape about seven inches high on the folded side. Cut it out and unfold it, and then fold it in half horizontally. The larger end of the oval will be the top of the head and the lower, the chin. Cut a neck and shoulders separately and place the head on the neck, either straight or tipped to one side. Place them both on a lightweight piece of typing or ditto paper. Now look in a mirror or at a friend's face and cut out two pieces of paper in the shape of the eye. Be sure to observe how the entire round circle of the iris is not seen because the lid covers a portion of it. Keep looking in the mirror or at a friend's face and cut out shapes for the eyebrows, nose, lips, and ears. Cut out some shapes or perhaps some fringed strips for hair. Remember that the tip of the nose and the line between the lips divide the lower half of the face in thirds. Let the cut shapes overlap and paste them in place with a minimal

amount of paste. Proceed to make a crayon rubbing as described for the sixteen-piece figure. A group portrait of an entire class of students may be made by arranging the cut-paper portraits beneath a long strip of butcher paper and making the crayon rubbings on it.

2. You may wish to apply a light food-coloring or watercolor wash over all, or parts of, your finished rubbing.

Understanding Artworks

Learning about MOVEMENT

With no movement, there is no life. Each tiny organism is in motion. The heart pumps in a regular beat and keeps us alive. Thanks to stop-frame photography, we can see the rosebud open to a full blossom in a few seconds or the butterfly emerge from the cocoon. Our eyes are attracted to moving things: the infant gazes attentively at the fluttering mobile suspended above its bed; we follow the antics of a frolicsome kitten. The beauty of a vapor trail streaking across the sky in the wake of a speeding plane compels our eyes to follow its moving line. We watch with delight the graceful and rhythmic movements of a ballet dancer.

The first artworks that we know about are those of the cave painters. These dynamic depictions show the motion of deer, horses, and bison running. It seems that throughout the history of art, artists have endeavored to catch and simulate motion and create the **illusion of movement** in their artworks. This has not always been easy. To be absolutely sure that you are drawing the legs of a galloping horse realistically, you would need to freeze or arrest the horse in one split second of its galloping movement, because the motion is quicker than our eyes can follow. In 1878, which was some years before motion picture cameras could be used to show a whole sequence of multiple images and thus stop action in a single frame, a California governor named Leland Stanford made a bet with a friend for $25,000 that a galloping horse at times has all four hoofs off the ground. He hired a photographer named Eadweard Muybridge, who set up twelve still cameras, each one connected to a thread that was stretched across the racetrack. As the horse ran down the racecourse, the threads clicked the shutters on the cameras and enabled Stanford to win his bet. While cameras today with their high speed lenses can clearly show split-second arrested motion, photographers sometimes deliberately move the camera to make details indistinct to enhance the feeling of great speed and energy. Perhaps you have seen other pieces of art whose theme was athletes or racing cars and whose streaking blurs conveyed a vibrant sense of the illusion of movement.

Figure 3.17 Marcel Duchamp, *Nude Descending a Staircase.* *Philadelphia Museum of Art, Pennsylvania. Louise and Walter Arensberg Collection.*
The cinema was in its infancy when Duchamp discarded completely the naturalistic appearance of a figure, keeping only the abstract lines of some twenty different static positions in showing the successive action of descending. This artwork was the hit of the Armory Show and was interpreted as Futurism by thousands of Americans.

The **Futurists** were a group of Italian artists led by Umberto Boccioni that, beginning in 1909, were obsessed with speed and the sensation of motion itself. Boccioni endeavored to show that living things go through constant change and growth. He liked to show everything happening at once. To do this he created paintings and sculptures with circular forms that roll like waves, colliding and reacting with each other, rather than depicting the more visually realistic movement of a blurred image made with a slow-motion camera.

Figure 3.18 Rosa Bonheur, *The Horse Fair.* *Metropolitan Museum of Art.*
This enormous canvas is alive with the illusion of motion. The artist lived in the 19th century and was once called "the world's greatest animal painter." She was the first woman artist to receive the Cross of the Legion of Honor. She was always concerned with anatomical accuracy in her art and visited slaughterhouses, attended cattle markets and horse fairs, and even dissected animal parts obtained from butcher shops.

Figure 3.19 W. H. Brown, *Bareback Riders.* Reverse: Steamboat in Rough Seas; Date: dated 1886; Cardboard: .470 × .622 (18½ × 24½ in.) *National Gallery of Art, Washington, D.C. Gift of Edgar William and Bernice Chrysler Garbisch.*
A rather stiff and static illusion of movement is portrayed in this charming circus painting by an American naive or primitive artist. How does it differ from Bonheur's *Horse Fair?*

Figure 3.21   Bridget Riley, *Current,* **1964. Synthetic polymer paint on composition board, 58⅜ × 58⅞.**
Collection, The Museum of Modern Art, New York. Philip Johnson Fund.
This British artist chose to explore the possibilities of optical movement inherent in curving lines. She thus created a new mode of perceiving and experiencing motion.

Figure 3.20   Umberto Boccioni, *Unique Forms of Continuity in Space.* **Bronze (cast 1931), 43⅞ × 34⅞ × 15¾.**
Collection, The Museum of Modern Art, New York. Acquired through the Lillie P. Bliss Bequest.
This bronze sculpture by a leading Futurist artist shows the blurred effect of rapid movement through the use of mechanical curves, broken contours, and a number of shifting planes. Futurists believed that art should be forward looking, express modern technology, and ignore past traditions.

Other artists have investigated ways of making colors and shapes themselves seem to move backward and forward. Victor Vasarely, known as the **"father of Op art,"** has been a leader in painting **optical illusions.** He and other **Op artists** sought to make paintings seem to move by taking advantage of the way our eyes see things. When you look at one of his paintings for a few minutes, you'll see colors and patterns that begin to bulge, buckle, swell, and retreat. Nothing is stable; everything moves. Colors change. Bridget Riley creates movement by making her paintings undulate, push out, whirl, and push back. She achieves a sense of depth that moves up and down on the surface of the painting. She places dots, lines, or circles

with a mathematical regularity, the resulting effect being one of circles and lines that dance and move. She takes advantage of the optical effect called the "afterimage."

Some artists plan their artworks with more than the illusion of actual movement in mind. Their artworks themselves actually move. Alexander Calder's **mobiles** were inventive and pioneering in their explorations of movement. Artists that are most concerned with actual movement in the two-dimensional area are probably those that are involved with making **films** and **video productions.**

In addition to creating an illusion of movement, artists use combinations of the different elements in their artworks that will cause the **viewer's eyes to move** or sweep over the composition in a particular manner. This kind of movement directs our eyes to the focal point or causes our eyes to sweep along an important visual channel that includes all areas of the picture plane and leaves no dead or void spots. To do this the artist exploits the direction of a line or utilizes the compelling force of a path made by the placement of repeated shapes or colors.

	Color	Line	Shape/ Form	Texture	Space	Value
Movement						

Turn to the **Color Gallery** and select several artworks to use with this chart. Analyze them to see how each artist created movement through one or more of the elements of art.

Producing Artworks

Varying a Cut-Paper Shape to Show Movement

The student will create a pleasing shape that will be used as the basis for a cut-paper composition, varying its size, placement, and color to show movement.

1. For practice in cutting shapes, take a 6-by-9-inch piece of paper and a pair of scissors. Remember to place the paper deep into the V-shape of the blades and to turn the paper as you cut rather than turning the scissors. First make straight angular cuts, entering the piece of paper at one side and making continuous short and long cuts until you have explored and exited the paper at its opposite side. Then take another piece of paper and make only curving cuts, entering and exiting the paper in the same manner.

2. Now take some more paper and practice cutting out some geometric shapes of various kinds. Cut freely; do not draw the shapes first. Then make some free-form shapes. Then make a shape that is a combination of free-form and geometric. Keep your shapes fairly simple, not complex.

3. Select one of the shapes that you like best. Select three different colors of paper and make several more of the same shape, **varying either the color of the shape or the size of the shape.** Make some small, some medium size, and some large.

4. Place them on a piece of black or colored paper, 9″ × 12″. Let some of the shapes overlap. Let some of them be grouped closely together to show movement. Try to place a series of small shapes so that they move your eye around the composition. When you are satisfied that your arrangement of the shapes creates a feeling of movement, paste the shapes down on the background paper.

Figure 3.22   Alexander Calder, *Mobile.*
National Gallery of Art, Washington, D.C.
On display in the central courtyard of the East Building of the National Gallery in Washington, D.C., is Alexander Calder's giant red mobile, which actually moves, creating constantly changing relationships of its parts.

In *The Starry Night* by van Gogh in the **Color Gallery,** we see the triangular shape of the tall, dark cypress tree on the left echoed by the tiny, centrally placed church spire, stabilizing the spirally rolling movement in the night sky. Let your eyes move along the curves, following Vincent's definitive and characteristic brushstrokes, starting on the left and moving in a dizzy roll to the horizon on the far right. Then follow the gentle diagonal movement of the hills downward to the left and back to the cypress and thence upward again to the starry sky.

Figure 3.23 Henri Matisse, *Dance.* **(first version) 1909 (early). Oil on canvas, 8′6½″ × 12′9½″.** *Collection, Museum of Modern Art, New York. Gift of Nelson A. Rockefeller.*

The artist simplified the human form, leaving out distracting details, to create an alternative, rhythmic motion of graceful curving figures and darker negative spaces for our eyes to follow.

Figures Showing Movement

The student will make a drawing of a moving figure or an animal based on a newspaper photograph, examining it for its action lines and rendering it with a series of elongated ovals.

1. Select several photographs from the newspaper that show action: athletes or dancers, racing horses, etc. Use a soft lead pencil, conte crayon, charcoal, or marking pens, and newsprint or manila paper. Look at the photograph and identify the action lines—the long, sweeping main line that usually begins with the head, extends through the torso, and extends on to one foot. Also look for the directional lines made by the arms and legs.

2. Draw these action lines roughly and quickly. They will serve as guides and should give the feeling of running, jumping, throwing, reaching, etc.

3. Use elongated ovals and let each part of the body be represented by one. Make a large oval for the upper torso (or chest) and a smaller one for the lower torso (or hips). Make two long ovals for each thigh and two more about the same length for the lower legs. Now make two long ovals for the upper

arms and two for the lower arms. Make two small ovals for the hands and two more about the length of the head for the two feet.

4. Skip around from one part of your figure to another as you progress, so that the different parts will fit together better. Then make an outline, giving a little attention to details of clothing.

5. Try several more action drawings of people and animals.

Showing Action with Foil Figures

The student will make a small sculpture of a figure by manipulating aluminum foil into a pose expressing action and movement.

1. Tear off a length of heavy-duty aluminum foil about 15″ × 18″. Place it flat on the table and with a scissors make five cuts as diagrammed.

2. Leave the foil flat on the table. First crumple the sides in at the top to form the head. Then crumple and squeeze the arm sections. Then crumple and squeeze the right side to form the body and right leg. Repeat on the left to form the left side of the body and the left leg.

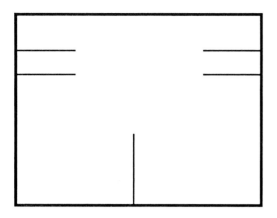

Made 5 cuts in a 15" × 18" piece of heavy-duty aluminum foil.

Figure 3.24 Pedro Ramirez Arrazola, *Painted Dog.*
The folk artist's innate love for, and understanding of, decorative pattern is evident in this hand-carved and delicately painted wooden dog from Oaxaca, Mexico.

3. Continue squeezing and manipulating the foil until you have formed a rather firm and solid figure. Then bend the knees, elbows, waist, and neck to show whether your figure is running, jumping, throwing a ball, etc. Mount on one or both feet on a small piece of corrugated cardboard with a stapler.

4. Place your foil mannequin in front of you and use it to help you draw a figure in action. Try to give it gesture and movement. Use oil pastels and felt pens for color and add clothing and environmental details.

Understanding Artworks

Learning about RHYTHM, REPETITION, and PATTERN

Rhythms and patterns are formed by repetition both in the world of nature and in artworks. From our early years, we respond to rhythm as well as create it. Small children clap their hands to the beat of music and quickly learn the words of singsong rhymes. Who can resist the toe-tapping rhythm of a polka or the strong beat of a marching band! Our lives are governed and surrounded by tempos, beats, and rhythms of all kinds—the rising and setting sun, our heartbeats, and flashing neon lights. We see visual patterns in the natural world as well as in artworks—on pineapples and cactus, on turtles, fish scales, and sea-shells. We identify as **rhythm a regular or harmonious pattern created by the repetition of lines, shapes, and colors.** Rhythm can create an exciting visual beat for our eyes to follow. Just as in music, rhythm and repetition in art can be smooth and flowing or they can be sharp and staccato. It depends on the effect the artist is trying to create.

Figure 3.25 Grant Wood, *Stone City, Iowa.*
Joslyn Art Museum, Omaha, Neb.
The artist, remembering that "cornfields in spring look like black comforters tied in green yarn," has painted the sprouting stalks in a gradated or progressive pattern that leads our eyes deep into the spatial depth of this landscape. Look for other motifs that the artist repeated. He developed and relied upon keen observational skills, researching old maps, atlases, Currier and Ives prints, family photos, and line drawings in Sears catalogs.

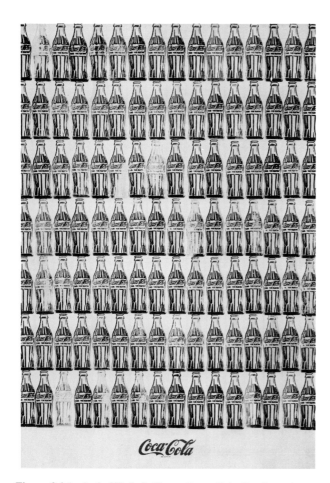

Figure 3.26 Andy Warhol, *Green Coca-Cola Bottles.*
Whitney Museum of American Art, New York. Purchase with
funds from the Howard and Jean Lipman Foundation, Inc.
Acq. #68.71
Monotonous, regular repeat of a single motif purposely makes
a statement about consumerism and contemporary life in this
artwork classified as "pop art."

Figure 3.27   Li-Ting, Hollow-legged tripod.
Chinese, Shensi Province, Early "Middle Western Chou"
Period, ca 950–900 B.C., bronze 61.203.
Cleveland Museum of Art. Gift from various donors by
exchange and the John L. Severance Fund.
Flowing, decorative design enhances the surface of this bronze
container, repeating endlessly, leading our eye in an intriguing
rhythmical pattern around the contours of this artwork.

Artists use **pattern** that results from visual repetition
of lines, colors, and shapes in a number of ways. In certain
artworks, the **repetition** of a unit called a **motif** creates a
decorative effect and often results in the kind of pattern
that we see in wallpaper, tile floors, fabrics, and the like.
The motif may be a line or shape or a combination of lines
and shapes. Pattern can provide **visual enhancement** to an
artwork, whether it is two- or three-dimensional, and provide **visual interest** and focus to an artwork. Sometimes
painters use a patterned area to **simulate texture,** and they
can also use a repeated pattern to **reveal the form** of the
object or figure beneath it. Notice how the pattern of
stripes on the woman's robe shows the contours of her body
in the warm and unified artwork *The Bath,* by Mary Cassatt, in the **Color Gallery.**

Pattern can also be a vital part of the **actual physical
structure** of an object: the material and its structure creates the pattern. Woven tapestries, baskets, and the brick-
work of a building are examples of ways in which pattern
integrates decorative elements within a structural function.

Repetition and pattern can be simple or complex. The
simple repetition of a regular motif or element creates a
regular pattern that is often used to embellish the surface
of an object. In this kind of pattern, the motifs that are
repeated, as well as the spaces between them, remain the
same. In regular allover patterns, the even distribution
usually follows one of several basic grids or networks that
form invisible guidelines for the placement of the motif.
Some of these networks are based on the square, checkerboard, bricks, a staggered grid, or they may follow a
half-drop or diamond arrangement. These guidelines may
not only be visible, they may form an important part of
the finished pattern of checks, stripes, lattice, etc. The
spaces between the network lines usually interlock or connect endlessly in any direction. This sort of allover repetition is referred to as a **tessellation.** The artist M. C.

Figure 3.28   Henri Rousseau, *The Equatorial Jungle*. [Date: dated 1909; Canvas; 1.406 × 1.295 (55¼ × 51 in.)] *Chester Dale Collection, National Gallery of Art, Washington, D.C.*
The primitive or unschooled artist usually has an innate and intuitive sense of the decorative beauty of repeated patterns. Notice the variety of leaf motifs that overlap and intrigue the viewer in this almost dreamlike jungle scene. Note how repeated fine lines in foreground simulate texture of fine grasses.

Escher visited the Alhambra in Spain early in his career and became fascinated with walls and floors that were covered with repeated tile motifs. He subsequently used the tessellation concept in designing numerous artworks that create illusions with their intriguing flowing patterns.

We can achieve variety and complexity within a pattern by changing the colors, positions, shapes, and their directions, or by changing the intervals or spaces between them. This **irregular** or **alternating pattern** is usually more interesting than a regular one since two or more motifs may be used instead of just one. Artists know that our eyes like the visual excitement of the unexpected and know that it adds suspense and surprise to an artwork.

Still another kind of repeated pattern shows a **progression** or **gradation** of the motif, perhaps in size or in the intensity of its color. This is an orderly step-by-step change of the elements or intervals. Here we may see the same motif steadily repeated but notice that it gradually becomes smaller or lighter in color and closer together.

However, not all visual rhythms that we see and make in our artworks are created by a regular arrangement of the motif and its intervals. A **random pattern** is often seen where there is no obvious order, either of the motif or the intervening spaces. We see random patterns of wildflowers on hillsides, puffs of clouds in the sky, or horses grazing in a pasture.

We can describe as a **flowing pattern,** those lines and shapes that are repeated in waving or curving arrangements. Our eyes tend to glide along with them in a rhythmic manner as the direction they take makes smooth and gradual changes, or perhaps abrupt and forceful ones. Leonardo was fascinated with the patterns made by waves and moving water and sketched his observations of them carefully. If we look at the curly ringlets of hair that frame the face of *Ginevra de'Benci* in the **Color Gallery,** we see how he made a visual connection between the moving currents and the repeated pattern that simulated the actual texture of her hair.

The strong and determined peasants-turned-soldiers in Orozco's *Zapatistas,* in the **Color Gallery,** form a repeated pattern with their pants, serapes, and sombreros. Our eyes are forced to surge forward with them from right to left as they move to conflict. The four women follow, the motif of their rebozos forming another rhythmic repeat, while the enormous horsemen behind them form a trilogy of repeated shapes.

Both two- and three-dimensional artworks make use of the decorative principles of rhythm, repetition, and pattern. Patchwork quilts, baskets, pottery and sculpture, jewelry, masks, and many other pieces of traditional tribal and ethnic arts are often richly embellished with surface patterns. Architects plan for a variety of pattern when they design a building. How they will arrange multiple units of windows and doors, and how the effect of the pattern created by bricks and tiles will interact and relate with other structural surfaces, are major considerations. Landscape architects plan different groupings of trees, walkways, ground cover, and rocks that will create a harmonious pattern of shapes, textures, and colors. City planners strive to achieve unity and order in their designs by arranging small units of houses and streets in a balance of irregular and regular patterns.

The artwork of young children often shows their innate love for, and understanding of, repetition and pattern. They may take delight in the rhythmic repetition of dots and lines to create a decorative border around the outside edges of a painting they have made. They may use it to show realistic or symbolic details of the objects they are depicting. On a more structured and conscious level, they can study the relationships of patterning in math and art by weaving and simple printmaking activities such as potato, eraser, or gadget printing.

Direct observation of city buildings or collecting photographs of city skylines provide stimulus for making artwork that emphasizes repeated patterns.

Student work: Cityscape designed with templates to assist in achieving a variety of repetition.

	Color	Line	Shape/Form	Texture	Space	Value
Repetition, Rhythm and Pattern						

Turn to the **Color Gallery** and select several artworks to use with this chart. Analyze them to see how each artist created repetition, rhythm, and pattern through one or more of the elements of art.

Producing Artworks

Designing a Cityscape with Varied Patterns

The student will use direct observation and photographs of buildings to create an imaginary city. The overlapping, flat, frontal arrangement of tall buildings will be drawn with a black marking pen on white paper, and will be embellished with a variety of different repeated patterns and then painted with watercolor washes.

1. Notice the different shapes of tall and short city buildings. Observe their rooflines. Notice how the closer buildings overlap those behind them. Look for different repeated shapes of windows, balconies, doors, and fire escapes, as well as different patterns made by bricks, tiles, shingles, etc.

2. Use a ruler and assorted templates (jar lids, small blocks of wood, plastic templates from art supply stores, etc.). Draw a large geometric shape of a building that is nearest to the viewer. Then draw other buildings behind and beside it, varying the rooflines. Fill most of the paper with your cityscape. Then cover the surface of each building with a different repeated pattern of windows, bricks, etc.

3. Mix watercolor washes and add color to your cityscape. Wet washes on wet paper are recommended for the blurry effect of skies; wet washes on the buildings and ground will be sharp and crisp. Let some of the white paper show to add sparkle and freshness. If you have used a water-soluble marking pen, the black lines will run when water touches them. They can add to the effect you may wish to create. Permanent marking pens are unaffected by watercolor washes.

Allover Patterns: Carving a Rubber Stamp*

The student will carve a design in an eraser, inking it on an office stamp pad and printing it as a repeated allover pattern.

1. Use a small white or pink eraser that you purchase in an office, school, or art supply store. These come in square and rectangular shapes. Draw around the eraser on tracing paper and fit a design into the shape. You may make a simple geometric design or find an idea for one in books that show leaf and flower motifs, Japanese family crests, heraldic symbols, Southwestern Indian pottery, Celtic art, snowflakes, M. C. Escher's tessellations, the Bayeux Tapestry, Mexican or Egyptian designs, etc. You might wish to base your design on your astrological symbol, or make a design for a business logo or a design using your initials.

*George L. Thomson, *Rubber Stamps and How to Make Them* (Edinburgh, Scotland: Canongate Publishers); Joni L. Miller and Lowry Thompson, *The Rubber Stamp Album* (New York: Workman Publishing).

Student work: Eraser print of angel motif is repeated in brick-like grid.

Student work: Eraser print of heart design is varied by alternating up and down arrangement in a close together manner.

2. Think in terms of raised (black) and cutout (white) areas. Go over the lines of your design with a soft lead pencil. Turn the paper over and attach it to the eraser with tape. Go over the lines with a sharp pencil. Your design will transfer to the eraser. The design should be in reverse on the eraser. Hold it up to a mirror to see how the printed image will appear. Words and numbers must be carved in reverse.

3. Now go over the fuzzy pencil lines on the eraser with a black-tipped pen. Use denatured alcohol on a tissue to rub off the pencil smudges. This makes the carving much easier, as the black lines of the pen will remain. Use linocutters or an X-acto knife to carve your design. Avoid making undercuts.

4. Make a test print by pressing the eraser onto a well-inked office stamp pad and then pressing it onto paper. Add stamp-pad ink if necessary. If you are not satisfied, you may wish to carve away more areas.

5. Use your rubber stamp to create an allover pattern by repeating it on a large piece of paper many times. You may choose to make a regular repeat first and vary it on another piece of paper by using a brick grid, checkerboard grid, etc. Use as paper for bookbinding or for wrapping paper. Try other variations with your stamp and create borders, notepaper, posters, labels, etc.

Pattern by Repetition: From Above, Looking Down

Taking a bird's-eye point of view, the student will design a landscape composition made up of what one might see from above, looking down, dividing the paper into areas that are then painted with repeated patterns.

1. Imagine yourself floating in a hot-air balloon and looking down. You may wish to find photographs in *National Geographic* to help you trigger ideas for your composition. You might see and include some of the following: fields with crops in rows, orchards, fence posts, cars on highways, cars in a parking lot, boats on a river, bridges, ships in a harbor, horses and cows and lambs in a field, scarecrows, windmills, telephone poles, a family of crocodiles or turtles, etc. Lightly sketch the main spaces and shapes with a piece of chalk.

2. Pour small amounts of tempera in an egg carton, using the lid to mix your colors. Then paint the large areas first and let the paint dry. Then add details and patterns in the different areas, using a small brush or a Q-tip and contrasting colors. Plan on having a center of interest. Try to include a variety of regular repeated patterns, irregular patterns, and gradated patterns to represent the rows of corn, fence posts, parked cars, boats, etc.

Understanding Artworks

Learning about VARIETY and UNITY

Would you like to live in a room in which the walls, floor, furniture, and window coverings were all covered with red polka dots of the same size? Or would you like to eat the same food for every meal, seven days a week, month after month? Would you enjoy hearing the same music played over and over again without interruption or any change to another selection? Our eyes, our taste buds, and our ears like variety and seek it out. We choose a solid blue color for a carpet, a floral pattern for the sofa, and perhaps a light tan for the walls. We consider the different textures

Figure 3.29   Cecilia Beaux, *After the Meeting.*
The Toledo Museum of Art. Gift of Florence Scott Libby.
A splendid and rich variety of textures and patterns is
dominant in this eloquent glimpse of a finely dressed woman
seated in an overstuffed chair. Notice the splashes of flowers
and the striped dress, the fine gloves and feather in her hat. A
variety of near and far and a variety of dark and light areas
are controlled and limited to portray a quiet scene. The artist,
Cecilia Beaux, married artist Thomas Eakins in 1884.

Figure 3.30   Louise Moillon, *Still Life with Cherries,*
Strawberries, and Gooseberries.
The Norton Simon Foundation, Pasadena, Ca.
A variety of different plump and rounded shapes is seen in this
fresh and delectable still life painted in 1630. Against a dark
background, the patterned bowls and basket contain a pleasing
variety of textures, color gradations and blends, and sizes. The
tiny sprig of gooseberries and droplets of water in the lower
center give contrast. Cherry stems and contours of leaves
create an interesting linear note, and the rounded shapes of
the containers are accented by the horizontal edge of the table.

in the same room, striving to achieve a harmonious
blending of woods and fibers. In planning our meals, we
select from a variety of vegetables and fruits, and we like
to try new foods and restaurants to relieve sameness and
monotony. As any good cook knows, different sauces on
the same vegetables can entice and intrigue our taste buds.

Variety is the principle of art that is concerned with
differences. There is a lot of artistic truth in the old saying,
"Variety is the spice of life," because the use of differences
and contrasting elements enlivens artworks. Lines of a

uniform width used throughout a composition might lose
our attention because their sameness would probably bore
us. Looking at the same shape used without variation
throughout a composition would probably be quite monotonous, and our attention would wander elsewhere.

Artists know that the same shape may be repeated in
a composition without any changes, but variety can be
achieved by using **different sizes** of shapes, **varying their
colors,** or their **surface texture or pattern.** Thick, bold lines
provide striking **contrast** with spidery, brittle lines. Variety can be shown within the confines of one color by using
it as tints in one area, as shades in another, and as dulled
tones in yet another. Different kinds of textures draw our
attention to various areas of emphasis.

In planning artworks, we need to keep in mind that
an excess of variety tends to create a feel of haphazard-
ness and even chaos. A lack of variety makes for boredom.
Somewhere between these two extremes, we strive to arrive
at a harmonious balance that will contribute to the feeling
of unity. In *Girl Before a Mirror* by Pablo Picasso in the
Color Gallery, we see an example of how the artist achieved
unity and harmony through the use of controlled and limited variety. He used a limited selection of bright colors
and explored differences through changes in the size and
placement of circular shapes. A variety of patterned areas
is tightly balanced against flat, plain spaces.

Figure 3.32   Joan Miró, *Woman in the Night.*
Solomon R. Guggenheim Museum, New York. Fractional Gift of Evelyn Sharp to the Solomon R. Guggenheim Museum, 1977. Photo: Robert E. Mates.
Variety is limited to achieve a unified effect in this painting. Black dots vary in size and placement and are connected to each other and other floating shapes by thin lines.

**Figure 3.31   Jacob Lawrence, *Daybreak—A Time to Rest.*
[Date: dated 1967; Tempera on hardboard; 0.762 × 0.610 (30 × 24 in.)]**
National Gallery of Art, Washington, D.C. Gift of an Anonymous Donor.
Variety is seen in the curvilinear plant forms that tend to frame the abstracted, foreshortened figure. Several stalks are resting places for insects in the foreground. Differences in contrast are noted between the dark, sleeping figure and other tones in the composition.

The feeling of unity may be described as being the way we feel when we look at a completed artwork, our own or that of a great artist, and know that nothing should be changed, added, or taken away. **Unity** is the principle of art that makes all the separate elements of an artwork look as if they belonged together. The arrangement of the different parts and elements of art are in agreement, each contributing to the overall effect. Nothing seems to bother us or distract our eyes as not seeming to be quite "right." We are able to concentrate on the entire artwork because no one part keeps demanding our attention. The different elements help and complement each other. Nothing "interrupts" our conversation with the artwork. The various parts are in harmony and in accord with each other. The colors match the feeling; the shapes interact with the mood. We are led around and through the composition by any one of several devices—colors, lines, or shapes that connect various elements and lead our eyes. For centuries the

triangle has been an underlying structure in many artworks that relates and unifies the figures or other elements in a painting.

There are several techniques that we may incorporate in our own artworks to achieve a feeling of unity. First, we can place different shapes and objects close together, **clustering and overlapping** them and **surrounding them with an area of negative space,** while at the same time minimizing the spaces between the shapes. Think how the appearance of a large pile of rocks contrasts with the same number of rocks scattered randomly over a large area.

Limiting the variety of colors, shapes, lines, or patterns within an artwork is a second factor that contributes to unity. Too many different elements can lead to a feeling of chaos. In his glittering presentation of the *Rouen Cathedral,* in the **Color Gallery,** Claude Monet achieves a unified effect by the consistent and overall sameness of his brushstrokes. The limiting factor of using only two colors, blue and orange, further tends to create a feeling of completeness and wholeness, and thus unity.

Now look at *Breezing Up* by Winslow Homer in the **Color Gallery.** The artist has achieved a feeling of unity in several ways. First, the overall effect of light and limited colors match the happy and relaxed mood. Then we notice that the color red has been repeated in a number of places: on the central figure in the boat and small touches on the other figures. The mast and sail are edged

Figure 3.33 Narciso Abeyta (Ha-so-dee), *Navajo Horses.*
Collection of the authors.
Horses show unity by their overlapping, clustered
arrangement, and variety by their different positions and
colors. Delicately painted plants provide fine details that
harmonize with the grace and movement of the horses.

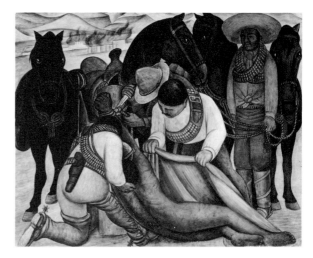

Figure 3.34 Diego Rivera, *The Liberation of the Peon.*
The Philadelphia Museum of Art. Given by Mr. and Mrs.
Herbert Cameron Morris.
Horses and figures are grouped closely together to give a
feeling of unity in this artwork that was created to evoke
feeling of solidarity and cooperation in fighting for
agricultural and land reforms in Mexico. Rounded, full forms
relate to one another to add to unified effect.

with red, and we even see reflected bits of red on the water
in the foreground. Now look at the horizon where Homer
has carefully placed two more boats to take your eyes into
the distance. He even edged the sails of the larger boat
with more red. The boats are tipped in the same direction,
with the figures in the large boat leaning in the other direction to provide balance, both actual and visual. The
skillful painting of the textures of splashing water and
scudding clouds adds to the overall unity.

	Color	Line	Shape/ Form	Texture	Space	Value
Variety and Unity						

Turn to the **Color Gallery** and select several artworks to
use with this chart. Analyze them to see how each artist
achieved variety and unity through one or more of the elements of art.

Producing Artworks

Stitchery: Limiting Variety to Achieve Unity

The student will make a variety of stitches with different
colors and textures of yarn to create a unified artwork on
burlap or other loosely woven fabric.

1. Use a piece (about 12″ × 15″) of plain or colored
   burlap, or any loosely woven fabric, through which
   a large needle may easily be used to pull yarn.
   Place masking tape around the edges to prevent it
   from becoming unraveled.

2. Select a theme, such as fireworks; earth strata; a
   spider's web; a volcano, above and below the
   ground; things that grow, above and below; jungle
   flowers, etc. You may want to sketch your idea on
   paper before you begin working on your fabric.
   Then you may want to sketch the main parts of
   your design on the fabric with a piece of chalk.

3. Choose appropriate colors and textures of yarns to
   match your theme. Limit the variety to no more
   than five different kinds. This will help give your
   stitchery unity.

4. Limit the kinds of stitches you will be using to an
   inventive use of the following: the **running stitch,
   cross stitch, blanket stitch, couching, fly stitch, back
   stitch,** the **chain stitch, satin stitch,** and **French
   knots** (see diagram). You can achieve variety by
   changing the length, size, direction, color, and
   placement of the stitches. Repeating them will add
   to the unity of your artwork. Let stitches overlap.

5. Place the stitches in such a manner as to have one
   area that is emphasized, thereby creating a center
   of interest or focus for your composition.

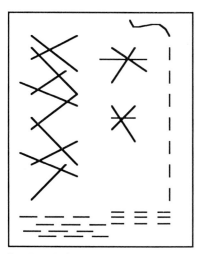

Running stitch and variations

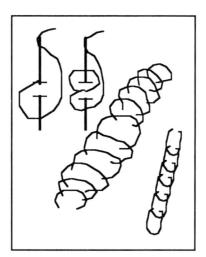

Chain stitch and variations

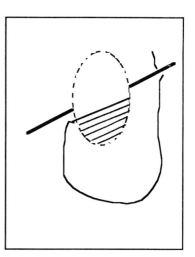

Satin stitch

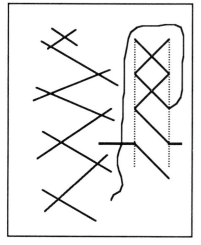

Cross-stitch and variations

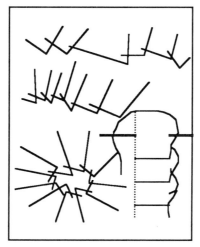

Blanket stitch and variations

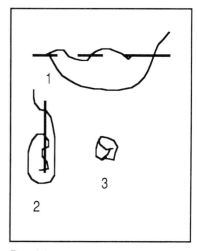

French knot

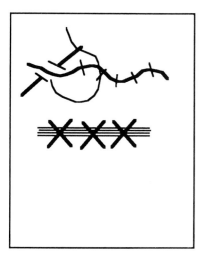

Couching variations

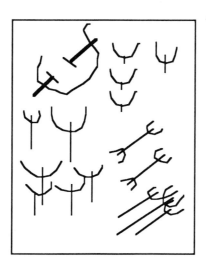

Fly stitch and variations

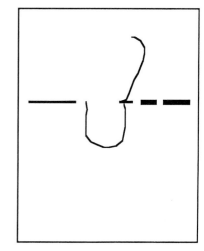

Backstitch

Weaving with Paper Strips

The student will weave a two-dimensional design with paper strips, using a variety of widths of paper strips, as well as a variety of colors and textures, in an effort to create a unified artwork.

1. Collect a variety of papers: colored, foil, shiny, velour, patterned wrapping paper, ribbons, brown paper bags, sandpaper, etc.

2. Cut 9-inch strips and 12-inch strips, varying the width.

3. Spread a half-inch strip of paste along one of the 9-inch sides of a piece of 9-by-12-inch construction paper. Then attach the 12-inch strips (called the **warps**) to the pasted area, side by side so they can be lifted up as you weave the 9-inch strips across. Select a pleasing variety of widths, textures, and colors of paper strips.

4. Begin weaving over and under the warp strips with the 12-inch strips. These are called **wefts**. Push the weft strips up to the top of the warp strips. You may weave in a random or a regular pattern, but try to create a composition that shows unity.

5. When you have finished weaving, the warps will be filled from top to bottom. Paste the warps and wefts down to the piece of construction paper upon which you pasted the warp strips.

Showing Variety and Unity with Chalk Dipped in Tempera

The student will dip the tip of colored chalk repeatedly in thick white tempera and make short marks on black paper to create a design that shows both variety and unity. Photographs will be used for visual information.

1. Use colored chalk that is designated for use on paper, not on chalkboards. Break pieces in half.

2. Dip the tip of a piece of chalk in white tempera and use a piece of black construction paper to practice making a variety of short marks: curving, straight, zigzag, circular, dots, etc. Marks may overlap. Keep dipping the tip of the chalk. Work to achieve a mark that shows the bright color of the chalk edged with the white tempera.

3. Decide upon your subject matter (fish, birds, fireworks are suggested). Dip the tip of the chalk repeatedly in the white tempera and keep making marks on the black paper until your composition is finished. The marks you make and the black background give your artwork a unified effect.

Setting Up for Direct Observation: Still Lifes, Costumed Models, and Landscapes

1. Sit comfortably **close to the subject matter** in order to perceive its details and relationships adequately. Try moving your chair until you have an interesting point of view.

2. Use your **viewfinder** to help you frame your composition. This will help you select your subject and place it within the format of your paper. The positive shapes bump the sides of the viewfinder, creating negative spaces that you can draw on your paper. Viewfinders eliminate distracting, irrelevant, and confusing elements in the environment.

3. Have the **supplies** you will need conveniently at hand.

4. Take time for a **visual analysis** of the subject matter.

   Look at the **proportions** and the relationships of **sizes** of various parts: larger than, smaller than, twice as tall as, wider than, the same as, etc.
   Look at the **relationship of the locations** of parts: halfway up, to the left of, below, in the upper right, in front of, behind, overlapping, etc.
   Look for inner and outer contour **lines.**
   Look for significant basic **shapes** of the principal objects and then of smaller parts of those objects: cones, circles, squares, rectangles, cylinders, etc.
   Look for different **colors** and different **values** of each color: where is the red darker, where is the lightest area?
   Look for different **patterns:** repeated shapes and lines, regular or irregular repeats.
   Look for **cast shadows.**

5. Decide if you will make a highly **realistic artwork,** interpreting what you see in a personal way. There are many personal ways to interpret what you see. For instance, if you apply paint with little overlapping daubs to create a feeling of sparkling sunlight, you will be painting as the Impressionists did. If you apply your paint with tiny dots, placing several colors so close together that your eyes blend the colors, you will be painting as the Pointillists did. You may create a **fantasy,** painting in a very realistic manner but creating an unlikely relationship or environment as the **Surrealist** artists do. You may choose to work as the Expressionists, emphasizing the **mood and emotion** of your subject matter. Or you may focus your attention on creating a more abstract artwork, emphasizing the **formal aspects** of color, line, shape, texture, etc. If you break up what you see into planes and cubes, creating a new structure from several viewpoints, you will be working as the Cubists do.

6. You may exaggerate and distort. You may change and delete and repeat what you see. You, the artist, will make decisions as you compose your artwork, selecting, refining, combining, eliminating, and repeating the elements you need to give meaning to your artwork and to create balance, pattern, direction, emphasis, and movement.

7. Make several different drawings or paintings of the subject matter, changing your viewpoint and trying to see it in a different way each time.

Still Lifes

1. A still life may be just one object or it may be made up of several items. Collect a variety of items that appeal to you for a **resource bank for still-life setups.** The following are suggested because of the variety of their shapes, colors, and textures, and because they have an appeal to most people.

   Fruit, vegetables: gourds, pumpkins, squash, apples, citrus, grapes, mushrooms, cross sections of oranges or cabbages, eggs, eggplants, broccoli, cauliflower, potatoes, etc.
   Flowers and plants: cactus, fresh flowers, twigs, dried plants, silk plants.
   Containers: bottles, jars, jugs, teapots, pitchers, bowls, ceramic items, baskets, etc.
   Tools, implements: spoon, typewriter, hammer, pliers, C-clamps, wrench, can opener.
   Other items: musical instruments, pipe, dolls, toys, gloves, hats, shoes, assorted antiques, feathers, butterflies, bones, shells, driftwood, mounted birds and animals, pieces of candy, ribbon, books.
   Backdrops: butcher paper, felt, fabric—plain and patterned, striped, or textured (lengths of fabric, blanket, shawl, beach towel, sheet).
   Lighting: floor lamp or tripod with strong bulb.

2. Hang the fabric on the wall behind the table and let it drape over the surface in a smooth or slightly rumpled manner. A backdrop eliminates distracting elements and can provide an interesting pattern for the background of your still life. It also helps unify the composition.

3. Select several items of differing height and width for your still-life setup. Have something tall and several items close together. Have something large and balance it with several smaller items. Try several combinations, moving and rearranging until you arrive at a pleasing and unified arrangement. Try to have a satisfying relationship of proportions. Let some objects stand in front of others. You may want to have some items grouped in an isolated position. Have a variety of textured objects and objects of several colors.

4. Give some thought to lighting. You can place a floodlight anchored in a tripod or a floor lamp on one side of the still life. This will create cast shadows and create highlights.

5. For making value studies and drawings in which the emphasis is on showing modeling and basic forms, spray with white paint items such as the following: plastic maple syrup jug, wine bottle, rolling pin, croquet ball, square and rectangular blocks of wood, pinecones, seashells, old cowboy boot, etc. This eliminates color and helps students to concentrate on drawing, shading, and showing modeling through tonal values.

6. When the class is drawing a single object—such as a turkey feather, pliers, wrench, or car keys—rather than an arrangement of still-life objects, each student should have an object in order to be very close to it. A **magnifying glass** provides a close-up look at details and makes for a larger-than-life composition for small items such as insects, seed pods, etc. A curved reflecting mirror can provide a pleasingly distorted image that is interesting to draw.

7. After choosing your materials, find the best viewpoint. Then use your viewfinder to focus on your composition and orient it to the format of your drawing paper. Make several small, quick thumbnail sketches of the outlines made by the shapes as a mass, shading in the solid parts. This will help you see the positive and negative shapes, their relation to the background, and their position on the paper. Next you may consider the individual shapes of the objects, drawing the contours of each as they overlap one another.

8. Blocking in the main vertical, horizontal, and diagonal lines often helps you get started. Then you can draw in the entire shape of the pumpkin or basket and more carefully delineate the roundness and contours. Observe the shapes made by cast shadows. Add details that characterize each object: the delicate gills on the mushroom, the woven texture of a basket. Add any decorative patterns you see in the backdrop. Use hatching, cross-hatching, stippling, and blending to create a modeled form. You might try filling in the background solidly to accent the individual shapes in the still life.

Costumed Models

1. Have the model wear several **costume items,** dressing as a character from literature, history, or another country. Costume items may include a hat or bonnet, scarf, cape, skirt, belt, sash, blanket, shawl, beads, crown, helmet, armor, bridal dress, etc.

2. Add interesting and appropriate **props:** a cloth-covered table beside the seated model's chair, a saddle, musical instrument, bicycle, large basket, ladder, cane, tennis racquet, fan, lasso, broom, sword, banjo, shovel, flowers, etc. Consider a fabric backdrop to soften or eliminate distracting elements.

3. Two models may pose together, seated and playing cards at a table, sweeping the floor, playing musical instruments, etc.

4. Think about the emotional aspects or the character and personality of the figure. Does he/she look tired, ferocious, humorous, wise, proud, arrogant, humble?

5. Look carefully at the gesture and posture of the pose. Use your viewfinder. Try several different points of view. Find angles and curves. Notice the relationship of the figure to the background. Decide if you will draw the entire figure, from the waist up, or from the shoulders up.

Land, Sea and Cityscapes

1. You will need a **drawing board** upon which you will tape your drawing paper. A viewfinder will help you select your subject and frame your composition in the same manner that a camera does. It will stop your eye from taking in too much from a panoramic view and will help you find a focal point. Start by selecting a subject with fairly shallow space, closing in on the main point of interest.

2. Try shifting your point of view so that the horizon is up high. Then try it down low before you decide which point of view best suits you. A high horizon line allows you to have a lot of ground space.

3. Let your eyes follow the lines and shapes that direct your attention to the focal point or points. It may be a road, fence posts, alley, side of a building, trees, edge of a lake or river, etc. Notice which shapes extend off the edges of the paper.

4. After you have chosen your scene, make quick thumbnail sketches to help you see how your composition looks on paper. Look for dark and light masses. Do any shapes in the foreground stand out against the sky? Will you use them to frame or be a focal point? Notice which direction the light is coming from and what effect it has on the objects in your composition. Dappled light is different from harsh light. Light at different times of the day casts different lengths of shadows and can contribute to the mood of your artwork.

5. Instead of a viewfinder, use natural framing provided by a window, a hole in a fence, an arched door, a gate, an entry hall, etc.

Questions and Activities

1. Select from the **Color Gallery** an example that clearly illustrates an aspect of each of the principles of art and defend the reasons for your choices.

2. Save all your examples from your Portfolio of Producing Artworks that relate to the principles of art and give them to a student that is not in your class. See if that student can select and name the principle of art that you focused upon in making your artwork.

3. Collect at least two photographs of nature from magazines and other sources that illustrate each of the principles of art. Mount them on a small posterboard or in a loose-leaf notebook, explaining how the principles of art are involved.

4. Make a small poster about the principle of balance. Collect photographs from magazines, travel folders, calendars, and such that demonstrate formal and informal balance, approximate balance, and radial balance as seen in nature and in artworks. Add labels and captions and use the poster to teach students about the principle of balance.

5. Make additional small posters in the same manner about the other principles of art. Collect photographs of both natural objects and artworks that focus on aspects of each principle of art. Then use your set in teaching students about the principles of art.

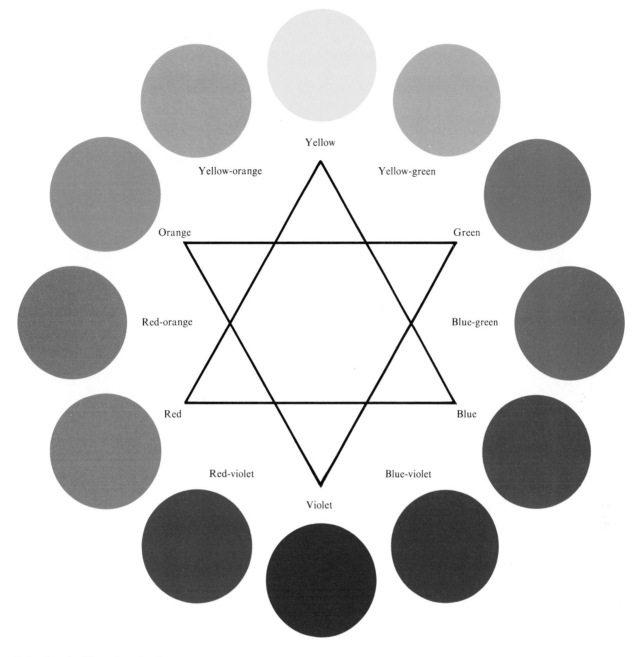

Colorplate 1 The color wheel.
From Ocvirk, Otto G. et al., *Art Fundamentals: Theory and Practice,* 5th ed. Copyright © 1985 by Otto Ocvirk, Robert Bone, Robert Stinson, and Philip Wigg. All rights reserved. Reprinted by permission.

Colorplate 2 Renoir, *Girl with Watering Can, 1876. Oil on canvas. 39½ × 28¾.*
Chester Dale Collection, 1962. National Gallery of Art, Washington, D.C.

Colorplate 3 José Ôrozco, *Zapatistas*, **1931.**
Oil on canvas, 45″ × 55″.
Collection, Museum of Modern Art, New York. Given
anonymously.

Colorplate 4 Leonardo da Vinci, *Ginevra de'Benci,* ca. 1480–
1481.
Oil and tempera on panel, 15⅛″ × 14½″.
Ailsa Mellon Bruce Fund. National Gallery of Art,
Washington, D.C.

Colorplate 5   Raphael, *The Alba Madonna,* **ca. 1510.**
Transferred from wood to canvas, diameter of 37¼″.
Andrew W. Mellon Collection. National Gallery of Art,
Washington, D.C.

Colorplate 6   Claude Monet, *Rouen Cathedral, West Facade*
Sunlight, **1894.**
Oil on canvas, 39½″ × 26″.
Chester Dale Collection, 1962. National Gallery of Art,
Washington, D.C.

Colorplate 7 Paul Cézanne, *Le Château Noir,* **ca. 1904.**
Oil on canvas, 29″ × 38″.
Gift of Eugene and Agnes Meyer, 1958. National Gallery of
Art, Washington, D.C.

Colorplate 8   Georges Seurat, *Sunday Afternoon on the Island of La Grande Jatte.* **1884–86. Oil on canvas, 207.6 × 308.0 cm.** *The Art Institute of Chicago, Helen Birch Bartlett Memorial Collection, 1926.224.*

Colorplate 9   Pablo Picasso, *Girl Before a Mirror,* **1932.**
Oil on canvas, 64″ × 51¼″.
Collection, The Museum of Modern Art, New York. Gift of
Mrs. Simon Guggenheim.

Colorplate 10 Thomas Eakins, *Max Schmitt in a Single Scull. Metropolitan Museum of Art. Purchase, 1934, Alfred N. Punnett Fund and Gift of George D. Pratt.* (34.92)

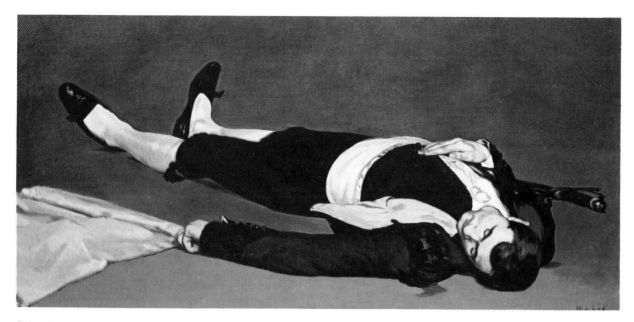

Colorplate 11   Edouard Manet, *The Dead Toreador,* **1864.**
Oil on canvas, 29⅞″ × 60⅜″.
Widener Collection. National Gallery of Art, Washington,
D.C.

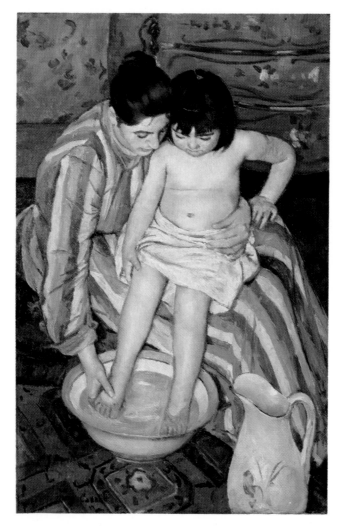

Colorplate 12   Mary Cassatt, *The Bath*, 1891–1892.
Oil on canvas, 39 × 26 in. (99 × 66.1 cm.).
The Art Institute of Chicago, Robert A. Waller Fund, 1910.2.

Colorplate 13   Pablo Picasso, *The Tragedy,* **1903.**
Wood, 41½ × 27⅛ in. (1.054 × 0.690 m.).
National Gallery of Art, Washington, Chester Dale
Collection.

Colorplate 14   Jan Vermeer, *The Girl with a Red Hat*, ca. 1660.
Oil on wood, 9⅛″ × 7⅛″.
Andrew W. Mellon Collection. National Gallery of Art. Washington, D.C.

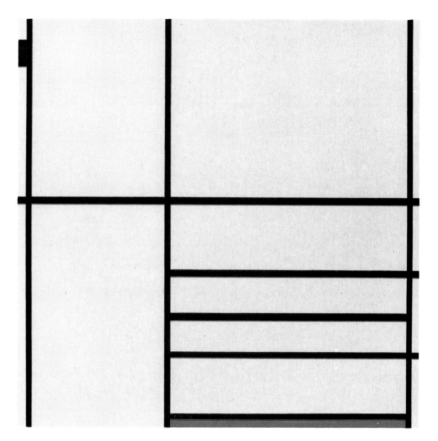

Colorplate 15 Piet Mondrian, *Composition II*, 1929.
Oil on canvas, 15⅞ × 12⅝ in. (40.3 × 32.1 cm.).
Collection, The Museum of Modern Art, New York. Gift of
Philip Johnson.

Colorplate 16   Franz Marc, *Yellow Cow,* **1911.**
Oil on canvas, 55⅜ × 74½ in. (140.5 × 189.2 cm.).
Solomon R. Guggenheim Museum, New York. Photo: Carmelo
Guadagno.

Colorplate 17 Marc Chagall, *Green Violinist*, 1923–1924.
Oil on canvas, 78 × 42¾ in. (198 × 108.6 cm.).
*Solomon R. Guggenheim Museum, New York. Gift of
Solomon R. Guggenheim, 1937. Photo: David Heald.*

Colorplate 18   Marisol, *Women and Dog,* 1964.
Wood, plaster, synthetic polymer, and miscellaneous items, 72″
× 82″ × 16″.
Courtesy Collection of the Whitney Museum of American Art.
Gift of the Friends of the Whitney Museum of American Art.

Colorplate 19 Winslow Homer, *Breezing Up*, 1876. Oil on canvas, 24⅛″ × 38⅛″. *Gift of the W. L. and May T. Mellon Foundation, 1943. National Gallery of Art, Washington, D.C.*

Colorplate 20   Vincent van Gogh, *The Starry Night*, 1889.
Oil on canvas, 29 × 36¼ in. (73.7 × 92.1 cm.).
Collection, The Museum of Modern Art, New York. Acquired
through the Lillie P. Bliss Bequest.

Colorplate 21   Henry Moore, *Reclining Figure,* **1939.**
Carved elm, 37 in. × 6 ft. × 30 in. (94 × 200.7 × 76.2 cm.).
The Detroit Institute of Arts, Gift of the Dexter M. Ferry, Jr.,
Trustee Corporation.

Colorplate 22 Albert Bierstadt, *The Rocky Mountains,* **1863.**
Oil on canvas, 73¼ × 120¾ in. (186.1 × 306.7 cm.).
The Metropolitan Museum of Art, Rogers Fund, 1907.

Colorplate 23 Vasily Kandinsky, *Painting No. 198,* **1914.**
Oil on canvas, 64 × 36¼ in. (162.6 × 92.1 cm.).
Collection, The Museum of Modern Art, New York, Mrs. Simon Guggenheim Fund.

Responding to Artworks: Art Criticism and Art History

4

Have you ever been puzzled, frustrated, or excited by an artwork? Learning how to look at paintings, sculptures, and examples of architecture and how to respond to them are essential elements in understanding and enjoying the important part of our cultural heritage that we call art. So let's investigate and practice ways of describing, analyzing, and interpreting artworks that will help us evaluate their importance and artistic merit, ways that go beyond taking a quick look and stating our personal preference (I like it, I don't like it) before moving on to the next painting in a gallery or museum.

When we talk about artworks, we clarify our thoughts. We are making a conscious effort to receive the communication that the creator of the artwork made. We strive to be in touch with the life of the artist. We come to know something of his/her personality, the culture and the time in which the artwork was created, and for what purpose it was created. Through further explorations in art history, we learn what other artists or artworks may have influenced the artist we are studying or how our artist may have influenced other artists. We take a second and then a third look at what we see in front of us and examine what we feel within us. Seeing, investigating, and then transforming into words may be a complex and difficult process, but it is one that is ultimately rewarding. Just looking at artworks is oftentimes not enough. When we search for words to describe and analyze them, we progress from **looking passively** to **seeing with greater discrimination and precision.** We move from being a casual, naive viewer to being one who is more sophisticated in perceiving and responding to artworks. We will share and compare our perceptions and enthusiasms, argue our points, and formulate our judgments with our classmates, because when we talk about art, we help others see the work as we see it.

Strategies that help us respond with understanding and appreciation of an artwork, rather than merely stating personal preferences, intermingle two important components: **art criticism and art history.** When we look at an artwork and think like an **art critic,** we have the visual information right in front of us. We can describe what we see, analyze it, and react to it. Our interpretation may be influenced by our own personal and unique background, our experiences and attitudes. When we look at an artwork and think like an **art historian,** we learn about the artwork from external sources. We are on a fact-finding mission in which we collect available evidence that may even include opinions of critics and historians. To increase our knowledge in this manner, we examine books and other source materials, listen to lectures, and perhaps question a docent in a museum. Art history helps us understand what people were thinking, valuing, believing, and doing at a given period of time. We may wonder why the artist painted in a particular manner and what meaning the art had or has. Responding to artworks is a simultaneous blend of both art criticism and art history components. Some artworks are only understood from the fact-finding of an art history search, but all artworks can be understood, enjoyed, and cherished on a higher level when we harmonize both strategies. Therefore, we will not insist on making a sharp distinction between art history and art criticism strategies but assume that most conversations with an artwork are blends of both. Art criticism and art history enrich and clarify each other.

The following outline encompasses both art criticism and art history strategies for learning from and about works of art. The points made will help us perceive and understand better what we see when we look closely at artworks.

Describing the Artwork

Art Criticism

We describe what we actually see before us. We state what art form we see, whether it is two- or three-dimensional, and whether the artwork is a painting, a drawing, a sculpture, etc. We decide if it has a vertical or horizontal **format** or even a round shape (called a **tondo**). We state if it is a landscape, a portrait, or perhaps an abstract work, etc. We state what medium was used (oil paint, watercolor, marble, etc.). We observe and comment upon the technical properties; that is, we may describe the manner in which paint was applied (thick, swirling brushstrokes; thin washes of color; or the repeated, overlapping marks left by the chisel on a wood surface). We make an inventory of the subject matter, noting the literal details of what we see. We note the pose of the figure, the angle of the head, the facial expression, and perhaps the viewpoint of the artist.

Art History

We describe the results of our fact-finding mission, stating the actual size of the original artwork if we are studying a reproduction of a smaller size. We relate where the artwork is located now and where it was originally meant to be housed, perhaps in a cathedral, a castle, or in the home of a wealthy seventeenth-century Dutch merchant. We tell the name of the artwork and the time and place in which it was created. We give the name of the artist and his/her birth and death dates. We make sure that we know the correct pronunciation of the artist's name. We consider biographical information that is pertinent to the creation of the artwork. We may tell the reason the artwork was made, considering whether it is based on some event in history or was created to inspire religious thought or to record how someone looked, or if it is the product of the artist's imagination. We might need to give sociological considerations to help us reap deeper understandings and ascertain what it tells us about the culture and time in which it was produced. The subject matter of Orozco's *Zapatistas* (**Color Gallery**) focused on agrarian reform and the efforts of farmers to unite and fight. Biographical research makes us aware of Picasso's early years in Paris when his works were marked by his own poverty. His haunting "blue period" from these years often depicts sad images of lonely, outcast people (see *The Tragedy* in the **Color Gallery**).

References to **iconography** (image writing) and **iconology** (image study) that we find in source materials identify specific images in artworks with symbolic content and meaning. For instance, a saint may be depicted by an object (**attribute**) that helps the viewer identify him/her (see "Symbols in Artworks", p. 151). The evangelist John the Baptist is identified with a cross made from reeds, while Luke, the patron saint of painters, is symbolized by a winged ox. It helps to know that artists used the symbol of a lighted candle to symbolize the shortness of life, ivy for eternal life, and that in Christian art, a dandelion stands for grief. **Iconology** helps us learn through literary and philosophical material the cultural attitudes and changes that give meaning and content to the artwork.

Analyzing the Artwork

Art Criticism

Analysis may be defined as the separation of the whole into its parts. We **identify the elements of art** and note how they were used in **ordering and controlling the principles of art**. In a **formal analysis** of an artwork, we look at the elements and principles of art that have given the painting, sculpture, or piece of architecture its **form** as well as its **content, meaning, and expression.** (In this context, the term "formal" analysis is not used as the opposite of "informal" or "casual"). Formal analysis goes beyond description by seeking to show *how* the composition works as it does.

There are many possible relationships between the elements and principles of art. An orderly system can help us determine how an artwork is put together. The charts at the end of each section on the principles of art can help us make observations that will enable us to make an orderly and detailed analysis of what we see in the artwork before us. Across the top of the chart are listed the elements of art. The principle of art is listed on the left. We may select any element, connect it with the principle, and then ask ourselves how this element is used. For instance, we may ask, are the **colors** in the painting **balanced** formally or informally? Has the artist used different thicknesses and kinds of **lines** to add **variety** to the artwork? How are the **shapes** distributed to create a feeling of **movement?** How does the simulation of **texture** create emphasis?

Art History

We compare and contrast the work with other works (by the same artist or by other artists) to determine its style, discovering what is unique and especially important about the work. **Comparing** two or three works of art is an effective technique that helps us identify **similarities** and **differences** in ways that artists have used the elements and principles of art. By looking back and forth to find resemblances or things the two works have in common, or to find ways in which they differ, we discover things we may have missed in a cursory glance at only one artwork.

Interpreting the Artwork

Just as two artists look at the same tree and render it in two entirely different manners, we can each look carefully and respond with different feelings to the content of the same artwork. Our response may be one of amusement. We may be soothed, uplifted, or repelled. We may sometimes ask ourselves questions we can't answer. Art critics, aestheticians, and art historians frequently find problems in endeavoring to interpret and understand something that they, at least for the moment, are unable to answer. Remember we are enlarging and extending not only our knowledge about artworks but our feelings as well. We may respond by feeling that the mood of the artwork is poetic or playful, joyous or sad. It may make us feel annoyed or hostile. It may remind us of a happy or frightening experience that we had long ago. It may be a narrative painting that causes us to wonder and to imagine beyond the actual subject matter that we see before us. We may feel uplifted by a religious artwork or inspired by a patriotic one. Our opinions may be swayed by an artwork that focuses on propaganda. We may enjoy an artwork for the gesture and movement of its realistic subject matter; we may delight in the exquisite colors, lines, and shapes alone. We may find that it touches upon the world of fantasy and dreams, and makes us ponder and ask questions that are hard to answer.

Some questions dealing with aesthetics that help us interpret artworks might be: Why do I feel as I do about this artwork? Why do I find the seascape (or portrait or abstraction) fascinating (or boring)? How did the artist use the medium and technique and arrange the elements and principles of art to evoke this response in me?

Art Criticism

We respond to the artwork emotionally and endeavor to understand how and why we react the way we do. We interpret with more than our eyes. Our memories, emotions, and values are brought into play as we endeavor to give coherence to our perceptions. We ponder upon what is in the work that evokes our feelings and sets the mood of the work—perhaps its colors, shapes, textures, or proportions. Perhaps the subject matter itself or the technical properties of the medium may cause our feelings to be aroused in the manner they are. We endeavor to find within the work of art evidence that supports our opinions.

Art History

We respond to the artwork by knowing how the artist was influenced by his/her time and place and by such significant events as a war or oppression. We respond more fully if we know the purpose the artist had in mind in creating the artwork—whether it was to inspire religious fervor, to record the demeanor of royalty, or to experiment in exploring new ways of seeing. The artwork may reach us more eloquently if we know significant factors in the artist's life and personality. In viewing some artworks, our study of art history will greatly help our understanding of what we see and are interpreting. For instance, many artists have depicted biblical events by painting the central characters dressed in clothing of their own time and in their own environment. In the seventeenth century, Rembrandt sought to show the human ministry of the Christian religion in this manner, and it is important to identify the images in these artworks in their symbolic context.

Judging the Artwork

Art Criticism

We make an evaluative decision about the artistic merit of the work as it relates to the following **styles of art.** Many artworks do not clearly fall into only one of the categories; they may be weighted in one direction but have overlapping emphases. We may decide that the artist was extremely successful and innovative in his/her handling of one or more of the elements and principles of art. We may particularly respond to the artist's successful handling of the medium. Sometimes we are in awe of the emotional impact or the fantasy or the mood of the painting, or we are uplifted and inspired by his message. We may want to compare any of these qualities with another artwork with a similar theme or one that was made in another time or culture. We may find that our friends are not always in agreement with our judgments and choices; however, remember that we are evaluating the artwork on many points that go beyond stating one's personal preference.

(1) **Representationalism; realism**—In these artworks, the emphasis is on the realistic presentation of the subject matter. The people, objects, or landscape look very real and may be considered an imitation of nature. (In the **Color Gallery,** see artworks by Bierstadt and Vermeer. Can you identify any other artworks that fall mostly in this category?)

(2) **Abstraction; formalism**—In these artworks, the emphasis is on the organization of the elements and principles of art. The artist was more interested in the lines, shapes, and colors (the formal design) than in the objects, people, or landscape itself. (In the **Color Gallery,** see artworks by Mondrian and Kandinsky. Can you identify any other artworks that fall mostly in this category?)

(3) **Expressionism; emotionalism**—In these artworks, the emphasis is on the intense feeling, mood, or idea related to the visual image rather than on the realistic depiction of the people, objects, or landscape. (In the **Color Gallery,** see artworks by van Gogh and Marc. Can you identify any other artworks that fall mostly in this category?)

(4) **Surrealism; fantasy**—In these artworks, the emphasis is on the imagination and the world of the subconscious. The artist often depicts objects in a very realistic manner but makes unusual connections and relationships. (In the **Color Gallery,** see artwork by Chagall. Can you find any other artworks that fall mostly in this category?)

Art History

We make a thoughtful evaluation of the factors that are related to the artwork's importance and its place in the history of art, arriving at objective conclusions. We comment on the influence the artwork may have had on the artworks of other artists or perhaps what artworks were forerunners of the piece we are viewing.

Responding to Artworks

Conversations with an Artwork

Asking and answering questions about an artwork is a strategy that involves more than expressing one's random feelings about an artwork and stating one's personal preferences, preferences that are often based on subject matter or how realistic an artwork is. The actress Jodie Foster once stated that she loves to be interviewed because it makes her know what she thinks. Of course, the interviewer asked appropriate questions of the interviewee to elicit this comment!

The following inquiries are examples of the kinds of questions that we may ask ourselves to help us get started in this seemingly complex process of describing, analyzing, interpreting, and judging art. They will help us know what we think about an artwork. They will ultimately help us understand and evaluate an artwork. They will be instrumental in "demystifying" the artist's production without destroying the "magical" qualities inherent in its creation. These questions are based on the use of critical thinking skills as explained in Benjamin Bloom's *Taxonomy of Educational Objectives in the Cognitive Domain.* **Such strategies ask us to:**

1. **recall information learned in a similar form (knowledge)**
2. **understand and interpret information learned in a different form (comprehension)**
3. **use information learned to relate or apply ideas to new or unusual situations (application)**
4. **examine and break information down into its component parts and identify its unusual characteristics (analysis)**
5. **communicate, generate, or develop something new and original from what is learned (synthesis)**
6. **make judgments and evaluate something based on either external or internal conditions or criteria (evaluation)**

Thus, some questions call upon us to list, describe, define, identify; others call upon us to explain, infer, sequence, classify, contrast, and make analogies; still others challenge us to forecast, predict, and hypothesize.

DESCRIBING THE ARTWORK

What is the subject matter (if any) and what is happening?

How large is the original and where is it now?

Who was the artist and when was it created? What is the name of the artwork? What is the medium?

What is at the top, bottom, and sides of the artwork?

If figures/portraits are seen, how much is shown and what is the stance?

Is the view three-quarter, profile, or frontal? What is the facial expression?

What is in the foreground, middle ground, background?

Describe how the artist showed the time of day in the landscape.

Where is the horizon?

Do we see diagonal lines and shapes?

Does the artwork show deep space?

Are the contours strong and definite?

Are the edges of the object shown with an outline, or are they separated by color, texture, or value differences?

How do the lines differ? same or different widths?

How does the tool relate to the surface of the paper (or canvas or wood or plaster)? (A pencil drawing on smooth paper is different from a pencil drawing on coarse, rough paper. Bits of rough paper show through when crayons or oil pastels are rubbed over it.)

Does the color imitate local color?

What is the light source? What is its direction?

How are the figures depicted in relation to the landscape itself: dwarfed by it, infused with it?

Where is the horizon?

3-D artworks (sculpture/crafts/architecture): Does the artwork have a utilitarian function?

What is the effect of surface quality (highly polished woodgrain, chisel marks, etc.)?

Is there a base, and what purpose beyond support does it serve?

ANALYZING THE ARTWORK

How is unity achieved?

How did the artist vary the color (shape, line, texture)?

Is there an illusion of movement?

From looking at several paintings in which artists used perspective, what can we infer about diminishing sizes?

Are the proportions realistic or exaggerated for expressive purposes?

What is the emphasis of the composition? (The arrangements of the parts are sometimes easy to see; at other times, a closer look is warranted.)

How did the artist use dark and light contrast?

Is there another artist that you know about that used balance in the same way this artist did?

Are there any circular, spiraling, or triangular elements that lead our eyes through the composition?

Do the lines denote movement and energy?

Could your eyes "take a walk" into the distance seen in the artwork, or is the space shallow and flat?

Why do you think the artist used these colors?

Does the effect of light make strong contrasts, with some parts brightly lit while other areas are in darkness?

Is the artwork unified by gradations and balance of light and dark?

What do repetition and pattern contribute?

How do the positive and negative spaces relate?

INTERPRETING THE ARTWORK

Is the person's personality, character, or mood revealed?

Why do you think the artist placed the horizon up so high? or low?

If we see symmetrical or approximate balance, does this give a quiet, rigid, or monumental effect?

If we see asymmetrical balance, what makes us feel that visual balance was achieved?

If the lines and shapes are mostly vertical, what feeling does this give us?

If the lines and shapes are mostly horizontal, does this make us feel peaceful and quiet?

Is the use of deep space exaggerated and expressive?

Does the light seem natural, or theatrical and dramatic?

Is the light used to focus on certain symbolic areas?

Is the environment frightening, inviting, or depressing?

Is the effect of color that of being symbolic, realistic, or decorative?

Does the artwork reflect an aristocratic life-style or a simple, domestic one?

Are symbols included? (Idleness, for example, may be symbolized by playing cards.)

JUDGING THE ARTWORK

Would you recognize this person in real life?

Is the landscape recognizable as a specific place?

For what purpose was the artwork made?

Which paintings are most realistic? Which are more abstract?

Which painting is mostly concerned with dreams and imagination?

Was the artist primarily interested in expressing a strong emotion?

Was the artist mostly concerned with formal aspects of arranging the lines, shapes, and colors?

Judge the artistic merit of the artwork, depending on which style of art it is most concerned with.

How did this artwork influence other artists?

Arrange the paintings in order, from those having the most repeated patterns to those with the least.

How do the medium and technique contribute to (or distract from) the overall effect?

If this artist had lived another one hundred years, how do you think his/her style might have changed?

Which artist do you think will be best remembered in the next one hundred years? Why?

Which of the paintings do you think shows the most imagination? the most feeling? the most unity in the arrangement of colors and shapes?

How do you think the painting would make you feel if the artist had used all warm colors instead of cool colors?

Is the surface quality of the objects dominant, or is the volume and form of the objects more important?

What does the artist's degree of skill in handling the medium contribute to the artistic merit of the work?

Chart for Analyzing Artworks

A few of the spaces have been filled in as examples of how to use this chart. Look at Marc Chagall's *Green Violinist* in the **Color Gallery** and see if you agree with these comments. Then select another artwork in the **Color Gallery** and make your own analysis of how the artist used the elements and principles of art.

Elements of Art

	Color	Line	Shape/Form	Texture	Space	Value
Balance			Houses and figures on either side of and below central figure give feeling of informal balance		Negative spaces are well balanced with positive	Dark and light values in comfortable balance
Emphasis	Unusual color of face catches our attention	Black line of bowstring and on violin directs our attention to face and hand	Triangular shapes, squares and half-rounds are emphasized			
Proportion	Secondary colors are in good proportion to neutral colors				Proportion of figures and houses in relation to violinist gives feeling of fantasy and shallow space	
Movement			Eyes are led to focal point by angular points of triangles in coat			
Rhythm, Repetition, Pattern			Square shapes on pants and windows make patterns			
Variety			Small dreamlike shapes of houses, figures, surrounding figure provide variety of images			Light and dark tones of purple provide pleasing variety
Unity	Limited number of colors (3) plus neutrals provide unity		Similar shapes repeated throughout composition			

Principles of Art

An Oral Presentation of an Artwork

A short oral presentation of an artwork can help you organize and clarify your thoughts and perceptions. Select an artwork from the **Color Gallery** and use art criticism and art history strategies to help you describe, analyze, interpret, and judge it. You will need to read about the artist in some of the reference books listed on pp. 155–156 to help you with aspects of art history. Then spend five minutes or more to present it to your classmates. The following is an example of how a university student responded to Vincent van Gogh's *Starry Night* (**see Color Gallery**).

This oil painting was made by Vincent van Gogh in 1889, one year before he died. The size of the original is 29 × 36¼ inches. It hangs in the Museum of Modern Art in New York. It is a nighttime landscape that is done in the thick, swirling brushstrokes that are characteristic of this artist. We see the sky taking up most of the picture space. The sky is filled with the circular, rolling, spiraling lines and shapes that represent the stars and moon. In the foreground, we see a sleeping village with the tall dark triangular shape of a cypress tree reaching upward on the left. Blue and yellow are the dominant colors. Since daytime scenes are far more prevalent as subjects for landscapes, we find a certain fascination in seeing a landscape at night.

Born in Holland in 1853, Vincent, as he signed his artworks and liked to be called, was a sensitive, lonely man who often alienated people by his behavior. He always wanted to help people but failed at being a minister, a missionary, and at working for art dealers. Only the last ten years of his life were devoted to art. During that time he sold only one painting, and that was for $80. He worked at painting with a fierce intensity, all the while conveying his thoughts and feelings in correspondence with his brother Theo, who supported him financially and emotionally.

Perhaps we see Vincent's longing for a family and a homelife in the peaceful village in the middleground with its church spire pointing upward and catching our attention. We observe his feverish brushstrokes in this painting and can see how he may have even squeezed the paint directly on the canvas rather than placing it on his palette first. This created thick layers of paint that add an actual texture to the artwork. We can almost visualize Vincent working on this painting as he stood in the field at night, candles blazing on his palette and around the brim of his hat to help him see.

The round circular shapes of the stars are repeated a number of times in the dark blue sky in a random pattern with the sizes varied. Our eyes follow the movement of the rolling circles and spirals in the skies. The dark cypress in the foreground tends to stabilize the turbulence. The lightest part of the picture is the haloed crescent moon on the right. It is balanced by the deep green cypress tree on the left, a shape which reminds us of a flame writhing upward as if it were trying to reach the heavens. The

gently rolling hills in the background behind the village seem restful and quiet and tend to lead our eyes to the cypress. We see a great variety of dark and light tones of both blue and yellow used throughout the picture. These were two of Vincent's favorite colors; he believed that yellow stood for love, warmth and friendship. The limited number of colors gives unity to the painting as do the uniform thick swirling brushstrokes.

We feel peaceful when we look at the sleeping village with its lights glowing in the windows even though the busy skies are alive with the restless energy of the stars. We feel uplifted, perhaps even somewhat protected, when our eyes are carried rhythmically upward by the dark form of the tree. We remember summer evenings and looking up at the clear skies and seeing stars that were especially bright. Although Vincent has painted the stars larger and more vibrant than we are accustomed to seeing them without the benefit of telescopes, he has conveyed his deep feelings. He once stated he wanted people to understand that he felt deeply and tenderly. This expressive work of art succeeds in touching our emotions and making us see night skies with perhaps a greater clarity than we would have without Vincent's special vision.

Talking with Children about an Artwork

Children like to look at artworks and respond to them. When reproductions of artworks are placed before them or when they visit a museum and study original artworks, dialogue can cause their perceptions to broaden. When they describe, analyze, and interpret and make aesthetic judgments about an artwork, they learn a new vocabulary, and repeated encounters with a variety of artworks will help children's skills in responding.

Large reproductions (often called study prints or posters), slides, books, and postcards of great artworks are available for classroom use and are relatively inexpensive (see Resources on pp. 157–159). Calendars with first-rate large reproductions of the works of famous artists are readily available. This accessibility presents an advancement from the past, when color reproductions were costly and limited in number. Nothing can take the place of seeing original artworks; however, the difficulty of visiting distant and foreign museums presents an obvious deterrent for many people.

There are certain educational advantages in using reproductions. When you visit a museum, you may see, for instance, one or two works by Winslow Homer. But with reproductions, students can compare five or six of his artworks; or the teacher may select five or six artworks by other artists that deal with the same theme. Students may then be called upon to compare works that illustrate the four styles of art, and to discuss how each artist used the elements and principles of arts and how they are affected by the mood and meaning of each artwork.

Large reproductions have advantages over the use of slides and overhead transparencies in elementary classrooms. Reproductions can be viewed in multiples in lighted rooms and left for extended periods of time for students to view.

When large reproductions are used in the classroom, it is important that the children are seated close to the work being described and analyzed, and that they know that it is a reproduction rather than an original.

The following dialogue suggests the sort of remarks and teacher-responses that could direct the students' thinking to a greater understanding of the artwork.

Sunday Afternoon on the Island of La Grande Jatte, by Georges Seurat (See Color Gallery)

T: Tell me what you see.

S: A lot of people.

T: Where are they?

S: On the grass. Maybe a park or something because I see some water, too. And I see a border, sort of like a frame painted all around the outside edge.

T: What are the people doing?

S: Just standing there or sitting. Oh, maybe walking. I see a lady with a little girl like she's walking toward me. They are really dresssed up for a day in the park. They look like real people, but their clothes look like they're from an old-fashioned movie.

T: Yes, that's how people dressed at the time the artist Georges Seurat painted this artwork, a little over one hundred years ago. Which people are the closest to us?

S: That man and woman on the right.

T: You're right. The artist made them larger than any other figures and placed them lower on the canvas. That makes them seem closer to us. Which other figures seem close to us?

S: Those three on the left that are sitting on the grass. They are looking out toward the water. Maybe there is a sailboat race or something going on. Looks like the black dog is eating their lunch scraps.

T: Those figures are in the foreground, too. Can you see how the artist, Georges Seurat, has painted a shaded area here? What else do you see in the foreground?

S: Oh, I see a little monkey and a little dog running toward the black dog.

T: Let's take a little walk with our eyes back into the distance and find some more figures. How are they like the figures in the foreground?

S: Well, they are dressed like them, they're looking out at the water, most of them anyway, and I see some more parasols. Most of the people seem real quiet. I don't think it looks like a noisy place. Maybe you could hear some quiet sort of music playing if you were there. Oh, I do see one little girl running.

T: Let's have several of you stand and sit in the same positions of the figures in the painting. Look carefully at the painting before you take a position. (*Time out for this activity.*)

T: Now let's look at the picture again and measure the figures you see in the middle ground. (Use a ruler or string and hold it upright to measure the height of the couple on the right; then the central figure with the little girl, and then a figure in the background.) Seurat painted the figures that he wanted us to see as farthest away the smallest. When artists do this, we say they have used diminishing sizes to show deep space. He also placed them higher up from the bottom of the canvas. They are also lighter in color value. Can you see any other ways he made the figures seem farther away from us?

S: We can't see any stripes or ribbons or anything on their clothes.

T: Right, he made the details and textures less sharp and clear. Let's look and see how many places Seurat used curving lines and shapes. (Let a student use a pointer to do this.)

S: The skirts, the parasols and hats, and even the tails on the animals. Oh, yes, the sailboat.

T: I'm glad you noticed that white, curving sail in the background. It is very much like part of the parasol. I think you may have noticed it because it was white, in contrast to the darker blue of the water. Can you find other places in the composition where the artist repeated white? This tends to add unity to the picture and lead our eyes around and throughout the complex organization. He has painted a shadow shape for almost each figure and that adds unity, too. Describe the colors you see. Are they the same as you would see in nature?

S: Well, I see a lot of green, I guess, but I see light greens, sort of a yellow-green and some blue-greens. Quite a bit of blue, too. Then I see that reddish-orange color on the clothing and the parasol in the middle. They're probably the same colors the artist saw.

T: Good. Red and green are complementary colors on the color wheel. They are opposites and contrast strongly with each other. Let's talk about the surface quality of the painting. Do you see it as being smooth or what?

S: It looks, well, kind of grainy when I think of the way most other paintings look, like the one by Gauguin we saw a few days ago.

T: Grainy is a good word, because Seurat invented a new way to put the paint on his canvas and he called it pointillism. He applied the paint with many tiny dots, one color next to another color, so that when he was done and you, the viewer, stepped away from the artwork, your eyes would mix the colors together. If a lot of white dots were applied with only a few blue dots, your eyes would see a light blue.

S: That must have taken him a long time. How large is that painting in the original?

T: It is 81″ × 120⅜″; that's about 8′ × 10′!

S: Wow! Did he make very many paintings during his life?

T: Only about sixty because he died in 1891, when he was only thirty-one, of a throat infection. He was working with another artist named Signac, who carried on the experiments with pointillism. Look at the way Seurat arranged the people and trees. It all seems very casual and lifelike, yet he was very careful to create a feel of visual balance. We call the kind of symmetry he used, informal. One side is not exactly like the other side. The two large figures in rather dark clothing on the right tend to balance the three seated figures and the dog on the left. Can you find other things that balance each other?

S: (Students use brush pointer)

T: What do you see as the center of emphasis in this painting? What leads your eye to it?

S: I see the lady in the center, the one with the little girl in the white dress. I think it's because she is in the center and is the only one facing us. Then, too, her red parasol contrasts against the green foliage of the trees above her.

S: I don't agree. My attention goes to the couple on the right. They're the largest figures. Their clothing is dark and the line of the parasol and cane kind of point to them.

T: Do you like looking at this painting?

S: Yes. There are so many things to see. My eyes keep moving back and forth, imagining what the people were saying. It looks like a warm day. It is almost like a photo, but then again the people all look like they aren't moving—like they're posing and still as statues. Most of the shapes and lines are vertical, the tree trunks and the people. Maybe that's why it looks quiet and peaceful.

S: And I like the new way Seurat painted, that pointillism. It's neat. Could we try making a picture like that . . . only not 8′ × 10′!

Visiting Art Museums and Galleries

Museums house many of the world's great artworks, even those that were created long before there was such a thing as a museum, because many works of art in the distant past were commissioned and created to serve purposes other than hanging in a museum. For instance, in the Western world, religious pieces were made for a populace that was largely illiterate to teach them Bible stories and to inspire them. These works were displayed in places of worship. Royalty hired court painters to record their likenesses, and these works hung in palaces. Today museums have special exhibits that bring together groups of major artworks from many different museums and private collections. Such exhibits may feature such things as a retrospective show of the lifetime accomplishments of a single artist or a number of works created during the same period of time.

Getting in the habit of making frequent visits to museums can be a lifetime source of enjoyment. Most of us live reasonably close to a major museum, and many people travel in America and abroad where wonderful museums await us.

Entering a museum for the first time, especially a large one, may seem bewildering, so don't overlook the maps and guides that are available at the front desk. These printed materials will help you know what kinds of works to expect and in which rooms they may be found. Often a visit to a museum is one in which you want to gain an overview of what is there, taking a look at the major galleries and rooms, letting some works attract your attention, and gaining a rather quick impression of the collections. After several hours you will probably leave with a satisfying feeling of exhaustion and saturation. You probably won't find it possible to take more than quick glances at each of the artworks on such a visit, but when you see one or two that you find especially appealing, linger and enjoy the experience. You will probably finish your visit remembering several magnificent artworks and begin planning when you will return for another look. Look for what appeals to you and build upon it, but keep your eyes open and find something you are attracted to that you never liked before. Go at your own pace. There is a limit to one's endurance, and it is advisable to either relax for awhile on a seat in a gallery or find the gallery cafe for a snack.

By reading the labels that are posted next to artworks, you can find the title of the work, the artist, the medium used, and other pertinent data. This may include a number that tells the date when the museum acquired the work, the date when the artwork was created, and the name of the present owners if it is on loan from another museum or a private collection. Some museums include additional information.

Another way to plan your visit to a museum is to select which gallery or collection you will focus upon. Most museums do not arrange their permanent collection of artworks in a chronological order, grouping them instead on a geographical basis or by schools of art. Thus, you will find in separate sections artworks from Egypt, Greece, or perhaps the Renaissance period. In addition to permanent collections, most museums have a gallery or two for changing exhibits, and a quick look at the museum calendar or program will tell you "what's on" at the time you are there. Some of the very popular so-called "blockbuster" shows may even require that you purchase a ticket in advance.

On a more leisurely visit you can use these approaches to absorbing an artwork that particularly appeals to you:

1. Stand before it and study all its parts (art elements); then close your eyes and see if you can reconstruct it. If your visual memory is faulty, open your eyes and reexamine the parts more carefully. Then close your eyes and try again. This technique makes you look more carefully at the artwork, really seeing it, and remembering it.

2. Take along a viewfinder and hold it before an artwork that particularly strikes your senses. Frame a significant detail and focus your attention on that part. You can try to find a painting-within-a-painting in this manner, one that particularly appeals to you, using your viewfinder to locate within its boundaries a center of interest and an arrangement that has a comfortable informal balance. After you have accomplished this, make a small sketch of what you see through the viewfinder. You will be taking home your personalized selection of your artwork.

3. Sketch the entire artwork. Art students, and artists as well, have always trained themselves by drawing from artworks. One frequently sees a student in a museum working at an easel, copying from a masterpiece. Even if you don't feel you are copying it very skillfully, your pen or pencil acts as a magnifying glass, focusing your attention on wonderful things that you probably wouldn't see otherwise.

By all means, visit the museum bookshop, either before you enter the galleries or afterward. By stopping there first, you will discover by looking at the postcards, reproductions, slides, books, and catalogs, which artworks the museum considers extraordinary enough to have reproduced. This might guide you as to what things you won't want to miss, or those works you didn't know were there. By purchasing these museum-shop reproductions, you are able to take your visual memories home in a tangible way.

The noted art historian Kenneth Clark has his own fine collection of original works of art in his home, but he also keeps postcard reproductions on his mantelpiece of works that currently fit his mood. If you read a catalog after you have seen the exhibit, your knowledge about the artworks and the artists will be enhanced.

Your visit to a museum may be one in which you are alone, with a friend, or with a group. There are advantages to each arrangement. If you are with a friend, you will each be discovering things and sharing what you see. If you are alone, there is probably a closer relationship between you and the individual artwork. Have you ever stood before a fine portrait of a seventeenth-century Dutch master and had the almost eerie feeling that the eyes of the person, long since dead, are gazing directly at you alone down through the centuries? Or perhaps you just let the pure visual impact of Kandinsky's vibrant colors drench you in a silent form of communication? Or you sense the eternal quality of Egyptian artifacts, or the lonely isolation of an Edward Hopper cityscape?

Alone or with friends, an audioguide can provide you with an individually guided and sequenced look at an exhibit. Through your own set of earphones, you are told upon which artwork to focus your attention and then are provided with interesting information. You can shut the tape cassette off at any time and linger longer before a particular piece of art or before one that has caught your eye but which was not included in the tape's monologue.

Group tours in a museum give visitors the opportunity to have the expert guidance of a trained guide called a **docent.** Such a knowledgeable museum lecturer can point out aspects of an artwork that the first-time viewer might miss, and pass along pertinent historical information about the artist and time period that gives the trip a special indepth quality.

If you plan on taking a group of children on a field trip to a museum, it is best to arrange with the museum ahead of time. The museum may send you a set of slides and written information to use in preparing the children for their visit. Upon your arrival, they will provide you with a museum docent that is trained in talking with children. Here we won't expect to see everything in one visit; rather we will expect to focus on only one exhibit and especially on several works of art. Young viewers need to understand that they may only "touch the artwork with their eyes," since the artworks are very valuable and can be damaged by touching. Many museums provide studio space for children to go to after seeing an exhibit and try their hand at working with a particular medium. In addition, museum worksheets are often provided for students to enable them to go on a guided "treasure hunt," searching for specific things in specific paintings. And, of course, a visit to the museum shop can give young viewers an opportunity to begin their own small-scale private art collection by purchasing postcard reproductions of the favorite artworks they have just seen.

Figure 4.1 Lecturers and docents make museum visits more meaningful and interesting. Henry Augustine Tate, Ph.D., Lecturer, Department of Education, Museum of Fine Arts, Boston, points out details in the painting by John Singleton Copley, *Boy with a Squirrel.*

Not to be overlooked as artwork is the museum itself. Many museums are spectacular pieces of architecture, and some are set in dazzling gardens and grounds that demand our attention. You will usually find outdoor sculpture to admire on the museum grounds. Notice the stately classical columns of the Metropolitan Museum in New York; be absorbed with the buildings that were once homes and are now museums, such as the Isabella Stewart Gardner Museum in Boston and the Frick in New York. Newer museums show styles of contemporary architects and reflect the times, such as the Guggenheim in New York, the Hirshhorn in Washington, D.C. and the Los Angeles County Museum. Contrast the new east wing of the National Gallery of Art in Washington, D.C. with the older part of the museum.

Some of the world's major museums have produced videos of "museum tours." For instance, the Metropolitan Museum, the Louvre in Paris, and the National Gallery in Washington show the viewer some of the finest works in the museums and at the same time give us a glimpse of the museums themselves (see Resources).

Thirty-Six Ways to Use Reproductions in the Classroom

1. Make a "magic paintbrush" by covering the handle of a regular brush with glue and sprinkling it with glitter dust; or make a "super paintbrush" by attaching two feet of dowel stick to the ferrule of a brush. Use as pointers. Use to show students how artists created brushstrokes. Use with young children as a magic wand to enable the child to have "magic eyes" and to see special things in the artwork.

2. Start a story about the reproduction and have each student add to the story after he/she is touched on the shoulder with the magic paintbrush.

3. Ask students to rename an artwork, or have them give it a name before you tell them what the artist named it.

4. Have the students "memorize" the painting for fifteen seconds; then turn it around and ask them to describe it. Or have them make up questions about it to ask other students.

5. Ask students what they would change in the composition of the artwork, what they would add or take away if they were the artist.

6. Ask a student to choose two reproductions and tell why these paintings belong together or what they have in common. Have students then tell how the two artworks are different from each other.

7. Ask students to enter the painting with their eyes and "take a walk." Have one of them use the magic paintbrush to show the path his/her eyes follow. See if other students "take a different walk."

8. Ask students to imitate a pose or imitate the facial expression of the person/s in the artwork. Have several students imitate a group pose, imitating the body positions of the figures in the reproduction.

9. Let one student "interview" the person in the painting, and have another student stand behind the reproduction and answer questions, pretending to be the person in the painting. If two or more people are in the painting, students may assume roles of each of them and have a discussion.

10. After a discussion of a reproduction or of a thematic grouping of artworks, play tic-tac-toe on the chalkboard. Divide class into two teams. Ask questions. Let teams take turns answering questions and placing an *x* or *o* for each correct answer.

11. After a discussion of a reproduction, let one student be a salesperson and let him/her have thirty seconds to "sell" the painting to the group, basing the sales pitch on the way the artist used the elements and principles of art, the way the artist expressed feelings, showed imagination, used art materials, etc.

12. At the close of a discussion of an artwork, have students take turns using one word or short phrase to describe it. First child says "bright colors." Second child says "bright colors and black outlines." Third child repeats and adds another word or phrase.

13. Use a piece of butcher paper the same size as the reproduction. Cut out several small openings so that they reveal details of the reproduction underneath. Then let students guess what the rest of the artwork might be. Before you remove the butcher paper, let students use crayons or marking pens and draw on the butcher paper what they think might be beneath it.

14. Write short, descriptive phrases on file cards that are appropriate to one or more of the reproductions that the class will be discussing. These may be such descriptive terms as: "mostly cool colors, strong vertical lines, lots of geometric shapes, very lonely feeling, lots of movement, most imagination, calmest feeling, emotional use of color, shapes with hard edges, saddest feeling, deepest space, greatest contrast in texture, monochromatic colors, lots of movement, unity shown by use of color, red draws attention to focal point, shapes with blurry edges, dull intensity of colors, greatest variety of simulated textures, implied lines, shallow flat space, definite contour lines, repetition to create pattern," etc. Choose six students to serve as "jurors" and give one of the cards to each one. Students will "award" their card to the artwork they feel should receive that descriptive phrase. They then must be able to explain or justify their choices.

15. Reconstruct the artwork; that is, have the students speculate as to what they think the artist did first in making the artwork. Then what did he/she probably do next?

16. Place a clear sheet of acetate or mylar over the reproduction. Then use a water-soluble black marking pen and draw on it. The teacher or student may choose to show all the round shapes; areas where artist used red; negative spaces; perspective lines; focal point; directional lines; contour lines, etc. Wipe pen marks off the acetate with a damp paper towel.

17. Bake a thick gingerbread cookie the full size of a baking sheet (or bake a sheet cake). Then use royal frosting or buttercream frosting and decorate it to be an "edible" duplication of a famous artwork.

18. Use small reproductions or details from larger ones. Make badges and have Friday serve as "Badge Day," with students selecting a badge and having friends try to guess who the artist is.

For Students

Students "adopt" an artist and do reading and research on the artist's life and work. They then may participate in the following activities:

Figure 4.2 A memorable student impersonation of Pablo Picasso was the result of reading and reflecting about this great artist's life and work.

19. Student writes a day in the diary of van Gogh, Renoir, Leonardo, etc.

20. Student impersonates the artist, or two students may stage a mock interview for the "Today Show," with one student interviewing the artist and one student impersonating the artist. Students may dress in costume.

21. Class writes a front page for a newspaper that might have appeared in the lifetime of one artist, or several artists who are living or who lived during the same period. They may record events that were happening at that time, along with a story about the artist and his/her contemporaries.

22. Students celebrate the birthday of one of the artists, coming to school in regular clothing plus a hat or headgear that was in style at the time that the artist lived or that is decorated in the manner of that artist's works. They may make paper banners related to the artist and his/her works.

23. Students bind a book, writing in it questions and answers about an artist, a poem they wrote about the artist, short bio, etc.

24. Students write the name of the artist vertically, one letter to a line. Then they write a short phrase that relates to that artist and his/her artworks:

C—Children and women were favorite themes
A—Attended Pennsylvania Academy of Fine Arts
S—"Simply and frankly American"
S—Saw her painting "hung on the line"
A—Accepted Legion of Honor Award in France
T—Traveled to Paris as a child
T—Treasured in America after her death in 1926

25. Students imagine the artist alive today and write about where they would take him/her and what conversations they would have if they could spend one day with him/her. What questions would they ask? What would they like to show him/her in today's America? How do they think the artist would react? What would they most like to tell the artist?

26. Two students imagine a conversation that would occur if their two artists could meet and talk to each other today. Would they argue? Upon what would they agree? Would they be surprised at anything? What themes would they paint about in today's world?

27. Students will use a large piece of paper and make a folded paper hat and decorate it to celebrate the works of one artist. Use cut paper, marking pens, paint, crayons, scrap material, etc. What symbols and motifs will they need to incorporate?

28. Each student chooses a reproduction and studies the artist and artwork. Then they write eight true facts, each one on a separate file card. They then write two false statements on two different cards. Cards are numbered on reverse side and put in an envelope. Envelope may be decorated in a manner related to the artist's work. The name of the student is written inside the flap. Students trade envelopes and try to find the two false cards. Consult with writer to see if they are correct in their answers.

29. Find a quotation by an artist in a reference book. Use calligraphy to make a small poster. Illustrate it in the manner of that artist. Design a border and use an illuminated initial to begin the quotation.

30. Students do research in reference books and create a chronological time-line on a long roll of paper, marking dates when key artworks were created. They should include important historical events, discoveries, inventions, births and deaths of important people, etc. Time-line may be illustrated with students' own drawings, clips from magazines, travel catalogs, etc.

31. Students make a painting or drawing "in the manner" of the artist they adopted, except they choose subject matter that their artist never tried. For instance, paint a penguin in the manner of Picasso. Paint a butterfly the way Renoir might have painted it. Paint a self-portrait as Catlin painted Native American Indians.

32. Student makes up a crossword puzzle about his/her artist.

33. Master Peeks of art—Select an artwork with a few large figures. Cover the reproduction with Saran wrap and rule it off in squares with a black marker. Then use a large, heavy piece of corrugated cardboard or foamboard. Rule it off in the same number of squares. These squares will be much larger than those on the reproduction. Have students paint it with tempera. When finished painting, cut out the face areas and let students peek through the openings to have their pictures taken. This is a good project for a school carnival or any fund-raising event.

34. Baker's dough mural—Select a reproduction such as Edward Hicks's *Peaceable Kingdom* or *Noah's Ark*. After studying it from the standpoint of art criticism and art history, students will make their own version of it using colored baker's dough. Use particle board, ⅝" thick, about 18" × 24", and cover it with chicken wire. Attach wood strips on the four sides for a frame. Mix baker's dough for the background. (4 cups of flour, 1 cup of salt, ¼ cup of liquid tempera, and water to make a soft dough—about 1½ cups.) Spread the dough over the panel with your knuckles and then with a rolling pin to flatten it. It should be about ½" thick. You will need one batch of dough for each 12" square area.

Figure 4.3 Detail from a Cubist artwork by Picasso is emulated by a university student who made a crayon drawing on white paper that was placed on a warming tray.

Assign different objects in composition to different students: animals, trees, people, etc. Have students use different colors of baker's dough to create small bas-relief figures. Use a scale of nothing larger than the palm of your hand. Students model figures on paper towels, bringing their finished objects to the panel for assembly. Spray background with water and attach figures, pressing gently in place. When finished, let panel dry thoroughly (probably several weeks); then cover it with Enviro-tex resin for a glossy, long-lasting finish.

35. Composite painting—Find a small reproduction of a famous artwork and cut it apart in small squares and have each student enlarge a square. Reassemble. (See directions on p. 19).

36. Warming tray art emulation—Use L-frames and place them on a reproduction, moving them until you find a pleasing and interesting detail. Then place a piece of white paper on a warming tray.

Hold it in place with a mitt, if necessary. Use a crayon and move the tip slowly over the paper, allowing time for the crayon to melt as it moves. Enlarge the detail you see in the L-frame. Emulate the strokes and technique you see in the master's work. Match colors, blend colors, etc. Use scrap crayons that have had the paper removed by soaking them in warm water.

Learning to Evaluate One's Own Artwork

Responding to our own artwork in a manner that requires us to examine what we have done by describing, analyzing, interpreting, and evaluating it can help us identify where our artwork is successful and where we might wish to improve our skills in the future. By writing a critique of our own process and product, we become more consciously aware of what we have accomplished and where our skills need to be enhanced.

After you complete one of the **Producing Artworks** lessons that follow each of the sections on the Elements and Principles of Art, you can evaluate your own progress by using the format that follows. It gives specific steps to guide you, along with a variety of vocabulary terms and phrases that will help you make a thoughtful critique of your own artwork. Follow this outline and write one or two pages. First describe what you actually see in the way of subject matter and technical properties, and then analyze the way you used the elements and principles of art. The next steps ask you to reflect on the mood or emotion that you have expressed, and then you will endeavor to relate the meaning of your artwork to the four styles of art. The final step gives you the opportunity to describe the best parts of your composition as well as thinking of how you could improve your artwork.

The following is an example written by a university student that used the outline as a guide for responding to a piece of her own artwork:

My artwork is a watercolor painting. I used thick paper and watercolor paints. Some of the brushstrokes are thin washes as in the sky, while others are very thick as in the stream. The objects depicted are trees, clouds, rocks, and a stream. It is a landscape painting showing a mountainside with tall trees and shrubbery, and a stream flowing through it.

When starting the artwork, I used a thin black marker to outline the objects. I used curvy, meandering lines for the clouds and stream. The trees were made of sketchy, hatched lines. All the colors I used were cool colors, shades and tints of blue or green. The green trees next to the bright blue stream express a happy and fresh feeling. The trees have sharp or jagged edges. Some of the branches are repeated shapes. The clouds and stream take a freeform shape. The water has a shiny texture that I created with dark and light blobs of blue. The clouds are billowy, and the sky is slick light blue. The greatest changes of value are found in the trees. Some of the trees are a bright green while others a more avacado tone. The river, by being smaller near the upper part and growing larger in the lower part creates deep space; the trees show depth by overlapping and this makes them look thick and dense.

The trees forming large shapes on the right side are balanced informally by some greenery and the descending stream on the left. Variety is shown by differences in the greens of the trees and in the thickness and thinness of blue in the stream. A flowing movement is seen in the water, and the thin brushstrokes in the sky also show cloud movement. The first thing I see in my artwork is the group of trees; they are most dominant because they are the largest mass of color and are centered in the composition. The proportion of the stream to the rocks is of a realistic scale. My artwork seems complete and harmonious.

I was mostly representing a landscape, working with L-frames and a detail of a photograph. The best parts of my artwork are in the way I used texture and color: the texture of the stream was accomplished by applying wet-on-wet washes; the variety of green tones in the trees was obtained by blending various intensities of green. I could improve my artwork with the use of less outline details on the clouds. I could also improve the rocks by my handling of wet-on-dry color washes and layering of colors. I used my imagination with my changes in brushstrokes for the clouds and the trees. My artwork shows a mood of relaxation, peacefulness, and tranquility and gives the feeling that no person has ever set foot on the hillside.

Evaluating My Own Art Production

1. *Describing what I see in my artwork:* the medium used; the size of the work; the technical properties (thick brushstrokes, thin washes of color, etc.); stating if the artwork is a landscape painting, still life, figure drawing, portrait, relief print, sculpture, etc.; describing the subject matter—the objects depicted (animals, figures, buildings, etc.)

2. *Analyzing the ELEMENTS OF ART*

   Colors—*What kinds did I use?*
   primary, secondary, intermediate, complementary, analogous, tints, shades, neutrals, warm, cool, bright, intense, dull, dark, light, glowing, soft, harmonious, flat, modeled, monochromatic, sad, happy, expressive, decorative, clashing, high-keyed, low-keyed, representational, realistic, symbolic, imaginative

   Lines—*What kinds did I use?*
   straight, horizontal, vertical, diagonal, curving, smooth, broken, fuzzy, blurred, spiraling, jagged, thick, wide, thin, sharp, graceful, contour, bold, long, short, thick to thin, continuous, meandering, sketchy, hatched, angular, nervous, energetic, delicate, strong, gesture, implied, actual, zigzag, outline, firm, hypnotic, tense, parallel, rough, branching, confusing, stable, stiff, dignified, calligraphic, perspective, realistic, abstract, decorative, gradated, converging

   Shapes/Forms—*What kinds did I use?*
   angular, circular, geometric, free-form, soft-edged, hard-edged, large, small, organic, gradated, repeated, outlined, natural, expressive, threatening, irregular, positive, negative, light, heavy, silhouette, decorative, symbolic, realistic

   Textures—*What kinds did I use?*
   rough, smooth, shiny, soft, metallic, fuzzy, feathery, bumpy, simulated, visual, actual, real, slick, grainy, fluffy, matte, inviting, impasto

   Space—*What kind do I see?*
   deep, overlapping, flat, shallow, distant/lighter, distant/smaller, distant/less detail, distant/higher, negative, perspective, realistic

   Value—*What kind did I use?*
   very dark, medium dark, light, gradated, dramatic, expressive, blended, hatched, crosshatched, stippled, modeled, distance, shadows, shading

3. *Analyzing the PRINCIPLES OF ART*

   Balance—*What kind did I use?*
   formal or symmetrical, approximate, informal or asymmetrical, radial, uncomfortable, casual, calm, comfortable, achieved by _____

   Emphasis—*What is the center of interest and how did I achieve it?*
   dominant, subordinate, less important, location, convergence, isolation, contrast, triangular, center, off-center, dominant, focal point, eyes, face, unusual or surprising subject matter, directional, eye-leading, pointers, texture, lighting

   Proportion—*What relationships did I emphasize?*
   bright to dull, large to small, dark to light, rough to smooth, realistic, distorted, exaggerated, unrealistic

   Movement—*What kind did I use?*
   actual, simulated, illusion, stiff, frozen, static, swinging, sweeping, optical, shifting, mechanical, flowing, random, progressive, regular, alternating, circular, dizzy, diagonal, downward, upward, triangular, animated, realistic, powerful, rhythmical

Rhythm, Repetition and Pattern—*What kinds did I use?*

decorative, motif/module, lines, shapes, colors, gradated, monotonous, dull, lively, realistic, flowing, surface enhancement, revealing form, structural, regular, irregular, random, intriguing, optical, simulating texture

Variety—*What kind did I use?*

color, line, shape, texture, value, size, contrast, placement, monotonous, dull, chaotic

Unity—*Does my artwork seem complete and harmonious?*

yes, no, somewhat, limitations of each element, harmony among elements, harmony between subject matter and style, overlapping, clustering, interlocking, repetition and variation of colors/shapes/lines

4. *Interpreting the mood or emotion of my artwork*

poetic, playful, humorous, vigorous, peaceful, joyous, sad, religious, narrative, propaganda, energetic, warm, loving, angry, recording a likeness, inspirational, restless, quiet, frightening, dreamlike, charming, mysterious, puzzling

5. *Describing the purpose and/or meaning of my artwork*

Realism/representationalism—My artwork is mostly concerned with representing what I saw.

Expressionism/emotionalism—My artwork is mostly concerned with telling about a feeling, idea, or an emotion.

Abstraction/formalism—My artwork is mostly concerned with colors, lines, shapes, textures, and values rather than subject matter.

Surrealism/fantasy—My artwork is mostly concerned with imagination, dreams, the subconscious and the world of the imagination.

6. *Evaluating the artwork*
   1. The best parts of the composition in my artwork are in the way I used _____ (Choose **two** of the art elements and **two** of the art principles and describe them.)
   2. The composition could be improved by changing the _____ (Choose an art element and an art principle and describe them.)
   3. The thing I like best about the way I used the art material is _____
   4. I was especially creative in the way I _____
   5. My artwork shows a feeling of (happiness, sadness, humor, etc.) because of _____
   6. This artwork could be compared/contrasted to another artwork: _____

Questions and Activities

1. Select an artwork from the **Color Gallery** and ask an elementary child to look at it with you. Ask the child questions that involve describing, analyzing, interpreting, and judging the artwork, as detailed in this chapter.

2. To more directly understand how a child responds to artworks, refer to recent studies about how children understand art, such as the book ***How We Understand Art*** by Michael J. Parsons (Cambridge University Press, 1987). Do your own research with children based on the model used by Parsons in his study. Compare your results with those of Parsons.

3. Investigate some other ways to become involved in art criticism, such as "A Phenomenological Methodology for Art Criticism" by E. Louis Lankford, *Studies in Art Education* 25 (1984): 151–58, or "An Art Criticism Questioning Strategy within the Framework of Bloom's Taxonomy" by Karen A. Hamblen, *Studies in Art Education* 26 (1984): 41–50. Compare and contrast these with the art criticism in this chapter.

4. Visit an art museum and then prepare a "treasure hunt" (study sheet) that could be used by a target audience of elementary children on a field trip. Think of specific questions that would guide them in seeking out visual information and that would help make their visit to the museum memorable and meaningful. You may include game-type activities, actual drawing, fill-in-the-blank, or missing spot (draw a portion from a painting and ask them to find its source). Include some activities or questions that will focus on looking at the museum as a structure in itself.

5. Collect postcards and inexpensive reproductions of artworks. Then read chapter 3 in ***Early Childhood Art (4th ed.)*** by Barbara Herberholz and Lee Hanson (Wm. C. Brown Publishers, 1990) and make several art games as described. Your game may focus on aspects of the elements and principles of art or on artists, artworks, and art history.

6. Read at least three "Looking and Learning" sections in *School Arts* magazine. Then select either an artwork from the **Color Gallery** or a famous artwork in an art book and write your own version of "Looking and Learning." Use the same format of: Looking Carefully, Comparing, Key Concepts, Resources, Biography, and Suggested Activities.

When Children Make Art

5

Inseparable Companions: Art Production and Art Appreciation

At any one moment, we experience a thousand things. We can hear a bird, smell the sea, touch a flower, taste peppermint, and watch the sun set—all at the same time. When people create art, they isolate small parts of that vast experience. They simplify and organize the world as they know it, and thus translate their experience into a personal visual statement.

Claire Golding and Al Hurwitz[1]

Children come into this world with the desire to draw; or, we might say, they have the impulse for art in their genetic fuel. Children are "intrinsically motivated in kindergarten through the third grade" and their "continual searching, experimenting, and questioning are striking evidence" of this fact.[2] We have all seen the results of art made by young children without instruction. They begin by making marks (scribbles) and proceed to make graphic symbols (geometric schemas). Some continue on to graphic representation (realism). Most children achieve this natural unfolding in their graphic expression in a sequential manner. The question, then, is how do we as teachers and parents instruct children in art in order to enhance and deepen their artistic growth? What is the content of art that children can learn through instruction? In the past, it was often thought that giving children materials and telling them to create was all that was necessary. Art educators today believe that it is necessary to provide instruction in both art production and art appreciation.

This position is expressed by Tom Anderson, who states "that expression in art and appreciation of art should be taught in close relation to each other is fundamentally sound; more insights will be gained in both areas when one is interrelated to the other. In addition, seizing opportunities to have one activity lead organically into another creates a sense of connectedness in the minds of students between making and perceiving art."[3] He further states

that he is referring to two different types of art talk. One is "largely for instruction to further students' artistic development," and the other is talk in relation to the formal qualities and thematic content of the larger realm of art appreciation. As students learn through study and instruction in art, they will learn about the expressive and formal content of artworks as well as growing in their own art expression. One area of the content of art—art production, criticism, aesthetic judgment or art history—is not given preference over another. They are all intermingled in the instructional period so that students learn to produce and understand art simultaneously.

Howard Gardner takes a similar position on the value and importance of art production when he says that "making art is central to artistic learning and . . . perception and reflection activities must be linked directly to student production of art." He sees school as a place that should develop different components of the mind and he believes that "artistic thinking—thinking in artistic symbols—is a distinctive way of using the mind." He says that all the arts represent separate sets of cognitive skills and "if we omit those areas from the curriculum, we are in effect shortchanging the mind." He strongly believes that art production should remain central in the teaching of art to young children: "That is, we think artistic learning should grow from kids doing things: not just imitating, but actually drawing, dancing, performing, singing on their own." Production is "central to our approach—and it's very different from just learning traditions from the past or just talking about art." He emphasizes that "production should be linked intrinsically to perception and reflection. Perception means learning to see better, to hear better, to make finer discriminations, to see connections between things. Reflection means to be able to step back from both your production and your perceptions. . . ." He urges questioning strategies that require the student to ask "what, why, and how well am I doing this."[4]

Three-dimensional construction toy called "Pablos" was used by student as subject for drawing.

Around the age of three, children start to simplify their scribbles and begin to make distinct shapes. The line closes upon itself and becomes an outline for a shape. Experimenting with crayons and pencils continues, and circles, squares, triangles, and crosses are made at random or for the satisfaction of being able to repeat a shape. The scribbling child is involved in the creative process out of pure intuition and kinetic energy, and without any help or direction frequently produces compositions pleasing to the eye.

The next stage of graphic discovery occurs when, as Morris states, "a few lines or spots are placed inside of the circle and then, as if by magic, a face stares back at the infant painter."[5] Once the symbol for the face is realized, the child attempts to enrich it by adding details—eyes, ears, hair, arms, and legs. Soon the child creates other images—the sun, flowers, houses, etc. These beginning symbols gradually become more detailed until, as Morris states, "accurate representation is achieved and precise copies of the outside world can be trapped and preserved on paper."

At about six to eight years of age, children's art becomes less of an exploratory activity and gives way to the more pressing need to communicate important ideas and feelings. At this time, children use lines and mostly geometric shapes to form their symbols. When they reach the age of eight or nine, the symbol gives way to more realistic representations of figures, objects, and space as children become more visually perceptive of how things really look.

Let's take a close-up view of each of the sequential stages of artistic growth in the child's life.

The Years of Manipulation and Discovery: 2–4 Years of Age

The scribbling stage is an action time in which the child enjoys movement and the arranging, cutting, and manipulating of art materials. Children at this point in their development are not attempting to make realistic images. The child begins by making marks on the table, wall, or paper, using any available instrument: crayon, pencil, chalk, or pen.

The child is delighted to discover how to make lines on any surface. If the child has an opportunity to practice scribbling, he/she will develop greater control over the direction of the lines he/she is making.

Generally speaking, children scribble between the ages of two and four, but some will start earlier and some will start later. In the beginning, they scribble in what appears to be an uncontrolled fashion. When children have had an opportunity to practice making scribbles, their marks become more controlled. Soon they gain enough control that they can make straight lines or curved lines whenever

Art production should be central to the art program because it provides, as Gardner says, a "distinctive way of using the mind." It is apparent that perception and reflection in both art production and art appreciation must be intermingled in art lessons in order to offer the greatest opportunity for the development of the child's artistic growth.

Blueprint for Artistic Growth

To be effective in teaching elementary art, a teacher needs to know how children develop in their art production. All of us have seen the scribbles made by young children of 1½ to 2 years of age. The author Desmond Morris says that the child is intrigued by the fact that something comes out of the end of the pencil. It is an unexpected bonus connected with the child's arm movement. Children will repeat the experiment over and over again until they either tire of the activity or the surface on which they are marking is covered.

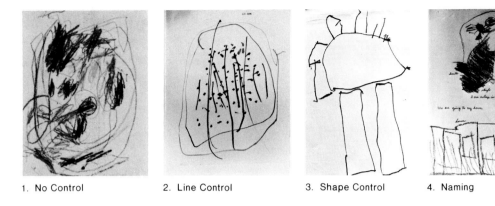

1. No Control   2. Line Control   3. Shape Control   4. Naming

Stages of scribbling: two- to four-years-old.

they wish. After children have scribbled in a controlled fashion for a period of time, they will begin to tell stories about their marks.

When children name their scribbles, they retain a mental image and think about concrete objects and events during the act of drawing. If children's visual attention is directed to observing detailed aspects of the environment, they will become more visually perceptive and more aware of objects and things. This includes touching, smelling, tasting, and listening, as well as looking at objects and things in their world. Kami and Radin state that "only after thorough sensory-motor acquaintance with real things does the child become able to reproduce actions in the absence of objects. Children need to internalize sensory-motor perception through art production so that they can form their own private images before they can be related and then constructed into their own world of private visual symbols."[6]

In summary, the child's artistic growth in its early years includes four recognizable scribbling stages: (1) no control when using line, which is not deliberately repeated, (2) line is now controlled and can be repeated, (3) shapes are now made and can be repeated at will, and (4) the child now names the mark or shape, sometimes before it is made and sometimes afterward.

The parent or other adult should remember that different children of the same age will be at different stages in their development. Some children will be slower in both their physical and mental development. Some children will have had many opportunities to manipulate art materials and have had much encouragement in their art activity. Children will demonstrate this in a more sophisticated way in their art production and in talking about their artworks.

The Symbol Stage: 4–8 Years of Age

To teachers and parents, it may seem as though the young child will never stop scribbling. Then one day the child begins to draw what an adult sees as a recognizable picture. The naming of the scribbling stage unfolds into crude

images that most adults can recognize. The producing of a recognizable symbol to which children give meaning is now a very deliberate and controlled act. The symbols produced tell us what events, people, or objects impressed them at a particular moment. Children will develop a variety of symbols for things in their environment, such as dogs, houses, flowers, and toys, but they will most frequently draw people. The first figure they draw will usually be of themselves, and then their parents, relatives, and friends. The first symbols in children's drawings do not always relate to other symbols in the same drawing or to a single idea. Children are very intent on drawing one symbol at a time, and only later in the symbol stage do they relate symbols to each other in a story fashion. This act usually necessitates a base or ground line on which objects are attached or placed.

Children have a certain logic in the way they depict and relate their symbols. The first symbols of figures in a drawing may all look alike, except the child may use a different color for each one to signify different individuals within that drawing. The most important figure symbol is often made larger than the other figures, and it usually represents the self. The ground line with objects placed on it represents the child's first attempts to depict space. The sky is at the top of the page, the grass or ground is at the bottom of the page, and in between is the air. As children develop and advance their spatial concepts, they will make X-ray drawings, fold-over drawings, and space-time sequence drawings. These logical interpretations of space are based on what the child knows rather than what the child sees.

At the beginning of the symbol stage, color is not yet related to objects. Later in the symbol stage, the first color relationships are established, usually blue for sky, yellow for sun, and green or brown for grass or ground. By the end of the symbol stage, visual realism begins to dominate and children begin to draw more of what they see rather than what they know. The geometric lines that they have been using to make their symbols gradually give way to more realistic lines that depict their concept of the actual

"I am on a trapeze" by 5-year-old.

"I am feeding the birds" by 6-year-old.

object they are drawing. For example, students will no longer be satisfied with depicting a symbol for an eye—a circle and a dot—and will attempt to draw the eye as they see it. A flat green can no longer stand for grass, clouds are no longer colored blue on a white sky, objects in the distance are now higher up on the page, and the figure is no longer the largest object on the page. This is the critical point at which students begin to be more aware of how things look in the real world and to sense a discrepancy between what they see and the symbols they have been using to represent them. The stage of realism begins.

Realism: 9–12 Years of Age

This stage is generally thought of as the last outpost for childish pictures composed of symbols. The beginning of a newfound realistic approach to making pictures begins at about eight or nine years of age. Students at this time may still retain the remnants of the uncritical blissfulness of childhood fantasy, but their thinking about what they see and how they make their art changes dramatically. The geometric symbols with which they were satisfied in their earlier artworks no longer suffice. Children begin to show in their drawings that they perceive that the sky meets the horizon and that objects can overlap each other and create new spatial effects.

They want to be able to draw figures that are more realistic, figures that are drawn with a greater sense of correct visual proportion and less exaggeration of body parts. More attention is given to the hair and clothing of the figures they draw. Correct colors are seen on objects

"I am all dressed up for a party" by 8-year-old.

and people. More perceptive children will attempt to shade objects, to draw shadows, to show motion, and to make distant objects smaller will less detail. Visual space and perspective begin to dominate their picture making. Figures are drawn smaller than previously in relation to the size of the paper. Students often show objects overlapping and extending off the page.

During the realism stage, as in other levels, there can be a mixture of stages in a single artwork.

"Running on the playground" by 11-year-old.

"Skipping rope" by 9-year-old.

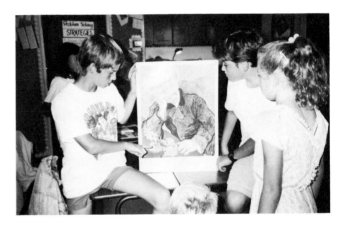

Students respond to artworks by describing, analyzing, interpreting, and judging.

"Doing exercises" by 10-year-old.

Most children of this age will benefit by close observation of the objects they wish to draw. They can be encouraged to gain the visual information that they need not only from actual objects, models, and landscapes, but by photographs of them. A study of artworks can assist students in understanding how artists have perceived and depicted similar subjects, moods, and themes, as well as how they have used media and solved problems dealing with space, shading, color changes, and other aesthetic problems. This can be in the form of the real object, photographs, and fine-art reproductions. In our culture, if children of this age are to continue in their artwork, they will insist on learning realistic drawing skills, or in frustration they will stop drawing altogether.

Motivating for Artistic Growth

Motivations are the basic means that the teacher has of evoking artistic responses in elementary students. A motivation is comprised of a dialogue in the classroom prior to art production. The dialogue may be supplemented with, and enriched by, visual aids, actual objects, and models. Some motivational dialogues may include image-evoking stories and poems that the teacher has selected as appropriate to the focus of the lesson.

The erroneous idea that sharpening students' perceptual and media skills will somehow impose the adult's own view of the world on the children was perpetuated in the past by teachers who believed they were imposing themselves on the child's own vision. However, when children are denied appropriate guidance, they are unduly and needlessly handicapped in their artistic growth and in developing their own personal artistic style.

If students are to produce and respond to artworks, they need to be taught how to see and how to select with finer discrimination. The sequential growth of manipulative skills requires time and instruction if it is to flourish and be achieved. If too much change of media occurs, students will never master the world of tools and materials. Understanding the nature and degree of assistance each student requires is dependent upon the teacher's observation of individual children. It is helpful to keep a portfolio of each student's work to assess progress over the school year. In this way the teacher can note if the stages of development—in regard to depictions of figures, houses, and space, for instance—are in general alignment with those expected at that age level. For instance, a child that is drawing rather realistic figures running and throwing a football, but who persists in drawing the sky as a strip across the top of the paper, may be helped by the teacher to see clouds moving along behind the treetops.

Motivations need to be ongoing during the time the child is drawing. A teacher may notice that a child continues to draw objects very small even though the paper is quite large. This is usually the sign of a lack of confidence and/or knowledge about, and perceptual experience of, the subject. Such a student can be helped by the teacher in a conversation to realize how much more he/she actually knows or feels about the subject in a technique called *accretion,* which means extending, expanding, or adding onto the original tiny figure, house, or animal that the child has drawn.[7] Questioning strategies may be used by the teacher to direct the child's attention, memory, and/or perception: "What a fine rabbit! Do you remember what Alice did when she saw the rabbit? How tall was Alice? How big was the rabbit? Where was the hole she fell through? What happened next?" and so on. Or: "You made the lion look like he's roaring. Good for you! When we went to the zoo, do you remember what the lion's cage looked like? How big was it? Was there a tree in the cage? Was there another lion? How large was he? What animals were on the left, the right of the cage? Where did you walk next? What else did you see?" and so on.

Children have the inborn capacity to transform their primary means of knowing—that is, their experiences of feeling, thinking, and perceiving—into their own unique art forms. Motivations may have one or more emphases, which culminate in the child's art product. Motivations may underscore (1) viewing an object in detail, (2) recalling past experiences, (3) having empathy, (4) becoming involved with the formal aspects of the elements and principles of art, (5) delving into one's art heritage, (6) exploring feelings, fantasy, and the imagination, or (7) being inventive and experimental with art materials.

The articulate process of transforming perceptions, feelings, and thoughts into an art form can come about through a strong self-motivation; however, it is usually necessary for the teacher to provide motivation for the students and to help them order their impressions and concepts.

In responding to a motivation, students are challenged to reflect, to observe, to imagine, and to form their ideas. They are encouraged to be inventive, imaginative, and original. They are guided in exercising judgment and self-discipline as they choose and arrange their visual images.

Motivations, then, are both intrinsic and extrinsic in encouraging elementary students' artistic growth. Examples of two kinds of motivations that have different emphases are found in two well-known art textbooks for elementary students. *Art in Action,* Grade 1, Lesson 29,[8] focuses on lines and shapes and asks the six-year-old student to use a method of combining letters of the alphabet into a design, after looking at an abstract artwork by Stuart Davis. *Discover Art,* Grade 2, Lesson 41,[9] requires second-grade students to point out and identify the various shapes and patterns that they see in a photograph of a house, and then create a real or imaginary fancy house.

A motivation that calls upon students to remember, imagine, and observe what they see—as well as to give visual form to their observations and feelings about objects, figures, and places—may include the following aspects:

1. A **focus** that is clear to the students at the outset.

2. A **reproduction** of an appropriate artwork may provide a basis for involving the students in describing, analyzing, and interpreting its theme, its medium, its formal use of the elements and principles of art, its mood, etc., as it relates to the focus of the lesson.

3. Questions and discussion can activate thoughts and feelings that children already have about the subject, as well as provide them with new information. Discussion should encourage children's imaginative responses, helping them externalize and share emotions and moods so that they can transform their thoughts and feelings into concrete visual images in their artworks.

4. Questions and discussion related to **perception** can direct the students' attention to a sensitive look at the subject, sharpening their observation of what they see before them so that they perceive differences and similarities of shapes, colors, proportions, lines, and so on. Teachers should always use many photographs or the real object in relation to the motivation.

5. During the last part of a motivation, thought-provoking questions can help students formulate plans for what they will select from what they see and feel and how they will **arrange their composition.**

The following models are examples of this sort of motivation. They contain guided dialogues that teachers may use in stimulating students to give greater meaning to their artworks. The first four focus on the primary grades and the last four on the upper grades.

K–6 Motivations

K–3—If I Could Be a Bird

Focus: The students will imagine what sort of birds they would like to be if they could become one for a day, and make an artwork about their choice.

Reproduction—*Soaring* by Andrew Wyeth, Shorewood Reproduction #1765, or similar artwork.
How would it feel to be a bird with outstretched wings, soaring, dipping, and gliding above the fields and hills? Look at the feathers on the wings and tail of the large bird in the foreground of Wyeth's painting. Can you describe the shape of one feather? Can you see where the feathers overlap and make a repeated pattern? What are the shapes of the wings? the tail? the head? The smaller birds that are farther away echo the shape of the large bird. Can you describe the colors of the birds? Andrew Wyeth looked very closely at these birds and imagined how it must feel to fly.

Thinking and feeling—If you could be a bird for just one day, what kind of bird would you want to be? There are so many kinds! Would you be a dignified, magnificent bird like an ostrich, or a colorful flamingo or peacock? Or would you be a bird of prey—a hawk, eagle, or vulture? Or would you like to be a smaller bird—perhaps a hummingbird, a magpie, a woodpecker, bluejay, cardinal, or robin? If you like cold weather, maybe you would like to be a penguin. Maybe you will choose to be a hen or rooster, or a duck or goose in a pond. Maybe you'd like to be a parrot or a new kind of bird that no one has ever seen! Will you show your bird flying, yanking a juicy worm out of the garden, or chirping happily on a cherry tree branch? Will it be perched on a nest feeding its young or sitting on a telephone wire? Will you show it from the side or front?

Perceiving (shapes, colors, proportion, pattern)— Let's make a picture about our imaginary selves as birds. What colors will you choose for the body, the head, the beak, wings, tail, feet, and claws? Will your bird have a long body or a fat, round one? What shape will the head be? Will the body be larger or smaller than the head? Will there be a crest on the top of the head? What shape? What shape is its beak? Will it be open or closed? What shape is the eye? Some birds have long necks and some have short ones. Which kind will yours have? What sort of tail will your bird have? Will you make it spread out like a fan or drooping on the ground? What shape are its wings? Where are they attached to the body? Will you show the wings outstretched or tucked close to its side? Will you show feathers overlapping and making a pattern? How long will the legs be—longer than the neck or shorter? Make the largest parts of your bird first and add feathers, eyes, head, beak, feet, and all the other things you wish to include.

K–3—Halloween Witches Making Brew

Focus: By using their imaginations about this holiday, the students will make artworks that express their ideas about the Halloween symbol of witches making brew.

Reproduction—*Tree with Crows* by Caspar David Friedrich, Shorewood Reproduction #604, or similar artwork.
Can you almost feel the wind blowing through the bare, scratchy branches of this tree? Its trunk is tipped to one side and the twigs look brittle and dry. Can you see anything else tipped in the same manner? The tree is so large that part of the branches extend off the top and side. The branches almost seem to reach out and beckon the crows to alight on them. What colors did the artist use?

Would the picture give you a different feeling if the artist had chosen green tones? The crows are settling in its branches. Can you see some of the birds still in the sky? How would you like to be out on this hill Halloween night with your friends? Would you be a little frightened? Do you think the wind would be blowing? What noises would you hear? Halloween is a time when most people enjoy scary things because they know they aren't real, but they can pretend for one night and dress up as goblins and ghosts and witches.

Thinking and feeling—Listen to this recipe and see if you can guess what it is for.

3 teaspoons of powdered bat wing
4 cups of black cat fur
½ cup of dust from a haunted belfry
3 ghosts' eyeballs

Bring to a boil in a big, black kettle and stir with two feathers from an owl's tail.

Who would use this recipe? It's the time of year when witches are dusting off their cookbooks and stirring up potions and brews of all sorts. Do you suppose those witches are getting their brooms ready to ride on Halloween? How do Halloween witches dress? Would you like to dress up in costume and join them?

Perceiving (shape, color, texture, proportion)—Let's make pictures about witches on Halloween night making magic brew. Maybe they are going to gather under the tree in Friedrich's painting and exchange recipes or try out the one we just read. How tall are witches? Do you suppose some might be young and small, some tall, and some fat? What shape are witches' hats? What sort of hair do they have—soft and curly or coarse and stringy? What color is their hair? Is it long or short? Do you think witches ever comb their hair? What shapes will the noses be on the witches you draw? They can all be different shapes! Are their faces wrinkled? What shape are their ears? What sort of hands does a witch have? What about the fingernails? What shape are the sleeves of a witch's costume? Do you suppose their costumes are patched? Do witches' costumes billow out when they swoop across they sky on brooms? What do witches wear on their feet? How large do you suppose the kettle for the brew might be? How many witches can you draw standing around the kettle stirring? Will steam and awful odors be coming out of the kettle? Will you show some witches arriving a little late on their broomsticks with cats riding behind? What shape will the moon be—full or crescent? Will there be owls or bats or scary trees in your picture?

K-3—Bears in a Tall Tree

Focus: The students will draw several bears climbing a tall tree on a vertical piece of paper.

Reproduction—*Birds in Bamboo Tree* by Koson, Shorewood Reproduction #409, or similar artwork. The Japanese artist who painted these plump little thrushes placed them carefully in a bamboo tree. It is a tall painting, and the stalks are cut off at the top and bottom of the picture so that we just see a part of the bamboo. Where do your eyes go first when you look at this painting? The bamboo crosses at almost the same place where the birds are perched. The birds blend into the foliage. One has an open beak. We see the long, pointed shape of the leaves repeated a number of times around the birds. Where else? Can you find light and dark greens? The background is left plain so that the contrast of the bamboo and birds will have our complete attention.

Thinking and feeling—Did you ever see real bamboo growing? It is quite a bit different from trees that grow in the forest, like pine trees and redwood trees and oak or maple trees. How tall was the tallest tree you ever saw? Do you think you could climb it? Do you remember if the trunk was thick and the bark rough? Bears are good tree climbers. How are their feet different from yours? Why do you suppose bears climb trees? Why are good thick branches important to a bear when it climbs a tree? Where does a bear sit when it wants to rest? Can bears walk out on a heavy thick branch? Could a bear hang by its two front legs from a branch and then drop to the ground? Bears generally have two cubs. Who takes care of them and teaches them to climb trees? Did you know that bears can walk on their two hind legs as well as on all four? How do you suppose a cub feels when he gets way up high and looks down? What would he see down below? Do you suppose one of his parents might help him get down if he didn't know how? What would bears see when they climbed a tree? (squirrels, chipmunks, knotholes, bees, beehives, birds, bird nests, etc.)

Perceiving (color, texture, shape, proportion, space)—Let's make a picture about a family of bears climbing a tall tree. Have you ever seen live bears? How big are they? How big do you suppose a young cub is? Half as big as its parents? Have you seen pictures of bears? What color will you make them? There are black bears, cinnamon bears, and, of course, grizzly bears in forests. Are bears fat and shaggy? They do grow extra-heavy coats of fur in winter. How long are their legs—taller than their bodies or shorter?

What shape are their tails? (stub). What shape are their ears? (small and round). What about their noses? (rather long and pointed). How thick will you draw the tree trunk and branches? They will have to be strong enough to hold several bears. What shapes will the branches and leaves or needles be? What colors will you use to make the tree? Make your tree start at the bottom of a tall piece of paper and go all the way to the top.

K-3—Jumping Rope

Focus: The students will draw themselves and their friends jumping rope based on acting it out, observing, and remembering the movements and action involved.

Reproduction—*Sunny Side of the Street* by Philip Evergood, Shorewood Reproduction #871, or similar artwork.

Where are these boys playing? Have you ever played hockey? They are using those white sticks to hit the puck. We can also see lines drawn on the street that remind us of another game, hopscotch. How do we know that the boys in this painting are running and moving? (bent knees, kneeling, slanted bodies, etc.). The man and the other figures that are closest to us are the largest. They are in the foreground. Can you find them? How can you tell which ones are farthest away? (They are the smallest and highest up.) The yellow and orange colors make us feel as if the boys are having a lot of fun.

Thinking and feeling—Do you like to run and play games on the school ground with your friends? Or do you sometimes play by yourself? Jumping rope is something that we are able to do alone or with friends. It has been a favorite of children for many years. People once believed that the higher they could jump rope, the higher their crops would grow, so every year in the spring they had a jumping contest. Most children know singsong rhymes that they chant as they jump rope. Do you know any? Who can show us how to jump rope alone by turning the rope over your head? Can you jump rope as you run around the playground, or do you stand in one place? Can you jump on one foot? How many times have you jumped without missing? Did you ever cross your arms while you were jumping? Do you get out of breath? Can you feel your heart beat faster?

Perceiving (line, proportion, shape)—Let's draw a picture about jumping rope and try to show the figures in action. (*While child is demonstrating*) Where are his arms when the rope goes up? When it goes down? How high are they held? Are his elbows bent? How does he hold the handles? Does he bend his knees? Does he jump high? How is he dressed? Let's say a jingle with him and feel the rhythm. (*While children are demonstrating, two swinging rope, one jumping*) Are they swinging the rope with one of their arms or both? See how high their arms must go to make the rope go all around. How do they place their feet? Now look at the jumper. Is she bending her knees or jumping straight up and down? Is she jumping on one foot or two? How does she hold her arms? Does her hair fly up when she jumps? How are the children dressed?

Grades 4,5,6—A King or Queen

Focus: The students will observe a costumed model and develop skills in blocking in, contour drawing, and applying color in their artworks.

Reproduction—*Queen Elizabeth I* by Nicholas Hilliard, Shorewood Reproduction #211, or similar artwork.

Nicholas Hilliard painted this portrait of Queen Elizabeth I of England over three hundred years ago. She is wearing a very elaborate dress that is covered with jewels. She is wearing a number of necklaces, too. She even has jewels in her hair. Look at her collar. Her hand is bare of jewels. What is she holding in her hand? This red rose is a symbol of her family, the Tudors, and this means that as the queen she is protecting the land. Look at the wonderful way the artist painted the different textures. We can almost touch the different pieces of jewelry. We see her in three-quarter view; that is, we see both eyes and only one ear. The artist painted the background very flat and dark so that our attention would be totally on the queen and her magnificent clothing. Does her face seem almost masklike? Does she look friendly or aloof and royal?

Thinking and feeling—How would it feel to be a member of a royal family? You would have both privileges and responsibilities. There aren't very many kings and queens in this day and age, and they don't dress like Hilliard's Queen Elizabeth I did. She spent quite a long time posing while she was having her portrait painted. This was often done hundreds of years ago as royalty and other rich people wanted to have a record of how they looked and cameras hadn't been invented yet. Perhaps you remember about some kings and queens in storybooks. Have you read about good kings and queens, dignified ones, strong ones, selfish and mean ones?

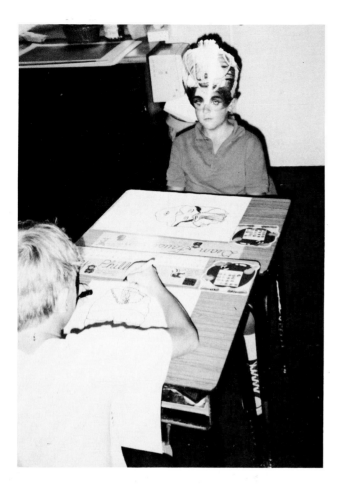

Students practice contour drawing by observing partner wearing a Victorian half-mask.

Perceiving—(Shape, color, pattern, texture)—Direct observation from posed model. Have two students model as a king and queen. They may stand or sit. They may wear improvised costumes—robe, paper crown, beads and jewelry, perhaps hold a flower or a scepter, etc. Have all the students close enough to one of the models to make good observations. They may use a viewfinder to help them focus upon a viewpoint and format. Use colored paper as background.

Let's look carefully at the model closest to you and think about how you will place your drawing on the paper. You may choose to draw it from the waist up or you may want to draw the entire figure. Some of you will be drawing a frontal view, while others will be drawing a profile or three-quarter view. A vertical format is probably the best. Image the model on your paper; that is, try to decide where you will place it so that most of the space on the paper is filled. Block in the big, important shapes of the figure first. Look at the top of the crown and make a mark with a piece of chalk near the top of your paper. Make more marks where you want the shoulders to be, the waistline, the arms, etc. Then draw in more edges and details, using contour drawing. **Keep looking at the model,** trying to see one part in relation to another part. You may want to exaggerate and distort some parts to create a special effect. You may want to make your king or queen look very powerful and strong or very rich and magnificent. When you are finished drawing your figure, use tempera paint or oil pastels for color. Look for the different colors that the model is wearing. Look for small shapes that can be repeated to make a decorative pattern. You can paint beads and jewels with a tiny brush or a Q-tip. (If you have some gold and silver tempera, make it available to students.)

Grades 4,5,6—Designing a Postage Stamp

Focus: The students will make a creative connection with social studies by basing their designs for commemorative postage stamps on events or persons in U.S. history.

Reproduction—*Washington at Yorktown* by James Peale, Shorewood Reproduction #964, or similar artwork.

The artist James Peale not only painted a portrait of George Washington but also shows us a historic moment in our nation's history. We see Washington posed triumphantly after the battle of Yorktown. He is standing on the battlefield among the fallen English banners and has one hand on a cannon. His horse and aide are behind him. Yorktown Harbor is in the background. Do you know what country the flag with the three *fleurs-de-lys* represents? (France). What does the blue flag with the thirteen white stars stand for? (thirteen colonies). Peale has painted George Washington very tall to give us the feeling of his heroic stature.

Thinking and feeling (Social studies connection)— What events do you think are very important in our nation's history? Which discoveries do you think are the most significant? What people do you think should be remembered and honored for their contributions in some field—science, inventions, explorations, sports, art, theater, military, music, government, etc.? You will need to use some reference books to get the right facts and visual information. If you collect postage stamps, you might like to bring some to class to show how artists have designed them as commemoratives. Look at them and you'll see how they usually have words and images combined in their designs.

Perceiving (line, shape, texture, value, balance)— Let's each design a postage stamp about someone or some event important in American history. We'll use a special kind of paper called Scratch-art (available in art supply catalogs). It is black on the surface, but when we scratch lines on it, a bright color comes through. You will want to include the words *US Postage* and *25¢* in the design. You may also want to include a brief phrase or title or the person's name. You can frame your design with a repeated motif that reminds us of perforations.

First make some rough sketches of your idea on a piece of white ditto paper or newsprint, 4¼″ × 5½″. Try arranging the images and words in different ways until you have made a pleasing and balanced design. Make your lettering neat and easy to read. Study examples of lettering in magazines. Then choose your best sketch and transfer it to the Scratch-art paper that has been cut to the same size. To do this, turn your design over and go over the lines with white chalk. Then tape it to the Scratch-art paper and go over the lines with a sharp pencil. White will transfer to the black surface. Now use a toothpick to scratch off the black to reveal the color underneath. Try to make different textures and patterns and to have a balance of dark and light areas. Use hatching, cross-hatching, and stippling to create different textures and values.

Grades 4,5,6—Landscape with a Mood

Focus: The students will use photographs of city, sea, or landscapes and create landscapes that convey moods and feelings.

Reproduction—*Landscape at Arles: The Orchard* by Vincent van Gogh, Shorewood Reproduction #1438, or similar artwork.
What do you see in this reproduction? It is a landscape of a peach orchard in the spring. Look how van Gogh applied the paint on the canvas. It is quite thick, and we can see the texture of his brushstrokes. What do you see in the foreground? the middle ground? the background? Most

landscapes have these three spaces. The closest things are near the bottom and are larger. As things go back in the distance, they appear smaller and have lighter colors and fewer details. Look how van Gogh has painted the fence in the foreground. He has made a pattern of repeated vertical lines and horizontal lines. The fence and the reddish path lead our eyes back to the right side of the picture, and then our eyes follow the more distant fence as it goes from right to left and draws our attention to the red-roofed houses. We see the white blossoming trees and a farmer bent over, working. Farther back are the blue hills. What do you see as the focal point? Can you almost smell the fresh spring air and the blossoms on the peach trees? Maybe it has just rained. Look at the bright colors of the road and path. Notice the sky. How would you describe the mood of this picture? Maybe you feel that it is calm and quiet. Maybe you feel that it is friendly and inviting and you would like to have a picnic here. Maybe you feel it is lonely.

Thinking and feeling—Look through a group of photographs of landscapes (or city- or seascapes) and select one of them. Does it show a place you have been or would like to be? What kind of weather do you see? Do different kinds of weather make you feel differently? Heavy storm clouds can almost be frightening. Sunny days can make us feel happy and like playing outdoors.

Perceiving (line, shape, emphasis, color)—Use L-frames to focus on a portion of the photograph you have selected. Then make a contour drawing of some of the important edges and shapes of the spaces and objects in the picture. You may change the positions and shapes of the things in the photograph to help you create a particular mood and feeling. Remember to have a foreground with larger, more detailed objects near the bottom of your paper. Remember to place small things in the background to create distance. Think about the mood you wish to create: happy, lonely, scary, sad, etc. Then use watercolor washes or acrylic paint to complete your picture. Think of which colors you will use to convey a particular emotion—warm colors, cool colors, dull and dark colors, etc.

Grades 4,5,6—Abstraction: A Still Life

Focus: Students will look for the essential shapes contained within a still-life arrangement and use them for creating an abstract design of colored paper.

Reproduction—*Guitar, Glass, Fruit Dish* by Pablo Picasso, Shorewood Reproduction #1334, or similar artwork.

Look at the variety of shapes in this abstract still life by Picasso. The negative and positive shapes fit together so neatly that we could put a piece of lightweight paper over it and trace over each shape to make a jigsaw puzzle. What positive shapes do you see? There is a guitar shape, a glass shape, and a fruit dish shape. What else? What is the focal point? Can you find the shape of the tabletop? Do you think Picasso was more interested in suggesting the shapes of these objects or in painting them exactly as he saw them, as rounded, three-dimensional forms? How did Picasso balance this abstract design? Can you see any shadows that are important shapes? He has used flat, dark colors for the shapes that represent shadows. They are very important parts of the composition because of the way they fit together in Picasso's design.

Thinking and feeling—Let's choose some objects and set up a still-life arrangement. We'll choose something tall and something low. We'll choose something small and several round or oblong items. We'll have some objects in front of others. Think about selecting and arranging a variety of colors and shapes.

Perceiving (shape, space, emphasis, balance)—Let's make an abstract still-life composition with colored paper. You will be concentrating on the shapes of the objects rather then trying to make the objects look rounded and solid. Try not to draw the objects first; cut directly into the paper, concentrating on the essential shape of each object and making your cutouts large. When you finish cutting out one shape, try another, using another color of paper. Cut out some shadow shapes, too. You can exaggerate, distort, and change the shapes you cut so that your design will fit together in a balanced way. When you have cut out all the shapes you need, place them on a piece of paper, 9″ × 12″. Decide on a focal point. Let some pieces overlap; let some pieces extend off the edges of the paper. Try to make all the positive and negative shapes fit together like the pieces of a jigsaw puzzle. When you are satisfied with your arrangement, paste the pieces to the background paper. You may want to add some lines with a black marking pen.

Evaluating Artworks of Elementary Students

In responding to and evaluating students' artistic growth over a period of time, the following four areas should be considered by the elementary teacher.

1. **The degree of technical skill that is seen in the artwork.** This is the extent to which the student has shown an increasing mastery in handling and controlling a given material—puddles of an excessive amount of paint, messy handling of paste in cut-paper collages, etc. The artwork should be evaluated on the evidence seen of increasing skills over a period of time. Very young children are not expected to be highly developed in controlling materials, but an improvement in mastering materials, along with a desire to develop more control, are suitable areas to evaluate.

2. **The manner in which the student has organized the artwork.** This has to do with artistic considerations related to the elements and principles of design. When variety and unity are seen in an artwork, the colors, lines, shapes, etc., give us a feeling of completeness. The different parts are so organized that the work gives a feeling of wholeness, balance, and harmony.

3. **The extent to which the student has shown feelings and emotional qualities in the artwork.** This has to do with the expressive qualities of showing happiness, sadness, anger, etc., in an artwork. It is governed not only by the choices of colors and the expressive use of lines and shapes but by the subject matter as well.

4. **The degree of creative imagination and ingenuity that the student has shown.** This is seen when a student makes unusual connections, relating two ordinarily unrelated ideas, or when a student has depicted an original theme, worked in a humorous or insightful way, or found a fresh new way to express an idea, solve a visual problem, or use a material.

While it is most inappropriate to compare the artworks of several children in a negative manner, teachers can use questioning strategies when students complete a project to help each student understand not only what is pleasing and good about his/her own products, but what important things happened during the process of making artworks. Teachers will find that some of the following questions are helpful to use after an art activity. Select a few of the questions from this list, choosing those that apply to the focus of the art lesson. First guide the students to reflect on the process they have undergone in making their art. Then ask them to talk about the successful aspects of their art products and to evaluate those aspects that could be improved upon.

Helping Students to Perceive and Reflect on Their Artwork

Process

Can I use some new art words to describe how I made my art?

Did I take some careful looks at the real object (the horse, tree, figure, flower) that I was drawing and observe its contours (edges), dark and light areas, colors, textures, proportions, big and little shapes?

Did I think about how I was going to draw or paint my idea before I started?

Did I "image" my idea on my paper before I started?

Did I "play around" with my idea and make some small thumbnail sketches before I started on my big picture?

Did I enjoy working with this medium?

Did I experiment and discover any new ways to work with my art materials or tools?

Did I try to improve my skills in handling this medium?

Did I work hard and "stick with it" longer than I usually do?

Did I stop working on my art now and then and step back and "take a critical look"?

Did I follow the directions given?

Did I try to think of a new and different way to draw something that I have drawn before?

Did I try not to bother other students?

Did I cooperate in a give-and-take of ideas? (murals and group projects)

Did I clean up my work space and return materials to their storage places?

Would I like to repeat this art project?

Can I think of a different way I would draw this theme next time?

Do I know about a great artist that painted this same theme?

Do I know about a great artist that used this medium or technique?

Product

Did I fill the paper with my picture, keeping in mind the format and letting some objects touch the sides of the paper?

Did I make the figures (or important shapes) large enough for my idea?

Do I need more visual or kinesthetic information to help me tell about my subject?

Did I show the necessary action for my idea?

Is the idea I wanted to show clear and easy to see?

Would this picture fit better on tall paper, larger paper, smaller paper?

Could I make the ground or sky more interesting in any way?

Did I show enough details to express what I had in mind?

Did I include overlapping, where and if necessary?

Did I make a focus or center of interest? How did I do this?

Did I use colors that give my picture the feeling I wanted?

Would I use the same colors next time?

Would using lighter or darker values of a color tell my idea better?

Did I use a variety of large and small shapes?

Does my composition feel balanced?

Did I use several patterns for variety or decorative purposes?

Did I show any contrast of textures?

Did I make several different kinds of lines (thick/thin, long/short, straight/curving, broken/continuous)?

Did I make my negative spaces interesting?

Would some exaggeration or distortion have helped create a stronger feeling or emotion?

Did I place distant objects higher up and make them smaller if I wanted to show deep space?

Do all the parts of my composition harmonize and give me a feeling of unity?

Did I draw any of the parts of my picture in a new or different way?

If I could make this picture over again, what would I change?

Is the feeling or emotion that I was thinking about easy to see?

Would my idea have been more effective had I used a different medium?

Questions and Activities

1. Make a collection of artworks from scribblers and see how their drawings and paintings compare to those in the text. Talk with the children about their artwork after they have finished. Does this information add to your understanding of their work? If so, how?

2. Make a collection of drawings from children during the symbol stage and look for differences and similarities in how they use color, figure, and space.

3. Evaluate how children use the elements and principles of art in their artworks. Which element do they start with and use most of the time?

4. Collect several drawings from children at the realism stage and observe how children at this stage use the principle of emphasis. What new space concepts are beginning to develop during this age level?

5. Do some research on safety in relation to the use of art materials. For example, review the health hazards in books such as *Safety in the Artroom* by Charles A. Qualley (Worcester, Mass.:Davis Publications, 1986) or check with your own state's requirements regarding health standards in relation to art materials.

6. Write an art motivation for grades one through three stressing the emotional involvement of the individual in a personal experience. Before you write your motivations, review the ones in this chapter. Then look at the list of questions in the pamphlet *Quality Art Education* (National Art Education Association, 1916 Association Dr., Reston, Virginia, 22091) that a child must be confronted with in making an artwork. In most motivations, the child needs guided visual analysis of the persons and objects with which they are dealing in the proposed artwork. In addition, many motivations will be enriched by incorporating a study of one or more famous artworks that are related to the activity either by theme, subject matter, style, or media.

7. Read at least three "Instructional Resources" in *Art Education* magazine, then select an artwork and follow this format in writing a lesson plan.

A Narrative Timeline of Western Artworks

6

A Brief Guide to Western Artworks

T his brief **chronological** guide noting the major periods and styles of art and important artists begins with the earliest achievements of humankind and moves through the centuries to those artworks created in our time. It is presented here as a reference only, a point of departure for more in-depth information gathering of both visual and written materials. Numerous books and other resources are available that go beyond the scope possible within the confines of this book. Though most attention is given to those artistic achievements of the **Western** world, the student should also be aware of the **Eastern** art world with its rich history of remarkable artistic accomplishments. Today's culturally diverse population needs to be acquainted with **popular** art forms as well as those of **folk artists** around the world. The importance of the **traditional arts** of Africa, Australia, Latin America, and other regions must not be overlooked. A study of **ethnic** art forms from the world over can help us gain insights and enrich our own lives. In addition, students need to develop a sensitivity to the art forms that surround us and make up the quality of our lives—the design of shopping centers and malls; landscaping on highways, parks, and homes; the design of containers, utensils, and packaging; jewelry, furniture, clothing, cars, magazines, photographs, advertisements, and films and video.

When Art Began

Discoveries in fairly recent years, the first being in 1875, have revealed the earliest attempts made by human beings in **prehistoric times** to represent their ideas and feelings in visual forms. The first paintings from these hunting economies were done about thirty thousand years ago in the Old Stone Age. They are found on the roof of the Altimira cave in Spain. Other caves in Spain, as well as some in France, have revealed marvelously painted animals. The people that made these wondrous depictions of bison,

Figure 6.1 Bull, ceiling painting, 18′ long, caves of Lascaux near Montignac, France, ca. 12,000 B.C. © Robert C. Lamm

horses, deer, boars, and elephants, as well as symbolic figures of themselves engaged in the hunt, most certainly didn't call their works "art." They were probably made in an effort to control the enormous, fierce creatures upon which they depended for survival and from which they obtained meat and furs for clothing. These Stone Age hunters had no horses and only the crudest weapons. It's hard to understand how such lifelike images, many depicting animals in motion, could have been created in the dark underground caves. Perhaps the artists were initially inspired to make these images when they observed the bulging contours of the stone interiors of their caves; when they traced a few lines of the creatures, they imagined they saw a more tangible form. In these paintings, we often see arrows and spears pointing at the animals. They used natural colors—pigments they found in different earths, charcoal, and such—and mixed them with fat, blood, and egg or plant juice. They made brushes of animal fur, feathers, moss, and leaves. These early folk also fashioned simple stone and bone tools for utilitarian purposes, and even in these earliest implements, we see the special need that we humans have to embellish and make beautiful the objects we deem primarily to be practical. During these prehistoric times, both human and animal figures were carved from horns, stones, and other materials. The famous *Venus of Willendorf,* with her broad hips and breasts, represents fertility and was probably called upon to insure the survival of the tribe.

Artworks in Ancient Times

When people learned to use such metals as bronze and copper, about 3000 or 4000 B.C., civilization as we know it began. Caves were abandoned and shelters built. Food was grown and domestic animals raised for use. Reading and writing were invented for keeping records and exchanging information over distances. People lived in larger communities, even cities. Ancient art reached through several cultures, some contemporary with each other. Many of these ancient peoples lived near the Mediterranean Sea and Middle East Asia, extending as far as China and Japan. They all left magnificent marks of artistic achievements.

One of the best known of these early civilizations appeared about 3500 B.C. in **Egypt.** The Nile River made the Egyptians prosperous, and the surrounding deserts and the Mediterranean protected the inhabitants. Their civilization, with its art and architecture suggesting stability and permanence, changed little for more than three thousand years, making it not only one of the earliest but the most long-lived civilization in history. Most of what we know of ancient Egypt comes from the royal families' tombs, since the Egyptians' belief was that life on earth, at least for the nobility, would continue after death. Thus, mummies were preserved and tombs painted with scenes of the pleasures of daily life. One can wonder at the size and exactness of the pyramids, one of which is made up of more than two million blocks of stone, each stone weighing more than 2½ tons. The world was fascinated when the untouched tomb of Tutankhamen, brimming with remarkably rich artworks, was discovered in 1922.

Egyptian art is divided into three major kingdoms: the **Old Kingdom,** the **Middle Kingdom,** and the **Empire.** The **pyramids of Giza** are examples of the powerful architectural accomplishments of the first period, a time when the belief was that existence on earth was preparatory to life hereafter. The **pharaohs** represented deity figures on earth, and the tombs they built contained stone sculptures, pottery, jewelry, and useful objects they would need in the afterlife. The Egyptians believed that spirits of their gods dwelt in certain animals and birds such as the cat and the hawk, and they worshiped these images. An Egyptian pharaoh is often shown in the form of an animal, or at

Figure 6.2   Portrait head of Queen Nefertiti, ca. 1370 B.C., New Kingdom. Eighteenth Dynasty. Painted limestone, ht. 20″. *State Museums West Berlin.*

least with some features of an animal. For example, the **sphinx** has a human head and the body of a lion. The Egyptians often depicted a beetle or **scarab** pushing the sun across the sky in the manner of a dung beetle pushing its egg in front of it. The magical powers of the scarab in a piece of jewelry from Tutankhamen's tomb was thought to protect the dead pharaoh.

The art of the Middle Kingdom and the Empire was characterized by elaborate temples built in honor of the ruling emperors. The artist, architect, and builders worked together in constructing these edifices, making decorative colonnades, walled surfaces, furniture, and implements. Sculptural forms were often a part of the structural support of a building. Also attributed to this splendid age are magnificent examples of metalwork, furniture, pottery, and glassware. The most famous of these temples were uncovered at **Luxor** and **Karnak.** Some of the memorable artworks from Egypt include a bejeweled sculpture portrait of **Queen Nefertiti** wearing an ornate headdress and the coffin cover for King Tutankhamen, dating to 1340 B.C. and made of gold and semiprecious stones. **Hieroglyphs** (picture writing) on the walls of tombs and on scrolls contain figures and objects that represent words or sounds. Architecture and sculpture were the major art forms, with some paintings surviving today on the walls of the tombs.

Figure 6.3 Iktinus and Kallikrates, Parthenon (viewed from the northwest), ca. 447–432 B.C. Akropolis, Athens. © Robert C. Lamm

The typical Egyptian stance for figures shows a profile view of the head, arms, and legs, and frontal views of the body and eyes. Important people were painted larger than slaves and servants.

During this time, Mesopotamia (the land between the Tigris and Euphrates rivers, now Iraq) was occupied by the **Sumerians, the Babylonians, the Assyrians, and the Persians.** It was a melting pot of different cultures, each passing on its religious beliefs, customs, knowledge, and skills. The land was flat, and the people built shrines on top of manufactured mountains. Here they placed offerings to the gods whose forces they believed controlled the universe. They also placed images of the rulers and priests that they believed could ask the gods for mercy and favors.

In this "land between the rivers" in the valley watered by the Tigris and Euphrates, the **Sumerians** recorded accounts of how they believed their world began, stories with which ancient Hebrew writers were almost surely familiar when they wrote parts of the Old Testament. They developed a **cuneiform system** of writing. It was also here that the world's first legal codes were made. This Middle Eastern nation lacked wood and stone in any quantity, and thus the Sumerians used mostly sun-dried clay bricks in their constructions. They built temples and palaces replete with relief sculpture, metalwork, and frescoed murals. They seemed to be more concerned with the here and now than with life in the next world. These accomplished builders explored the possibilities of the archway in their architectural constructions. They made glazed tiles for wall decorations. Their most notable achievement in palace construction was a colorful tower called a **ziggurat.** For the most part, Sumerian art tells us about a vigorous artistic society.

The main accomplishments of **Assyrian** art date from 1000 to 600 B.C. and are seen in the architecturally magnificent palaces that house many fine sculptures and wall paintings. The militant warlike nature of the people was reflected in their art, with scenes of battles, wounded animals, and monsters found in both sculpture and wall paintings. We see traces of Sumerian art but on a much grander scale. Unlike the stiff, stylized approach seen in the art of the Egyptians, the Assyrians expressed life with vigor and brusqueness. The Assyrians destroyed and rebuilt Babylon; its luxury under King Nebuchadnezzar was legendary, and the **Hanging Gardens** became one of the **Seven Wonders of the World.** The walls of the city boasted glazed bricks depicting huge reliefs of fierce lions.

The **Minoans** on the island of Crete and the **Mycenaeans,** who lived on the nearby Greek mainland, developed civilizations between 2000 and 3000 B.C. that were quite different from those of Egypt and Mesopotamia. These two groups were fishermen, seafarers, traders, and pirates. The ruling classes lived in fine palaces and villas complete with bathrooms and walls that were covered with bright paintings. Though they built no temples, they worshiped a mother goddess and sacrificed bulls to her. A double axe and the horns of a bull are seen as symbols that often marked their shrines. Bull leaping was a popular sport that was practiced by both young men and women. A famous wall painting from Crete, dated 1500 B.C., shows an acrobat grasping the horns while another athlete is seen somersaulting over the bull's back. Women played an important part in the Minoans' religious ceremonies. A well-known terra-cotta figure shows an elaborately dressed, bare-breasted woman holding a snake in each of her upraised hands. The Mycenaeans built massive stone walls to protect their cities and in time conquered the Minoans and absorbed a good deal of their culture. Disaster came about 1100 B.C. in the form of earthquakes, fires, and invasions by armies from the north. The glories of these lands are remembered in **Homer's** epic poems.

Another ancient civilization was that of **Persia,** with its exciting examples of woven and ceramic ware that can be traced as far back as 5000 B.C. Persian rugs are still regarded highly today and continue to delight and fascinate individuals around the world.

Moving across the seas, we learn of another culture that, some fifteen hundred years before Columbus sailed to the New World, flourished in Central America. The **Mayas** had developed a writing system, a refined and notable architecture, and spectacular achievements in the world of mathematics and astronomy. Though they lacked metal, wheels, or beasts of burden, they built towering temples and developed agriculture. Most of the art of the Mayas is related to the gods they believed controlled the sun, rain, wind, water, and such. Corn was the basis of their life, and every stage of the crop's growth was marked with religious ceremonies. The corn god was the most revered of the deities, and many statues of him were placed in tombs and temples. When their civilization declined, the **Aztecs** of Mexico and the **Incas** of Peru came into dominance, the latter being in control until the Spanish conquerors in the sixteenth century brought horses and cannons and took over their lands.

Classical Artworks

The art of the ancient Greeks and Romans is called **Classical art.** The art of Greece began to flower around 600 B.C. Today we can find traces of their marvelous architecture and sculpture. They built marble temples with vividly colored details like nothing ever seen before to honor both gods and goddesses. The well-known **Parthenon,** built in the fifth century B.C. under the leadership of the statesman Pericles, was sacred to Athena and stands on the **Acropolis,** a hill that overlooks Athens. Although painting was supposedly one of their most important arts, it has been all but lost to us. Their ceramic wares with painted depictions tell us much of their way of life. Greek art influenced the entire world, and the Romans borrowed it almost entirely. During the Middle Ages, both the Romanesque and Gothic cathedrals drew upon the Greek influence. In our cities today, we find many public buildings, banks, and architectural landmarks, such as the Lincoln Memorial, that were influenced by this ancient civilization. One can find numerous examples of either **Doric, Ionic,** or **Corinthian** columns on buildings in cities all over the world.

About 600 B.C., **Greece** emerged into a new era that marks the birth of Western civilization and art. The people no longer worshiped animal gods but fashioned gods in their own image that had the traits of humans, both bad and good, and could be understood in human terms. A marble statue (originally painted with bright colors) of a youth, Kouros, was made early in the development of Greek sculpture, 525 B.C., before anatomy was clearly understood. Their artists studied anatomy and understood how muscles and bones control the body positions, and their sculptures seem like perfect living beings because of the Greeks' belief in ideal proportions. Two of the most famous sculptures are *Winged Victory* (the goddess Aphrodite) and the *Venus de Milo,* both made late in the Classical period and showing lifelike figures of perfect beauty. Some of the names of Greek sculptors are known to us, the most influential including Phidias, Myron, Praxiteles, Polyclitus, and Lysippus. Nude males competed in the **Olympic games,** held every four years in honor of the gods, with the victors being celebrated in sculpture and painting.

At about the time Greece was reaching its most glorious period, the **Etruscans,** with their fierce warriors and skilled metalworkers, came into power in Italy, north of

Figure 6.4 *Exekias, Achilles Slays the Amazon Penthesileia.* **Black-figured neck-amphora, ca. 540 B.C.** H. 16⅓ in. *Reproduced by courtesy of the Trustees of the British Museum.*

the Greek colonies. They worshiped a number of different gods and placed all the things in tombs that they deemed necessary in the afterlife. We know that music and dance were important to these peoples from the paintings on the walls of the tombs. The rulers wore purple robes as symbols of office and laid out their cities on a gridiron plan, which the Romans, who followed them, were to do also.

The Etruscan city-state of **Rome** was organized in 753 B.C. The legend goes that the abandoned twins Romulus and Remus were suckled by a she-wolf, and when they were grown founded the city of Rome where they had been found by a shepherd. A famous bronze sculpture commemorates this legend. The Etruscan rulers were overthrown about 400 B.C., and the **Roman republic** was established. Within a few centuries, the Romans, with their talent for government and their desire to conquer, expanded into the largest empire ever known in the world. They borrowed ideas from all the peoples they had conquered; however, they replaced the ideal image used by the Greek sculptors with a realism that showed every sagging muscle and wrinkle. They were great engineers, constructing roads, waterways, and public baths. Their

Figure 6.5 Colosseum, Rome (aerial view).
© Robert C. Lamm

engineers were the first to use the **arch** and **concrete** in constructions, and Imperial Rome had many **triumphal arches** that were built to celebrate victories. Enormous crowds filled the amphitheaters, such as the **Colosseum** in Rome, to see chariot races and gladiators. On the walls of the interiors of villas and houses of the aristocracy were paintings of landscapes, still lifes, animals, and religious and historical subjects. The best known of these survive in the cities of **Herculaneum** and **Pompeii** because they were covered with volcanic ashes in A.D. 79 and thereby were preserved for centuries.

Imperial Rome gradually lost its power over a large part of the Western world after several hundred years of peace, and by the fifth century, the Dark Ages began.

Artworks in Medieval Times

Medieval art comes from the **Middle Ages,** a period that occurred between ancient and modern times—that is, the thousand years between the fall of Rome and the beginning of the Renaissance (the fifth to the fifteenth centuries A.D.). Economic and social conditions were such that during these Dark Ages, people had to devote full time to survival. The Church was the binding source of artistic inspiration and achievement. Its power was felt in law, science, economics, literature, and in the Crusades, military expeditions that sought to reclaim the Holy Land from the Muslims.

Until A.D. 313 Christians were a persecuted sect in the Roman world, but when the emperor **Constantine** was converted, Christianity was established as the official religion of the Roman Empire. He moved his court from Rome to the town of Byzantium, which was renamed Constantinople. Here the distinctive **Byzantine** style of art developed. **Mosaics** rich with decorative patterns showed figures with long faces and strange gestures. Paintings were

flat and decorative, with figures representing saints and holy people, as well as the emperor and empress, depicted in frozen, rigid positions. These images are called **icons,** and in the eighth century, people called **iconoclasts** (image breakers) disapproved of them and destroyed all they could find. Such artists as **Cimabue** and **Duccio** worked with stiff, formal patterns and flat backgrounds typical of the Byzantines. The flat handling of paint and the decorative style may have been influenced in part by a desire to discard the paganistic influences of Greece and Rome, where realism and man had been considered of utmost importance.

The Roman Empire in the west was overrun by barbarians in the fifth century A.D., and learning for awhile continued only in the monasteries. Because the printing press hadn't been invented yet, and most people couldn't read anyway, art was used by the Church to instruct and inspire the people. Monks kept the glow of culture alive with their **illuminated manuscripts** of sacred and scholarly texts. They worked in scriptoriums, copying the Bible in Latin by hand on fine **parchment** called **vellum** (animal skin). Decorations and pictures in the margins and for initial letters were called illuminations. **Gold leaf** beaten so thin that you could see through it, and sometimes with a pattern pressed into it, was stuck on these paintings and illuminated manuscripts. The **Book of Kells,** made in Ireland about A.D. 800, is a beautiful example of this art form.

In the sixth century, Pope Gregory declared that paintings were useful for teaching people about the Bible. Altar pictures painted on three panels were called **triptychs.** Brightly painted sculptures and colorful stained-glass windows also were used to inform and inspire people. **Giotto's** innovative painting techniques, on both altarpieces and frescoes on church walls, foreshadowed the coming Renaissance.

In A.D. 800 the French king **Charlemagne** was crowned by the pope as the first Holy Roman Emperor. Charlemagne hoped to restore his Christian homeland to the glory and grandeur of the past, so he imported scholars and artists. To guide them in their work, he brought in manuscripts and works of art from the ancient world. In the latter part of the Medieval years, **suits of armor** for knights to wear in combat or in tournaments were made by skilled metalworkers; other craftspersons wove **tapestries** filled with symbols and stories to hang on the cold stone walls of castles and churches.

Romanesque architecture, in vogue from the ninth to the twelfth centuries, is characterized by churches built of heavy masonry and having dark interiors. Toward the end of the Middle Ages, especially in the twelfth century, the old feudal systems began to deteriorate, and towns began to grow, towns that began as centers of learning, with the Church providing strong leadership. A style of architecture known as **Gothic** developed, particularly in France, and spread rapidly through much of Europe. (The term "gothic" has its roots in the Italian Renaissance, when it was used disparagingly to describe a style of architecture so barbaric that only the fifth-century invaders of Rome, the Goths, could have been responsible for its use. Gradually, "Gothic" lost its derogatory connotation.) Between the years 1175 and 1275, eighty cathedrals and nearly five hundred large churches were built in France alone. These splendid **cathedrals**—with their pointed arches, flying buttresses, sculptured images, mosaics, stained-glass windows, and lofty spires that rose higher than any structures ever had before—fitted the needs of a deeply religious society. The marvelous French **Cathedral of Chartres** housed eight thousand images in sculpture and stained glass.

Another notable artwork from this period is the **Bayeux Tapestry,** actually an embroidered pictorial account of the Norman conquest of England in A.D. 1066. It was made by a number of women, who stitched hundreds of figures on a 230-foot long fabric background.

As the Middle Ages came near its end, one thought was paramount in the minds of the lords constantly engaging in war between the city-states, that of insuring that future generations would remember their glorious battles. **Uccello** was the master of these military paintings. He painted an enormous work recalling a Florentine victory in 1456 for Cosimo de'Medici.

Artworks in the Fourteenth to Seventeenth Centuries

Renaissance and Baroque Art

The **Renaissance,** which means **rebirth,** took place between A.D. 1300 and 1600 and stands as one of the greatest periods of artistic development that the world has ever known. Classical art and the ideas of ancient Greece were rediscovered during this golden age, and artists ceased making the flat, decorative symbolic images that were prevalent during the Gothic days. Portraits were often painted in profile, like the heads seen by the Italian artists on Greek and Roman coins. The Italians sought to revive the glorification of the independence and nobility of man. Even though they continued to paint religious subjects, they placed the emphasis on the lives of human beings and their accomplishments on earth. Two of the most notable artistic developments that date from this period include the discovery of **perspective** (how to create the illusion of depth on a flat surface) and **chiaroscuro** (shading from light to dark to show modeled forms). Artists practiced ways of showing objects as they appear to our eyes. They studied nature and anatomy to learn how the body works so their artworks would be more lifelike.

Earlier, in the thirteenth century, the Florentine painter **Cimabue,** who died about 1302, had begun changing some of the old Byzantine methods by making

Figure 6.6   West facade, Chartres Cathedral, ca. 1142–1507. © Robert C. Lamm

figures express a feeling of movement in their gestures and faces and by adding a new monumentality or largeness to his artworks. He retained the gold background and patternlike arrangements of figures and objects. It remained for the great artist and architect **Giotto** (ca 1276–1337) to break away from the Byzantine tradition and lay the foundation for the Renaissance. In his scenes of the lives of Christ and Mary, he showed real emotions, naturalism, and human warmth. He shaded the figures and put deep shadows in their clothing. He painted with **egg tempera,** a medium that uses an egg as the binding agent for powdered pigment and that was perfected by the fourteenth-century Florentines. (Egg tempera was the dominant

Figure 6.7 Giotto, *Lamentation*, 1305–1306.
Fresco, 7'7" × 7'9". Arena Chapel, Padua.
Photo © Alinari/Art Resource.

medium for painting until oil paints almost completely replaced it in the sixteenth century). People had been accustomed to dark colors in the Byzantine panels, and the clearness and brightness of Giotto's works gave the impression of soft daylight on a scene and paved the way for those artists who came later.

An active commerce gave Italy money to sponsor art on a magnificent scale. Both painters and sculptors created lifelike portraits of recognizable individuals. No longer was the artist thought of as little more than a capable worker, as he was during the Middle Ages. **Master** artists, who belonged to **guilds,** took on youths as **apprentices** in their workshops. Most artworks were **commissioned** by church officials, the nobility and ruling classes, or wealthy merchants. The most important patrons of the arts were the **Medici family.**

Noted artists of the **Italian Renaissance** included a sculptor called **Donatello** (ca 1386–1466). His *David* was the first life-size, bronze, freestanding nude since ancient days. It combined Classicism with realism. **Masaccio** (1401–1428), revolutionized painting in his short lifetime. In *The Tribute Money,* a famous **fresco,** he placed solid, modeled figures in a landscape that had great depth. (Frescoes, in which pigment is applied to wet plaster, was a popular medium during the Renaissance. Large murals painted in this manner could be viewed from any angle without glare. They also were washable. Assistants helped the artist since the work was done in sections and had to be completed while the plaster was still wet.) It is thought that Masaccio learned perspective from **Filippo Brunelleschi** (ca 1377–1446), a great Florentine sculptor and architect. **Lorenzo Ghiberti's** (1378–1455) bronze designs

Figure 6.8 Leonardo da Vinci, *The Last Supper,* ca. 1495–
1498.
Mural, oil and tempera on plaster, 14′5″ × 28′.
*Refectory of Sta. Maria della Grazie, Milan. Photo, Alinari/
Art Resource.*

for the massive doors of the Baptistery in Florence won a
landmark competition and assured him a place in history.

Sassetta's (ca 1392–1450) delightful paintings are
small, narrative, and remind us of medieval book illustrations. The paintings of **Fra Angelico** (ca 1387–1455), a
priest, were made in the traditional manner of the early
Renaissance, with decorative patterns and lesser concern
for perspective. By the mid-fifteenth century, **Andrea del
Verrocchio** (1435–1488) was producing innovative and
important sculptures, painting, and metalwork in his
studio, attracting many young artists, among them **Leonardo da Vinci. Andrea Mantegna** (1431–1506) used perspective and foreshortening in a daring and startling
manner. **Sandro Botticelli's** (1444?–1510) *Primavera* and
the famous *Birth of Venus,* with their flowing rhythmic
lines, are examples of his masterpieces.

With the Italian **High Renaissance** came such artists
as **Leonardo da Vinci** (1452–1519), often called the
greatest genius who ever lived. He made scientific studies
and invented all kinds of machines, such as submarines
and helicopters, that were only realized hundreds of years
later. Only a few of his pictures remain to us, partly because his creative mind liked to experiment with different
materials and try different ways of painting rather than

using the traditional ones. He painted *The Last Supper*
at the end of the fifteenth century. He perfected a distinguishing way of showing lights and darks called **sfumato,**
which means smoky or misty. His *Mona Lisa* is probably
the most famous painting that was ever made.

The influence of the Italian Renaissance spread
throughout Europe, with artists from northern Europe
coming to Italy to learn and returning to their homelands.
The center of art and culture moved from Florence to
Rome during the sixteenth century. The popes saw to it
that artists worked to glorify the city with their paintings
and sculpture. **Michelangelo** (1475–1564) took four years
to paint 342 figures from the Bible on the ceiling of the
Sistine Chapel. Regarding himself primarily as a sculptor,
he at first refused to accept the pope's assignment. He developed a monumental style of painting solid, three-
dimensional–looking figures.

Other artists of great importance included **Raphael**
(1483–1520), a very popular young painter that died at
the age of thirty-seven from overwork, who was known as
the painter of "sweet Madonnas." He also painted murals
in the Vatican. **Bellini** (ca 1430–1516) was one of the first
Italian painters to use oil on canvas. (Artists from Flanders had visited his city and from them he learned of
Flemish experiments with oil paint and painting on canvas

Figure 6.9 Michelangelo, *Pieta,* **1498–1499/1500.**
Marble, height 68½″.
St. Peter's, Rome. Photo, Alinari/Art Resource.

rather than on wood panels.) **Giorgione** (ca 1478–1510) and **Titian** (ca 1488–1576), the most famous of all Venetian painters, were students in Bellini's workshop. About this time, artists began using canvases instead of wood panels. Mastering the oil technique, Titian painted with warm, rich colors on huge canvases, sacrificing details for the sweeping effect of the entire painting. His rich colors were built up with layers of contrasting glazes. He enjoyed the esteem of popes and princes and helped make full-length portraits fashionable. Giorgione, one of the first artists to paint small pictures for private collectors, died at the young age of thirty-two. His great contribution was that of integrating figures and the landscapes to create moods that were filled with a poetic reverie. He had a great influence on Venetian painting, most especially on the young Titian.

It was unusual for sixteenth-century women to have careers in art or otherwise, but **Sofonisba Anguissola** (1532/35–1625) became the first well-known woman artist. She and her five sisters came from a wealthy Italian family and were well educated. Sofonisba not only painted self-portraits but created a new kind of picture that showed people in scenes of everyday life. She was invited to paint for King Philip in Spain. Two other women that achieved success as artists during this time were **Lavina Fontana** (1552–1614) and **Artemisia Gentileschi** (1593–1652).

Lavina's father taught her to paint, and she became the first woman to make paintings for large public places. The pope invited her to Rome to paint religious works. Many fashionable people had her paint their portraits because she was so skilled in showing their fine clothing and jewelry. Many people feel that Artemisia is the greatest of Italian women artists. She often depicted powerful and courageous women from ancient myths, the Bible, or history. Some of her artworks were over six feet high.

Veronese (1528–1588) made paintings that used cool, clear colors and showed many figures, richly dressed in silk, velvet, lace, and jewels. He arranged the figures in large compositions with elegant backgrounds of classical antiquity, nature, or Venetian interiors. His sumptuous style set the standards for eighteenth-century Venetian decoration.

Jean Fouquet (ca 1420–1477/81) was a French court painter. His portraits are monumental in construction, full and rounded in contour, and well composed, ranking him among the first Renaissance painters north of the Alps and making him the founder of a tradition in France that was to be developed in the sixteenth century.

The last great sixteenth-century Venetian artist was **Tintoretto** (1518–1594). His works anticipated the coming Baroque style. He worked directly on his canvases without making sketches or underpaintings first. He even distorted and exaggerated shapes for the sake of the composition and the drama of the scene.

Much of what we know about these Renaissance artists comes from the writings of **Vasari** (1511–1574), an artist himself who gathered his information by traveling all over Italy. His first work was published in 1550 and was followed by an enlarged edition in 1568.

The **Late Renaissance** dates from about A.D. 1530 to 1600. The art done during the High Renaissance was thought to be so perfect that it was hard for young artists to improve upon the past. So some of them broke Renaissance rules and distorted the figures and spaces in their compositions; the result was very dramatic and the style was called **Mannerism. Parmigianino** (1503–1540) achieved this effect in his *Madonna of the Long Neck.* Other Mannerists attracted attention by exaggerating the proportions of the human figure and showing their subjects in unusual postures.

A **Mannerist** painter known as **El Greco** ("the Greek") (1541–1614) came to Venice from Crete to study art. He later moved to Spain, where the Byzantine art he had seen in Crete and the masterpieces of the Renaissance in Italy blended with the grimness of Spanish art to influence his work. He made many realistic yet mystical religious works, as well as portraits of the aristocracy, with a style of elongated figures that was easily recognizable as the work of El Greco. Typical of these is *The Burial of the Court Orgaz.* His dramatic *View of Toledo* shows a moody storm raging over the city.

Figure 6.10   Pieter Brueghel, the Elder, *The Wedding Dance,*
ca. 1566.
Oil on panel, 47 × 62 in.: 119.38 × 157.48 cm.
Courtesy of the Detroit Institute of Arts. City of Detroit
Purchase.

The Renaissance also took place in **northern Europe,** in **Flanders** (now part of northern France and Belgium), and Germany in the fifteenth century. Here artists made paintings filled with details and jewel-like colors. Italian ideas spread there later. Ghent and Bruges were centers for the wool and weaving trades, and many people—merchants and aristocrats—had money to spend on paintings.

Here **Jan van Eyck,** who died in 1441, is generally credited with developing a new technique of painting with oils. He started a trend in realism that depicted details with a minute precision that was to be typical of Flemish painters for many years. This came about because oil paints—due to being a mixture of dry pigments, oil, and sometimes varnish—lengthened the drying time and let artists work at a more leisurely pace. He produced an enormous altarpiece for the cathedral in Ghent, Belgium. Many **Flemish** artists used the techniques of Renaissance Italian painters; others continued with the Flemish tradition of **genre**—scenes from everyday life. **Hieronymus Bosch** (1450?–1516) had a vivid imagination and invented weird, grostesque creatures in his works. **Pieter Brueghel the Elder** (1525?–1569) worked in the Flemish manner but used perspective and other Renaissance techniques in his depictions of stout, rustic peasants at work

or enjoying life. His two sons also became artists, having been taught by their grandmother since he died when the boys were very young. Their names were **Jan Brueghel** (1568–1625) and **Pieter Brueghel the Younger** (1564–1638).

Rogier van der Weyden (ca 1399/1400–1464), influential early Flemish painter, worked in an extremely natural manner, using warm colors, subtle tonalities, and emotional presentations of religious scenes. **Lucas Cranach** (1472–1553) is remembered for his late Gothic mythological scenes and landscapes with figures, the latter showing precise technique and details of German clothing and landscapes. His paintings are quite small, decorative, and jewel-like.

In the sixteenth century, the Reformation split Europe into Protestant and Catholic countries, and many Protestants felt that religious art was a form of idol worship. So without the patronage of the Church, artists in northern Europe turned to nonreligious subjects such as landscapes, still lifes, portraits for the wealthy merchants, and scenes of everyday life.

Important German painters of the sixteenth century were **Albrecht Dürer** (1471–1528) and **Hans Holbein the Younger** (1497?–1543), whose father was also an artist.

Figure 6.11 Albrecht Dürer, *The Painter's Father,* **1497. Oil on panel, 20 × 15¾ in.** *The National Gallery, London.*

Figure 6.12 Hans Holbein the Younger, *Edward VI as a Child.* **Date: Probably 1538. Oil on wood; 0.57 × 0.44 (22⅜ × 17⅜ in.)** *National Gallery of Art, Washington, D.C. Andrew W. Mellon Collection.*

Dürer has been called the northern Leonardo because he was a learned man in many fields and had traveled to Italy. He is said to have been vain and handsome and painted many self-portraits. He was one of the first great engravers. **Holbein,** well-known internationally, made many portraits, especially in England where he painted members of the royal household of King Henry VIII, as well as designed jewelry, hall decorations, and costumes for pageants.

The seventeenth century is generally known as the **Baroque** period in art. (The word is thought to be derived from the Portuguese *barroco,* meaning an irregularly shaped pearl. It is also believed to have been named after the founder of the style, Federigo Barocci [1528–1612]. It was first used abusively to describe grotesque objects.) Baroque art was well suited to large-scale pictures of the sort we would find in churches and palaces. Ceilings were often painted with people, horses, and chariots that, viewed from below, appeared to be floating in the air, an effect that was called **illusionism.** It was the dominant style of

art in Europe from about 1550 to 1700. It is a style of art characterized by dynamic, often violent movement, flamboyant emotion, unusual curving compositions, swirling figures, dramatic lighting, and exaggerated gestures. It is typified by elaborate and ornate scrolls, curves, and other symmetrical ornamentation.

Baroque art began in Rome and extended from Italy to the Catholic countries of Europe—Flanders, Holland, France, and Spain. **Caravaggio** (1573–1619) used strong contrasts of light and dark to make exciting portrayals of people. The French artist **Claude Lorrain's** (1600–1685) **classical landscapes** show hills, plains, and the ruins of Rome with tiny figures of people. Notable artists include **Peter Paul Rubens,** the greatest of Baroque painters (1577–1649). Rubens was also an international diplomat with boundless energy. His works were in such demand

Figure 6.13 Peter Paul Rubens, *The Assumption of the Virgin*, ca 1626. [Date: c 1626; Wood; 1.254 × 0.942 (49⅜ × 37⅛ in.)]

National Gallery of Art, Washington, D.C. Samuel H. Kress Collection.

Figure 6.14 Diego Velázquez, *Maids of Honor (Las Meninas)*, 1656.
Oil on canvas, 10′5″ × 9′.
Prado Museum, Madrid. Photo, Alinari/Art Resource.

that he developed a "factory" of helpers. **Anthony van Dyck** (1599–1641) ranks as one of the greatest of all portrait painters.

Other notable artists of the seventeenth century included **Diego Velázquez** (1599–1660), one of the greatest of all Spanish painters. He was a court painter to King Philip IV of Spain, and he made use of rich, harmonious colors. His remarkable brushwork could create remarkable illusions of rich fabrics and flesh. Later the French Impressionists admired the manner in which he made small, roughly textured brushstrokes that showed the play of light on a surface.

During the seventeenth century, Holland became a rich, powerful, independent Protestant country. While Catholic countries had fostered and utilized art as a part of worship in their churches, the Protestants did not approve of religious paintings, and the churches were very plain. However, prosperous merchants, bankers, and other citizens wanted, and could easily afford, art for their homes. They frequently had their portraits painted, singly or in groups. Since Holland was a farming country, a popular subject for painters was domestic animals and landscapes. Genre paintings showing the interiors of tidy,

comfortable Dutch homes were often painted. Some artists specialized in still lifes showing fresh flowers, food, and dishes. A great deal of Holland's wealth came from sea trade, so pictures of ships and the sea were popular.

Frans Hals (1581/85–1666) has been called the first great painter of the seventeenth-century Dutch school. His portraits—with their quick, flashing brushstrokes—almost seem to be spontaneous snapshots showing exuberant people with dancing eyes, happy laughter, and joyful gestures. **Jan Vermeer** (1632–1675), though only thirty-two of his artworks remain for us today, handled light in such a way as to influence the Impressionists of the nineteenth century. He painted humble scenes of daily life, mostly showing one or more people in cheerful, sunlit rooms filled with household objects. Vermeer was also an art dealer, one of a number of people that bought pictures from artists and sold them for a profit.

Pieter de Hooch (1629–1688) was an important genre painter who usually depicted interiors of Dutch homes that showed rooms and receding rooms with a precise perspective. His colors were softly warm and the scenes quiet in atmosphere.

Several women achieved measurable success at this time in northern Europe, the most famous probably being **Judith Leyster** (1609–1660). She expertly painted still lifes, genre scenes, and portraits in her native Holland. She married an artist but kept her maiden name, signing her works with her initials J. L. and a star that stood for her last name "Lodestar." It was thought for many years that some of her works had been created by the artist Frans Hals. While in her twenties, she became the only female member of the Haarlem painters' guild. In Germany, **Maria Sibylla Merian** (1647–1717) combined art and science by creating paintings and writing books about insects and plant life. She even traveled to South America with one of her daughters and lived in a jungle where she could paint flowers, birds, and insects. **Rachel Ruysch** (1664–1750) watched her father, who was an anatomy and botany professor, and became interested in flowers and insects. She and her husband were invited to be court painters for a German ruler. She made many beautiful paintings of fruit and flowers.

The French artist **George de la Tour** (1593–1652) is noted for his night scenes that are dramatically lit by candles and torches. They are primarily religious subjects seen in quiet moods.

One of the most remarkable artists of all time was the Dutch painter, **Rembrandt van Rijn** (1606–1669), whose amazing talents captured human emotions in ways never seen before. The happy and sad times of his long life are visually chronicled by his many self-portraits. He built up a painting with many layers of color and showed important areas dramatically lit by a brilliant light. One of his first important commissions was for a group portrait called *The Anatomy Lesson of Dr. Tulp.* His best known work is another enormous group portrait called *The Night Watch,* in which he painted the figures grouped in an informal arrangement. He also painted Bible stories and scenes from ancient history.

Artworks in the Eighteenth and Nineteenth Centuries

Called the Age of Enlightenment or the Age of Reason, the eighteenth century was a time when people found happiness and freedom through the exercise of reason in all matters. Authority was fearlessly questioned and long-held conventions that had governed lives were discarded. Political and social revolutions took place. The American Revolution of 1776 was followed by the French Revolution of 1789. Napoleon's victories and defeats brought about world-shaking developments. People in Mexico and other Latin American countries were also striving for greater freedom. The Industrial Revolution was changing lives.

Leadership in art now changed from Italy to France. Societies were formed in order to have exhibits of paintings, some sites later becoming public galleries. Private collections were built by rich connoisseurs. Academies were founded in European capitals, and they held exhibits and taught students how to paint according to strict rules. The monumental grandeur of Baroque art lingered into the early part of the eighteenth century before it gave way to the more informal styles that were to follow. Fewer palaces and more modest homes were built, and in turn the smaller rooms needed smaller paintings. Subject matter became more varied, with French artists picturing carefree courtly life while other artists emphasized life among the common folk.

The gentry in England had itself portrayed enjoying the quiet life of its country homes, while the first great English artist, **William Hogarth** (1697–1764), painted the seamier side of society. The British liked to visit Italy, so Italian artists painted views of their native country to sell to them. Well-to-do colonists in America wanted portraits of themselves painted.

A style called **Rococo**—characterized by free and graceful movement, playful lines, rich colors, ornamentation, and decorative grace—superseded the formal grandeur of the Baroque. It began in France, and its extravagant, decorative scrolls and rock and plant motifs soon spread to all the fine and decorative arts.

Jean-Honoré Fragonard (1732–1806), one of the greatest of the Rococo artists, painted myths, gallantry, and landscapes. His works appealed to the high-living upper classes in France, and he was one of the first French artists to sell his works directly from his studio rather than from a public exhibit.

François Boucher (1703–1770) moved almost exclusively in the world of the French court. He decorated royal architecture and became the most popular painter of his day, with his influence extending not only to painting but to interior decoration, tapestries, and porcelain. He painted historical and mythological works, portraits, and pastoral scenes, for which he is most famous.

The Flemish born **Antoine Watteau** (1684–1721) was one of the greatest of Rococo artists and was a court painter to King Louis XV. He was one of the first to break away from the grandeur of the Baroque, but his career was cut short when he died of tuberculosis when he was only thirty-seven years old.

The first artist to explore the special uses of chalk and make pastel portraits popular was **Rosalba Carriera** (1675–1757). When a French art collector invited her to leave Venice and come to Paris, she introduced pastel portraits to France and was invited to become a member of the French Royal Academy of Painting. She was also a member of the Academy in Rome.

Jean-Baptiste-Siméon Chardin (1699–1779) painted still lifes and pictures of ordinary people doing their domestic routines or enjoying simple pleasures, his goal being to show goodness and truth in everyday life.

Elisabeth Vigée-Lebrun (1755–1842) made portraits of most of Europe's royalty, including Marie Antoinette, the queen of France. She painted over nine hundred portraits during her long life and is remembered as being one of the best portrait painters of the late eighteenth and early nineteenth centuries. Her fame caused her to be one of the only three women invited into the French Royal Academy of Painting. Only the best artists were asked to join the academies, where they could study and exhibit. Another woman who became a famous artist during this time was **Angelica Kauffman** (1741–1807). Though born in Switzerland, she traveled as a young girl to Austria and Italy with her artist father. Later she created many history scenes and helped introduce Neoclassicism. At this time it was thought that only men could paint historical artworks, but she refused to accept this idea. She also made many portraits of royalty, became wealthy, and was asked to be one of the founders of the British Royal Academy.

The popular Venetian artist **Canaletto** (1697–1768) was the leading view-painter of the eighteenth century. His output was prolific and included panoramic views of cities, canals, churches, bridges, and palaces that included much photographic detail.

Francisco Goya (1746–1828) was the official court painter of the king of Spain. He continued to paint after he lost his hearing in mid-life, but Napoleon's invasion, with its mercilessly cruel killings, changed his artworks. He showed a profound disillusionment with human beings.

During the eighteenth century, more works of art were revealed by excavations in Pompeii in Italy, which stimulated a new interest in the Classical works of the ancient world. Called **Neoclassical,** this style of art was in strong contrast to Rococo. Its interior design and architecture seem plain and simple when compared with Rococo. Artists chose Classical subjects and painted in the style they thought the ancient Romans would have used. The most illustrious Neoclassical painter was **Jacques-Louis David** (1748–1825), a Frenchman chosen by Napoleon, who saw himself in the role of a great empire builder in the tradition of ancient Rome. He commissioned David to so portray him, thus sparking a revival of the heroic grandeur of the Classical past. David's history painting, *The Oath of the Horatii,* created a sensation when it was first exhibited. It tells a story of self-sacrifice for the higher good. It shows young men swearing to their father to fight to the death while the grief-stricken young women are positioned on the right. Instead of the two states engaging in battle, the three young men will fight the three Alban brothers.

William Hogarth (1697–1764), one of the most original and influential of British artists, was the son of a schoolmaster who, during the boy's youth, was put in prison for debt, an experience that marked Hogarth's later art production. He is best remembered for making a series of storytelling pictures and a series of engravings in which he ridiculed the outlandish behavior he observed in Britain's upper classes. He was perhaps the first artist to use his art for social criticism and to direct his work to a large, unsophisticated public. He was also an excellent portrait painter.

Another English artist, **Thomas Gainsborough** (1727–1788), was both a landscapist and portraitist, often placing his figures in light, feathery landscapes. In *Blue Boy,* he shows his profound appreciation and understanding of van Dyck and Rubens. His work is in contrast to the ideals of his great rival, **Sir Joshua Reynolds** (1723–1792). Reynolds's works were influenced by the Venetian and Flemish Baroque painters. They are composed harmoniously and are completely unified, never being merely pretty or sentimental. He sought to raise the standing of art and artists. He often dressed up his subjects as characters from myths and ancient history.

During the first half of the nineteenth century, three important art styles were prominent. The first, **Neoclassicism,** continued to serve as a reaction to the Baroque and Rococo styles of art, rejecting traditional subject matter and looking to the Classical art of ancient Greece and Rome and to the Renaissance for inspiration. The second, the **Romantic** movement, took the place of the rigid and orderly conventions of the Classical school. It was a freer style of art in which the artist depicted historical and literary scenes of dramatic action, melodrama, and heightened emotion. Romanticists thought that showing feelings

and emotions was more important than anything. They chose strong colors and dramatic effects and were inspired by the concept of liberty and anything dramatic, heroic, exciting, exotic, or mysterious. Credit is generally given to **Théodore Géricault** (1791–1824) for creating the Romantic style. He emulated Rubens's exuberant works and showed much spontaneity in his drawing and painting. His *Raft of the Medusa,* telling of a frigate that sank in 1818 and lost many lives, was painted when he was twenty-seven and made him famous. He influenced **Eugène Delacroix** (1798–1863), whose numerous artworks showing horses testify to his ability to portray dynamic action.

A favorite theme of the Romantic painters dealt with showing the power and grandeur of nature—lofty mountains, storms, and rough seas, with human beings seen as small and defenseless. The English painter **Joseph M. W. Turner** (1775–1851) tried to give the viewer a feeling of being present at a scene rather than showing how it actually looked. He painted in watercolor as well as oils.

The English landscapist **John Constable** (1776–1837) gave realistic views of the countryside, painting directly from nature. His works influenced the **Barbizon school** of landscapists, a group of artists that were a part of the Romantic movement that lasted from about 1820 to 1850. Working near the village of Barbizon in France, they sketched out-of-doors and completed their artworks in their studios.

The third major style of art during this time was **Realism.** About 1850 artists began to show the commonplace without disguising the harsh realities that industrial progress had left untouched, such as peasants working in the fields. Here artists found objects and events around them to be suitable subjects, rather than choosing to express the exotic, romantic world of the Romantics. These artists observed and painted peasants and working classes, whose lives were difficult and unromantic.

Eugene Boudin's (1824–1898) paintings are light and tender in quality, fresh in color and in the portrayal of light and reflections on people and landscapes. He painted luminous skies and gave peaceful impressions of a pleasant landscape. He was admired by such artists as Corot, Courbet, Sisley, Manet, and Monet.

Other artists working during this period in artistic history were the following: **Jean-François Millet** (1814–1875) called himself the "peasant of peasants." He devoted himself to scenes of rural life. **Honoré Daumier** (1808–1879) was widely known for his political cartoons and today is considered one of the foremost French painters of his century. He was a confirmed **Realist,** but to stress the true character of his subjects, resorted to distortion. **Gustave Courbet** (1819–1877) was the foremost exponent of Realism and exerted an immense influence on modern art by his emphatic rejection of idealization, painting the world as he saw it, even its unpleasant and harsh side. He

Figure 6.15 Jean François Millet, *The Sower*, ca. **1814–1875.**
Oil on canvas, 40″ × 32½″.
Gift of Quincy Adams Shaw through Quincy A. Shaw, Jr. and
Mrs. Marian Shaw Haughton. Courtesy, Museum of Fine
Arts, Boston.

sometimes applied his paints with a palette knife and worked with a few somber colors. The landscapes of **Jean-Baptiste-Camille Corot** (1796–1875) reflect his love of nature. His early **luminous** paintings from nature greatly influenced future landscapists and place him among the more original artists of the nineteenth century.

The French artist **Rosa Bonheur** (1822–1899) was one of the most popular artists of the nineteenth century. There was even a doll in her likeness created for little girls. She loved painting animals and did it so well that royalty all over Europe gave her medals for her work.

American Artworks

During this time, art served a variety of purposes in fast-growing America. Reynolds's teaching of the importance of historical painting had a great influence on the American artist **Benjamin West** (1738–1820). West, one of the early Neoclassicists, had trained briefly in Philadelphia and then left in 1760 to study in Rome. Three years later he settled in London, where his studio soon became a gathering place for American students abroad. His painting of *Penn's Treaty with the Indians* shows figures

dressed in the clothing of their day rather than in the Roman togas fashionable with the Neoclassicists.

John Singleton Copley (1738–1815) was one of the greatest American artists of the eighteenth century. He was largely self-taught and made excellent likenesses of his countrymen, including a portrait of Paul Revere, showing him in his work clothes and holding a silver teapot he was making. **Gilbert Stuart** (1755–1828) is famous for his portraits of George Washington, one of which appears on the one dollar bill. **Charles Willson Peale** (1741–1827) was one of several family members, both male and female, who were artists. His niece, **Sarah Miriam Peale** (1800–1885) was the first American woman to support herself with the money she earned painting.

The most extraordinary painter to spring up from America was a Pennsylvania Quaker named **Edward Hicks** (1780–1849). Trained as a coach-and-sign painter, he is most famous for his religious works, especially the approximately seventy variations on the theme of a peaceable kingdom in which animals and people live peaceably together. The figures in West's painting of William Penn signing a peace treaty with the Indians, and Richard Westall's engraving, incidentally, served as prototypes and inspiration for Hicks's artworks.

Albert Ryder's (1847–1917) almost mystical scenes of the ocean—with their strange, often yellowish, lighting—were painted in a manner that paralleled the Romantic style. **George Inness's** (1825–1894) early work was influenced by the Hudson River school, but later, after contact with the Barbizon school, he abandoned precise detail for a broader style, using glowing light and indistinctly massed forms that gave a mystical view of nature.

The American artists **William Michael Harnett** (1848–1892) and **John Frederick Peto** (1854–1907) carried realism to the point where the objects they painted seemed like real objects rather than painted images. This kind of art is called **"trompe l'oeil,"** meaning to trick the eye.

John James Audubon (1784–1851) pictured the birds of America in their natural habitats in a highly realistic and beautiful way. At nearly the same time, **George Catlin** (1796–1872) turned from his law practice to devote his life to the portrayal of American Indians. **George Caleb Bingham** (1811–1879) painted Missouri River genre scenes showing male figures as they relaxed, danced, made music, fished, played cards, or held conversations.

Jacksonian democracy had created a new pride in the American wilderness. **The Hudson River school** was composed of an unorganized group of artists that depicted the newly perceived grandeur and beauty of America and produced our earliest landscapes. The best of these was probably **Thomas Cole** (1801–1848), who first traveled along the Hudson River in 1825 to sketch the Catskills. He later walked through the Adirondacks, the White Mountains, and the old Northwest Territory to make his

Figure 6.16   George Caleb Bingham, *Fur Traders Descending*
the Missouri.
Oil on canvas, 29 × 36½ in.
The Metropolitan Museum of Art, Morris K. Jesup Fund,
1933. (33.61).

artworks. His view of the countryside was highly emotional and patriotic. One of his followers was **Asher Brown Durand** (1796–1886), whose landscapes show the engraver's close attention to detail and are remarkably true to the American scene. **Frederic Church** (1826–1900), the only student of Cole, made large and spectacular landscapes.

Other Americans focused their efforts on other aspects of the American frontier. **Albert Bierstadt** (1830–1902) made grandiose interpretations of the American landscape, most notably the Rocky Mountains and further west. **Frederic Remington** (1861–1909), foreseeing an end to the "Wild West," painted its cowboys and Indians amid scenic grandeur. Likewise, **Charles Russell** (1865–1926) spent years as a trapper and cowboy, drawing and painting the frontier life he saw around him for amusement in idle moments. It wasn't long before his works began to surprise him by selling, and when he married a shrewd woman, she persuaded him to settle down to art. **William R. Leigh** (1866–1955) roamed the vast country on horseback, sketching as he went and painting the vanishing West until he died.

The American **James A. M. Whistler** (1834–1903) lived and worked abroad. He was a socialite, a celebrated wit, and the first American artist to belittle the importance of subject matter, claiming art was for art's sake.

Figure 6.17   James McNeill Whistler, *Arrangement in Gray*
and Black, No. 1, **ca. 1877.**
Oil on canvas, 57″ × 64½″.
The Louvre, Paris. Cliché des Musées Nationaux, Paris.

He stressed formal, decorative patterns, calling his famous painting of his mother *Arrangement in Gray and Black.* His younger American contemporary, **John Singer Sargent** (1856–1925), also spent much of his life abroad, painting portraits of fashionable people. When he painted for his own pleasure, he created dazzling watercolors.

Winslow Homer (1836–1910) is probably best known for his paintings of the sea. He lived on the rugged Maine coast and worked in both oils and watercolors. His career began as a lithographer, and later he recorded scenes of the Civil War for *Harper's Weekly.* He also painted many genre scenes of childhood.

Thomas Eakins (1844–1916) paid unblinking attention to facts when he painted, recording honestly and precisely the reality he saw and remarking at the beauty of the wrinkles he saw in an old woman's skin. His interest in anatomy is reflected in one of his celebrated works, *The Gross Clinic.*

Edmonia Lewis (1843–1909) made marble sculpture that reflected her feelings against racial prejudice and slavery. Her father was black and her mother was a Chippewa Indian. She was the first black American to become known throughout the world as a sculptor.

In the latter part of the nineteenth century, **Nathaniel Currier** (1813–1888) and **James Ives** (1824–1895) formed a partnership to produce inexpensive lithographs that recorded nineteenth-century life in America. More than four thousand of these **Currier and Ives prints** were issued, and they depicted steamboats, trains, landscapes, newsworthy events, and life on the frontier.

Impressionism and Post-Impressionism

During the 1860s, a group of painters came together in Paris. They had several common bonds. They were more interested in showing atmospheric effects by the way they used light and color than they were in the subject matter they were painting. Because they were mainly interested in light, they insisted on painting in the open air. They avoided using black because they said we rarely see it in nature, so they painted shadows made of other dark colors. They worked on scientific color theories. They developed a style of making tiny brushstrokes laid side by side and often in contrasting colors. The viewer's eyes would blend the colors from a distance. The effect was that of showing people and landscapes shimmering in sunlight and dazzling colors. The Impressionists also shared a common struggle for a number of years to be accepted by the critics and public. When they were rejected from showing their works in the prestigious **Salons,** the official exhibitions of the **French Royal Academy,** they joined together and sponsored eight of their own shows.

Figure 6.18   Camille Pissarro, *Boulevard des Italiens, Morning Sunlight.* **Date: dated 1897; Canvas; 0.732 × 0.921 (28⅞ × 36¼ in.)**
National Gallery of Art, Washington, D.C. Chester Dale Collection.

Edouard Manet (1832–1883) shocked people with his colorful contrasts and unusual techniques. He was an inspiration for younger artists that would be working in the Impressionist style. When one of his paintings was first exhibited, a man tried to slash it with his cane.

Claude Monet (1840–1926) exhibited a seascape named *Impression: Sunrise.* An art critic derisively called the group of artists "Impressionists," but the artists adopted the name for themselves. He painted about forty pictures of the facade of the Rouen Cathedral under many different lighting conditions. He worked rapidly, seizing a particular moment by not mixing different colors on his palette before applying them on his canvas. His rapidly applied strokes of pure colors allowed the eye to blend them. The Impressionist **Camille Pissarro** (1830–1903) studied with Corot before meeting Monet in 1859. He was a kindly father figure who helped younger artists and introduced them to his friends.

Edgar Degas (1834–1917) specialized in painting ballet dancers and horses, being fascinated with motion. He preferred to paint indoor scenes and even had a wooden horse in his studio to serve as a model. He was interested in a new invention, a portable camera, that could capture unposed action and take pictures from unusual angles. He worked closely with **Mary Cassatt** (1845–1926), an American artist who was born into a wealthy Pittsburgh family. Cassatt lived and worked in Paris, and is especially known for her portraits of women and children. She is responsible for helping the Impressionists gain acceptance in America because she urged her wealthy friends to purchase their works.

Pierre-Auguste Renoir (1841–1919) worked in his youth at a porcelain factory. He is well known for his shimmering effects of light and for his pictures of young women and little girls. **Alfred Sisley** (1839–1899) spent most of his life in France painting landscapes with a delicate sensitivity and careful compositions. **Berthe Morisot** (1841–1895) was the first woman to join the Impressionists, and she persuaded her brother-in-law, Manet, to take up **plein air** painting (painting outdoors). She shared the Impressionists' love of iridescent light but did not use the short, broken brushstrokes that they did. Instead, she developed a fragile, feathery technique. **Alfred Sisley** remained faithful to Impressionism throughout his life but captured the movement of foliage, shimmering water, and textures of cloudy skies rather than only recording atmospheric changes in light.

The **Post-Impressionists** were artists that became dissatisfied with Impressionism. They had other visions they wished to explore and express. One of the first was **Paul Cézanne** (1839–1906). He felt that the flicker and shimmer of light on the surface of objects did not describe the solidity of natural forms. He felt that everything in nature was basically a cone, cylinder, or cube, and he worked hard to apply his brushstrokes in a manner that would convey this idea of solid forms. (His method of building up simple geometric forms was pursued later by Pablo Picasso and Georges Braque in a style known as **Cubism.**) He liked to paint still lifes because they didn't move, as people that modeled for him did, and he could concentrate on their basic forms. He also made many paintings of a favorite landscape, Mont Sainte-Victoire.

Vincent van Gogh (1853–1890), though awakened to the brighter colors used by the Impressionists when he first came to Paris from Holland, soon reacted against the realism of the Impressionists. He put strongly contrasting colors such as blue and yellow next to each other to express his intense feelings more vividly. He spent time in the south of France producing landscapes, flowers, and portraits. His works are easily identified by their thick, swirling brushstrokes. His short, ten-year career as an artist ended tragically when he shot himself at the age of thirty-seven.

Van Gogh was a friend of another artist, **Paul Gauguin** (1848–1903). Gauguin gave up his family and a successful career as a stockbroker in Paris to become a full-time painter. Most of his time as an artist was spent in the South Seas, where he applied brilliant arbitrary colors smoothly in large, flat areas that were separated by dark lines. He liked to paint exotic subjects of native women set in tropical surroundings, "drawing from nature by dreaming in her presence."

Georges Seurat (1859–1891) was a superb draftsman who invented a new method of painting using lots of small dots. It is called **pointillism.** Seurat had studied the science of color and knew that if he painted many tiny dots close to each other, they would mix in the viewer's eye. **Paul Signac** (1863–1935) also worked in this manner.

Henri de Toulouse-Lautrec (1864–1901) observed and drew the life in music halls, theaters, circuses, and cabarets of Paris. Born into a wealthy, noble family, he had a normal torso but stunted legs due to childhood accidents. He excelled not only in painting and drawing but in lithography, making posters that advertised music hall performances.

Henri Rousseau (1844–1910), until he retired in 1885, worked as an official in a Parisian tollhouse and hence is often known as "Le Douanier." He is usually categorized as **primitive** or **naive,** never having had any formal art training. He never waivered in his own belief in the grandeur of the contribution he would make to French art. Ridiculed by the public and critics, Rousseau was acclaimed by a number of his artist peers, and his work continues to find delighted responses from Surrealists, Pop artists, and the public today. His exotic jungle fantasies were based on the sketches he made in the botanical gardens and zoo of Paris. He had a superb intuitive sense of design and detailed pattern.

Artworks in the Twentieth Century

Diversity, rapid change, and all kinds of "isms" mark the artworks of the twentieth century. Classifying artists into these "ism" compartments can be confusing because artists don't always fit neatly into a style, and if they do, they may not continue in that mode for all of their careers. It is best if we endeavor to understand and enjoy each artwork in its own right. However, an overview of some of the leading schools of art, identifying some of the mainstream artists of the twentieth century, can clarify for us the overlapping and dynamic trends and movements that took place and are still taking place both in America and abroad.

Artists have always been cognizant of the social and cultural events taking place around them. They have also been influenced by artists that preceded them and by artists that are their contemporaries. In turn, they influence other artists' works. This is especially true in the twentieth century.

Very early in the twentieth century, many artists stopped depicting objects that were recognizable and used colors, lines, and shapes to express their ideas and feelings, a kind of art that is often called **abstract.** One very important style that grew out of Post-Impressionism was **Expressionism.** These artists liked to use violent colors and distortions, exaggerating the shapes of the things they painted.

Figure 6.19 Pablo Picasso, *Guernica,* **1937.**
Oil on canvas, 25′5¾″ × 11′5½″.
The Prado Museum. Madrid. Photo, SPADEM/ARS, New
York.

At the beginning of the new century, **Cubism** was born. This revolutionary new movement was sparked by **Pablo Picasso** (1880–1973) and **Georges Braque** (1882–1963). Their compositions no longer just represented natural objects but created new shapes and forms, showing different planes and viewpoints all at once. Picasso created in many different styles and in a variety of media during his long, productive life. Born in Spain, he spent most of his life in France. His early works fall into his "Blue period," which was soon replaced by his "Rose period." He is probably the most influential artist of the twentieth century. Braque, in addition to working with Picasso on Cubism, added unrelated elements to his work, a technique known as **collage.** He often mixed sand with his paints and had a distinct palette of colors that utilized blacks, grays, dull greens, and browns. The Cubist works of **Juan Gris** (1887–1927) emphasized constructive rhythms and abstract components, as opposed to the more intuitive methods of visual analysis used by Braque and Picasso.

Just before the turn of the century, a group of young painters called **the Eight** opposed the standards and restrictions of the National Academy of Design in New York and began trying to create a distinctly American art form that later became known as the **Ashcan school.** Before the twentieth century, painting in America had mostly consisted of portraits and landscapes based on styles in Europe.

Led by artist and teacher **Robert Henri** (1865–1929), the group painted the urban life of the alleys, backyards, slums, and harbors. **John Sloan** (1871–1951) had started as a newspaper illustrator, and his artworks possess a feeling of immediacy and a quick instinct for showing relevant details. Other artists in the Eight were William J. Glackens, George Luks, Everett Shinn, Arthur B. Davies, Ernest Lawson, and Maurice Prendergast.

Edward Hopper (1882–1967) showed the lonely desolation of empty streets and isolated people, and of lighthouses and seacoasts, in his starkly realistic scenes in which the effect of light provided a dramatic element. **George Bellows** (1882–1925), though not one of the Eight, used great psychological insight in showing the drama of street life and popular sports. The independent spirit of the Eight spread after 1908 and culminated in the **Armory Show** in 1913.

The **Armory Show** has been called the starting point of modern American art. **Alfred Stieglitz** (1864–1946), a brilliant early twentieth-century photographer, had since 1905 run various avant-garde galleries in New York that had advanced American and European work. The Armory Show was held in New York by a group of artists wanting to promote new developments and to challenge the American tradition of representational painting. About thirty thousand people saw the show, about one-third of the works

Figure 6.20   John Sloan, *The City from Greenwich Village*.
[Date: 1922; Canvas; 0.660 × 0.857 (26 × 33¾ in.)]
National Gallery of Art, Washington, D.C. Gift of Helen Farr Sloan.

shown being foreign. The European section was meant to point out the evolution of modern art. It included works by Delacroix, Corot, Courbet, Goya, Ingres, and a number of the Impressionists and Post-Impressionists. Some of the works came as a shock to the public. For instance, **Marcel Duchamp's** (1887–1968) *Nude Descending a Staircase* created a furor. In this artwork, he depicted a female form in a manner that suggested rapid motion as seen in multiple-exposure photography. One critic likened it to an explosion in a shingle factory.

Maurice Prendergast (1859–1924) was one of the American painters that helped organize the Armory Show. Painting in oils and watercolors, he applied paint in small spots of bright color in a manner similar to the Impressionists. A critic derided his work as "spotty canvases" and "artistic tommy rot." His success later was considerable, and he felt vindicated and remarked that he was "glad they've found out I'm not crazy."

Soon a number of modern artists emerged in America. One of the most original of the avant-garde was **Marsden Hartley** (1877–1943), who had been influenced by the bold, bright colors of the German **Blue Riders.** His usual theme was the rugged coastline and mountain terrain of New England, but he also painted patterned, textured abstractions in an almost mosaic manner, showing militarism and flags. **Arthur Dove** (1880–1946) combined an advanced degree of abstraction with mystical images of natural forms. **John Marin** (1870–1953) often represented the rugged coast of Maine and the towers of Manhattan in his spontaneous watercolors marked with

slashing brushstrokes. Colorful abstractions showing a strong geometric structure were developed by **Charles Demuth** (1883–1935) in the 1920s. The Italian-born American painter **Joseph Stella** (1877–1946) painted a dynamic series of kaleidoscopic views of the Brooklyn Bridge and often painted mechanical and city themes.

Futurism was an Italian art movement that began in 1909. One of its key artists was **Umberto Boccioni** (1882–1916). The Futurists were concerned with incorporating the dynamism of speed, motion, and modern technology into art. **Giacomo Balla** (1871–1958) captured the comic movements of a little dog on a leash in a manner that reminds us of stop-frame photography.

In Germany in 1919, the **Bauhaus**—a school of architecture, design, and craftsmanship—was founded by architect **Walter Gropius.** Its goal was to reunite all forms of artistic efforts—sculpture and painting, as well as the applied and decorative arts—and to reintegrate them into architecture. It introduced a new concept of art based on the craftwork that was inspired by the memory of the old craftsmen's guilds. Before the school was closed by the Nazis in 1933, it had exerted an enormous and lasting influence. Its teachers included Kandinsky, Klee, Feininger, Moholy-Nagy, Albers, and others.

In 1905–6 a small band of young architecture students in Dresden formed a group called **Die Brücke** to create a modern artistic community. They were fired with an aggressive zeal and were concerned with the social role of art. They were excited about the expressive distortions and simplifications of primitive art. Their works were often angular, harsh, and crowded with details in which they created psychological tensions. Important founders of this movement were **Ernst Ludwig Kirchner** (1880–1938), **Karl Schmidt-Rottluff** (1884–1976), **Max Pechstein** (1881–1955), and **Emil Nolde** (1867–1956).

Other artists working during this time include **Suzanne Valadon** (1865–1938), who became a painter after an accident that occurred while she was working as a circus acrobat. She worked with strong lines and bright, contrasting colors in her paintings of landscapes and still lifes. **Maurice Utrillo** (1883–1955) was Valadon's son. She brought him postcards of city scenes and painting materials while he was being treated for alcoholism at the age of eighteen, so he took up painting. He is known for his paintings of street scenes, many of which show thick brushstrokes and white tones.

Édouard Vuillard (1868–1940) is mostly known for his harmonious, decorative, and quietly domestic scenes, in which patterns, objects, walls, and people blend together in soft, subdued colors. **Pierre Bonnard** (1867–1947) joined the Nabis (prophets) in 1891. His works are known for their fresh colors and his delight with ordinary objects and events. **Lyonel Feininger** (1871–1956) painted in a distinctly personal style that is both Cubist and architectural in derivation. His buildings, cityscapes, and seascapes are constructed of translucent, overlapping geometrical planes.

Wassily Kandinsky (1866–1944) was one of the most important artists of the early twentieth century. After giving up a law career in his native Russia, he moved to Germany and turned to art. He soon became a leader of a group called the **Blue Horseman or Blue Riders (der Blaue Reiter)**. (The name was taken from a picture by Kandinsky.) These artists believed that art should be as abstract as music, that it need not have a single specific style but a variety of forms in which artists manifested an "inner desire" with complete freedom from the constraints and conventions of the "fine" art of Europe. Before long, Kandinsky abandoned representation totally, using bright colors and free brushwork. He became known as the **"father of abstract art."** Other leading figures in the Blue Rider group were **Franz Marc** (1880–1916), who showed animal life in broad, abstract planes and brilliant colors that bore no relation to nature. **August Macke** (1887–1914) was also a founder of the group but was killed in World War I. **Alexei van Jawlensky** (1864–1941), although never formally a member, was close to the aims of Der Blaue Reiter.

Germany came to be the natural home for Expressionism. **Ernst Barlach** (1870–1938) made prints and sculpture showing the whole range of emotions from despair to ecstasy. His friend **Käthe Kollwitz** (1867–1945) had sympathies for the poor and oppressed in her lithographs and sculpture, as did Barlach; however, her personal art often showed sad and suffering women (her only son was killed in World War I and her grandson in World War II).

The independent spirit of German artist **Max Beckmann** (1884–1950) is manifested in the stark, heavily outlined, massive figures of his paintings, and in his numerous self-portraits.

The Norwegian artist **Edvard Munch's** (1863–1944) artworks, many almost like recurrent nightmares, are mostly expressive images dealing with his feelings of death, since the deaths of his mother and older sister had had a profound effect on his youth. He made paintings, woodcuts, and lithographs.

The **Fauves (wild beasts)** were led by **Henri Matisse** (1869–1954). They were so named because of the distorted forms and the violent, unrealistic colors they used for people's faces and figures. Later Matisse made many paintings in which the rich, decorative patterns remind us of the Persian carpets that influenced him. He is also famous for his cut-paper collages. Others associated with the Fauves included **Georges Rouault** (1871–1958), who later turned from bright to more somber colors. He had been apprenticed in a stained-glass shop in his youth. Dark outlines in his artworks separate areas of color and remind us of stained glass. As a devout Catholic, he frequently chose religious subjects. **Raoul Dufy** (1877–1953) arrived at his characteristic spontaneous style around 1910. His oils and watercolors of race tracks, fashionable resorts, landscapes, and flowers showed bright colors and calligraphic brushstrokes.

Maurice de Vlaminck (1876–1958) was an energetic giant of a man whose early works were painted in brilliant orange, red, and blue. He experimented with Cubism and showed a preference for pure whites and deep blues. After 1915 he began painting strong, stormy landscapes, overcast skies, and lonely villages in a turbulent style. **André Derain** (1880–1954) began as a **Fauve** (Wild Beasts) and was principally concerned with line and color—especially pinks, blues, and violets. He later concentrated more on form and structure and experimented with Cubism, Impressionism, and the styles of van Gogh, Gauguin, and Cézanne.

Amedeo Modigliani (1884–1920) was born in Italy but spent most of his short life in Paris. He distorted and elongated the forms in his paintings and sculptures, having been inspired by African sculpture as well as the works of Cézanne and Picasso. The Dutch artist **Piet Mondrian** (1872–1944) carried the idea of using geometric shapes to the extent of using only straight lines and the three primary colors. **Fernand Léger** (1881–1955) developed a style in which he depicted people and objects reduced to machinelike forms. He chose to celebrate modern technological culture by using heroic scale and popular imagery. His works are usually created with bright colors and definitive black outlines.

The paintings of **Paul Klee** (1879–1940) are filled with signs and symbols that give flight to our imagination. He endeavored to capture the spontaneous gaiety of children's art. Another highly imaginative artist was **Marc Chagall** (1887–1985), who was born in Russia and who recalled the folktales and imagery of his native village in his fanciful and colorful artworks. He is not only remembered as a painter but as a designer of book illustrations, stage sets, and stained-glass windows.

First appearing in 1915 and losing its impetus by 1923, **Dadaism** (French for hobbyhorse, a title picked at random from a dictionary) symbolized a movement that was deliberately antirational and anti-art. It first occurred in Zurich and spread to New York. The original antimilitary protest developed into a complete rejection of the "falseness and hypocrisy" of culture's established values.

Figure 6.21 Salvador Dali, *The Persistence of Memory,* **1931.** Oil on canvas, 13″ × 9¼″.
Collection, The Museum of Modern Art, New York. Given anonymously.

In the 1920s a few artists began painting in a manner called **Surrealism.** The objects they painted seemed quite realistic, but the combinations of objects and details were unlikely, unusual, sometimes even nonsensical. They evoked our subconscious world and reminded us of dreams. **Odilon Redon** (1840–1916) is said to be a precursor of Surrealism in painting and in the exploration of the symbols of the subconscious. His works show delicate colors and expression, haunting and mysterious, which balance between the real and the unreal. **René Magritte** (1898–1967), a Belgian painter, juxtaposed natural objects and those of human origin in a style that featured scrupulous preciseness. He often creates an effect of disturbing ambiguity. **Salvador Dali** (1904–1989), flamboyant Spanish Surrealist, led an eccentric life-style and created a body of paintings in a meticulous style that almost appears three-dimensional. He has created jewelry, ceramics, and sculpture as well. **Giorgio de Chirico** (1888–1978) painted empty Italian cityscapes in which he placed a solitary figure or statue, often in conjunction with a train or lighthouse. Surrealists recognized him as a forerunner of their movement. The Spanish painter **Joan Miró** (1893–1983), a versatile and original artist, shows brightly colored, amoeba-like shapes and organic, linear creatures that float and wriggle, defying the laws of gravity. The works of the Dutch artist **Maurits C. Escher** (1898–1972) often abound in bizarre metamorphoses and optical illusions that blend elements of Surrealism with mathematics.

Ben Shahn (1898–1969) was a social realist artist working with paintings, prints, photography, and calligraphy. He came to New York from Lithuania in 1906. Written words and comments are sometimes included with his images in a delicate, spiky, linear manner.

Georgia O'Keeffe's (1887–1986) paintings reached the peak of her style during her years in New Mexico. She frequently painted enormous close-ups of flowers and bones as well as the vast landscape of the Southwest. She was born in Wisconsin and was married to the photographer and art dealer **Alfred Stieglitz.**

The American artist **Stuart Davis** (1894–1964) used bright, clear colors, simplified forms, and hard edges in his artworks. After 1940 his works were quite abstract, often with fragments of lettering and words and zany titles.

In the Depression years, the 1930s, **Grant Wood** (1892–1942) and **Thomas Hart Benton** (1889–1975) painted realistic scenes of life in the Middle West and became known as **Regionalists.** Their works celebrate the life of small towns and rural America. **Charles Burchfield** (1893–1967), also a painter of midwestern landscapes, based his early, rather mystical works on childhood emotions and memories of the world of nature. During the 1920s and 1930s, he painted more realistic depictions of American landscapes. After 1943 a Nordic mysticism was seen in the jagged shapes that created a menacing element in his works.

After World War II, the United States became the world center of painting with artists searching for originality and freedom of expression. The two main forerunners of **Abstract Expressionism** were Armenian-born **Arshile Gorky** (1905–1948) and German-born **Hans Hofmann** (1880–1966). Both immigrated to America. Gorky's works show a personal Surrealism verging on Abstract Expressionism with fluid forms coagulating and merging. By 1942 his very free calligraphic brushwork was often done with no figurative reference. Hofmann worked with forceful outbursts of color that spoke of his belief that paintings should be made with feeling, not with knowing. In 1934, he established highly influential schools in New York and Provincetown, Massachusetts, where he taught a number of students that became prominent in the 1950s. Most notable of these was **Helen Frankenthaler** (1928–), who often used washes of color, pouring and staining the thinned paint directly onto unprimed canvases. Her abstract artworks had no recognizable objects in them; instead, they glowed with color and movement. She married and later divorced **Robert Motherwell** (1915–), a pioneer in Abstract Expressionism.

Willem de Kooning (1904–) came to New York from Holland when he was twenty-three. By the 1940s, he had emerged as a leading Abstract Expressionist. The themes of women and landscapes preoccupied him. He usually worked in a vigorous style, using broad, slashing brushstrokes. Russian-born American artist **Mark Rothko** (1903–1970) was another leader of Abstract Expressionism. He is best known for his canvases that show large, horizontal bars of thinned pigments. **Frank Stella**

(1936–) began as an Abstract Expressionist but experimented in a number of ways. His works became more systematic and rigorously formal, some of them being as large as ten feet high and twenty feet long.

Swiss-born **Sophie Taeuber-Arp** (1889–1943) and the French artist **Jean Arp** (1887–1966), as a husband-wife team, influenced each other's artworks, sometimes designing works together. Sophie made some of her husband's paintings into woven tapestries. She used pure and simple geometric shapes painted with glowing colors. Jean is famous principally for his abstract sculpture.

Jackson Pollock (1912–1956) was a leading member of the New York school of **Abstract Expressionism.** He is best remembered for his later works known as **action painting.** In these, he worked with his canvas on the floor, pouring and splashing paint across the surface from all four sides to create an allover texture of lines and splatters. He was fascinated by Mayan glyphs and intrigued with Navajo sand painting because of the way it is painted, in large movements on the ground. **Mark Tobey's** (1890–1978) work paralleled the Abstract Expressionist movement, but he was highly influenced by Japanese Zen philosophy and painting. His works show a kind of calligraphic, spontaneous brushwork called "white writing."

The Western world in the 1950s was shocked and dazzled by the Abstract Expressionists working in New York. Not only the scale of their paintings, but their unorthodox behavior and the general aura of the movement often diverted attention from other trends in the world of art. A reaction against Abstract Expressionism occurred early in the 1960s when a group of artists in the United States rebelled against it and began depicting in their artworks images of commonplace things. These realistic pictures of everyday **popular objects** included dart boards, light bulbs, flags, comic strips, and pies and cakes. Some important **Pop artists** are: **Andy Warhol** (1930–1987), **Wayne Thiebaud** (1920–), **Jasper Johns** (1930–), **Roy Lichtenstein** (1923–), **Claes Oldenburg** (1929–), and **Robert Rauschenberg** (1925–).

In the mid-1960s, **Op art** emerged. This is a type of abstract art that exploits the optical effects of pattern. It frequently uses hard-edged black-and-white or colored compositions, which seem to vibrate and change their shape as we look at them. **Victor Vasarely** (1908–), born in Hungary, is known as the "father of Op art." British artist **Bridget Riley's** (1930–) closely packed, curving parallel lines create a strong impact on our eyes.

Josef Albers (1888–1976) began teaching at Black Mountain College and later at Yale North Carolina when the Nazis closed the Bauhaus in 1933. He was as concerned with the applied as with the fine arts and was responsible for one of the first laminated wood chairs. His nonobjective paintings were highly structured in their use of color.

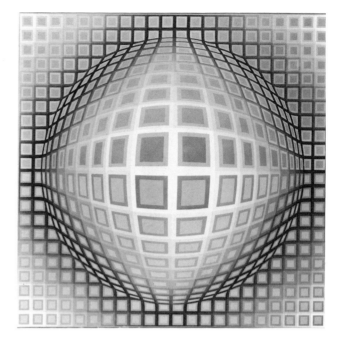

Figure 6.22   Victor Vasarely, *Vega-Nor,* **1969. Oil on canvas, 78¾ × 78¾ in.** *Albright-Knox Art Gallery, Buffalo, New York. Gift of Seymour H. Knox, 1969.*

Andrew Wyeth (1917–), the son of the illustrator **Newell Convers Wyeth** (1882–1944), has spent his life painting the landscape and neighbors of his home town in Pennsylvania. He uses watercolor and drybrush and has perfected the technique of egg tempera. He achieves a stark, highly realistic effect that often has a strange, eerie quality of loneliness.

British-born **David Hockney** (1937–) makes his home in Los Angeles and not only paints but makes enormous "joiners," photo collages made up of numerous single shots.

Anna Mary Robertson (Grandma Moses) (1860–1961), a celebrated primitive or naive painter, began to paint at age sixty, her first one-woman show being in New York in 1940. She painted in minute detail the scenes and events from the countryside that she remembered.

Photography, being communication, is a personal statement of an artist, and good photographs have recognizable styles in the same manner that paintings do. They may reveal the nature and character of their subjects while being carefully composed and sensitively designed. **L. J. M. Daguerre** (1787–1851) announced in 1838

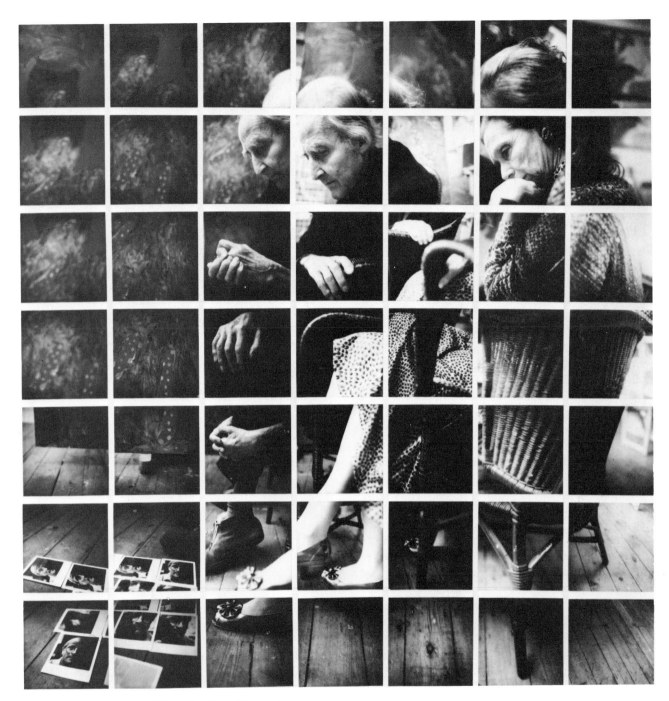

Figure 6.23   Noya and Bill Brandt with self-portrait,
*Pembroke Studios, London. 8th May, 1982. Composite
Polaroid © David Hockney 1982.*

the invention that bears his name, and photography entered the public domain. Several important names in the field of American photography are listed below:

Mathew Brady (1823–1896) showed the carnage of the battlefield in his Civil War photographs, thereby presenting the world for the first time with such images. He took many photographs of Abraham Lincoln that showed his strength, dignity, and nobility.

Alfred Stieglitz (1864–1946), after buying his first camera for $7.50, became dedicated to photography and to his New York gallery (where he displayed the work of other artists, including that of his wife, Georgia O'Keeffe). **Edward Weston** (1886–1958) made romantic, soft-focus pictures that gave him worldwide recognition before adopting "straight photography" and focusing on close-ups of peppers, roots, shells, and other objects. **Ansel Adams's** (1902–1984) landscapes of western America show fine details, a full range of tonal values, and great depth of field.

Berenice Abbott (1898–) captured the personality of her subjects in a number of fine portraits. She spent ten years photographing New York's architecture, transportation, and people. **Margaret Bourke-White** (1904–1971) photographed industry and cities as well as natural disasters and World War II. **Dorothea Lange** (1895–1965) made sensitive pictures of the Dust Bowl victims of the 1930s as they migrated to California to seek work. Her photographs helped bring about federal legislation to assist their plight. Several other notable photographers were **Imogene Cunningham** (1883–1976), **Man Ray** (1890–1976), and **Paul Strand** (1890–1976).

The invention of the elevator and the development of steel for structural skeletons helped make major breakthroughs in architecture. **Louis Sullivan** (1856–1924) was a turn-of-the-century American pioneer whose work led to the evolvement of the skyscraper. He observed that "form follows function" and led the way for architects to break from the past and rethink their designs from the inside out. **Le Corbusier** (1887–1965) solved urban design problems with steel columns and reinforced slab constructions. In Europe, a new international architecture evolved between 1910 and 1930 that rejected decorative ornamentation and traditional materials. **Walter Gropius** (1883–1969) used these principles in his building of the Bauhaus in Germany, a building that shows the interior and exterior simultaneously in opaque and transparent, overlapping planes. **Mies van der Rohe** (1886–1969) and **Philip Johnson** (1906–) designed and built the elegant, austere Seagram building in New York between 1956 and 1958, with vertical lines emphasizing the feeling of height and providing a strong pattern.

Frank Lloyd Wright, (1869–1959), one of the most influential American architects, designed bold and elegant homes and public buildings, often harmonizing his

Figure 6.24   Dorothea Lange, *Migrant Mother.* Nipomo, California. 1938. Gelatin-silver print, 12½ × 9⅞". Photograph. Collection, *The Museum of Modern Art, New York. Purchase.*

meticulous attention for design detail with nature and the surrounding site. **Buckminster Fuller** (1895–1983) was a forward-thinking inventor, architect, and structural engineer who developed the **geodesic dome,** having been inspired by polyhedrons found in nature.

Several important **Mexican artists** made significant contributions during the twentieth century. **Diego Rivera** (1886–1957), after spending a number of years abroad, returned to Mexico in 1921 and studied the traditions of Mexican folk art. He then experimented with Italian fresco techniques, painting overwhelming murals that sang of the triumph of work and the destruction of poverty and oppression. **José Clemente Orozco** (1883–1949) created savage caricatures dealing with the Mexican Revolution. **David Siqueiros** (1896–1974) was the most politically active, even being imprisoned and fighting in the Spanish Civil War. He exploited folklore and surrealist and symbolic effects, as well as using photographs and new techniques such as airbrushing. **Rufino Tamayo's** (1899–) best works are his easel paintings in which he blended European styles with Mexican folklore.

Figure 6.25 Alberto Giacometti, *Man Pointing,* 1947.
Bronze, 70½ in. high, at base 12 × 13¼ in.
Collection. The Museum of Modern Art, New York. Gift of Mrs. John D. Rockefeller 3rd.

The twentieth century has also seen important and significant developments in sculpture. **August Rodin** (1840–1917) is called the father of modern sculpture. Despite bad critical reactions to his first works, he began to win recognition and was commissioned to make a bronze door for a Paris museum. Though the door was never completed, some of his later works, such as *The Thinker,* were based on figures planned for the door. He constantly experimented with new techniques and ideas. He made sculpture of hands alone; sometimes he carved part of a body from a stone and left much of the block uncut and unpolished. **Constantin Brancusi** (1876–1957), born in Romania, explored his ovoid theme throughout his life,

abstracting into stone or metal the essence of physical life-forms. The American sculptor **Alexander Calder** (1898–1976), with his engineering background, created fantastic animated toys before he became widely known for his freestanding **stabiles** of metal and **mobiles** with moving elements.

The English sculptor **Henry Moore** (1898–1986) carved and cast enormous, massive reclining and seated figures, often using the theme of the mother and child. He was influenced by such natural forms as driftwood, polished stones, and shells, as well as archaic Mexican sculpture. In 1929 he began piercing holes through solid masses in his works to create negative spaces. He liked his works to be displayed out-of-doors. Also from England, **Barbara Hepworth** (1903–1975) moved from biomorphic to geometric forms, exploring the play of voids and solid masses and reducing her forms to very simple shapes with subtle finishes.

Marino Marini (1901–1980) of Italy depicted a theme, that of a horse and rider, many times. His images often show a primitive roughness, as if his figures had recently been excavated. **David Smith** (1906–1965) is known for his cubiform elements of stainless steel that he polished, abraded, and arranged at odd angles. Displayed monumentally against the sky, his sculptures command an extraordinary authority. **Alberto Giacometti** (1901–1966), Swiss sculptor, made cast sticklike figures of varying scale, often placing them in dramatic groups.

Louise Nevelson (1899–1988), an American of Russian origin, made sculptures composed of found objects, usually wood, arranged in boxes or shelves and occupying a wall taller than the spectator. The assembled sculpture is sprayed in white, black, or gold, which unifies the objects and reduces the shadows. **Duane Hanson** (1925–), American, has become well known for his life-size figures made of fiberglass resin. They are realistic to the smallest detail and are dressed in real garments and often hold real props. As a child, **Marisol** (1930–) often traveled to Venezuela and New York with her wealthy French parents. Her brightly painted sculptures of boxy figures are made of wood plaster and found objects, and they satirize contemporary customs and manners. **Judy Chicago's** (1939–) enormous *Dinner Party* tells women's history through thirty-nine place settings, each dedicated to a great woman in the past. Chicago has also written books and made films.

African American Artists

Americans of African descent have made artistic contributions since **Joshua Johnson** (1765–1830) made his family portraits, which have a charming, modern appeal. Some of his works are in the National Gallery, but most are retained by descendents of the original families that owned them.

Working in the Hudson River school, **Robert S. Duncanson** (1817–1872) was recognized in his own time as an outstanding landscape painter whose works are romantic and mystical. **Edward M. Bannister** (1828–1901) felt compelled to be an artist after reading in a newspaper that while "the Negro may harbor an appreciation of art, he is unable to produce it." He refused to accept patronage to study in Europe and developed a landscape style in the Hudson River tradition, winning a gold medal at the Philadelphia Centennial Exposition. Also winning an award at the Philadelphia Exposition, sculptor **Edmonia Lewis** (1843–ca 1900) exploited racial issues in the Neoclassic style. **Henry O. Tanner** (1859–1937) was a student of Thomas Eakins and was the first black American artist to achieve an international reputation when he was elected to the French Academy. **Horace Pippin** (1888–1946) taught himself to paint, but unlike his French counterpart, Henri Rousseau, was acclaimed in his own lifetime.

Four black artists born near the turn of the century were **Hale Woodruff** (1900–), **Richmond Barthe** (1901–), **Lois Maillol Jones** (1905–), and **Hughie Lee-Smith** (1915–). Woodruff's most famous work is a three-panel series showing a slave revolt on a Spanish ship in 1839 with the slaves being returned to their homeland by John Quincy Adams and other abolitionists. Barthe is a prolific sculptor. Jones paints cityscapes in the spirit of Cézanne and designs textiles. Lee-Smith paints, with the precision of Surrealism, aging city neighborhoods where old buildings stand isolated and empty, with one or two figures that seem alone and depressed.

Working with paint and photographic fragments, **Romare Bearden** (1914–1988) made collages that reflect life in the rural South and in the northern cities. **Jacob Lawrence** (1917–) uses strong silhouetted patterns and narrative subject matter, and is deeply dedicated to black history in America. Like Woodruff and Lawrence, **Charles White** (1918–) worked during the Depression for the WPA Art Project. He was a strong social critic, working in the style of Mexican muralists Rivera and Siqueiros.

Norma Morgan (1928–) is noted for her "magic-realist" etchings and copper engravings. A leading member of a movement called Blackstream, **Benny Andrews** (1930–) makes powerful works that attack American junk culture and show that African American artists are creating art as uniquely American as jazz.

Figure 6.26   Joshua Johnson, *The Westwood Children*, ca. 1807.
Oil on canvas, 41⅛″ × 46″.
Gift of Edgar William and Bernice Chrysler Garbisch, 1959.
National Gallery of Art, Washington, D.C.

Figure 6.27   Horace Pippin, *Victorian Interior*, 1946.
Oil on canvas, 30″ × 28¼″.
The Metropolitan Museum of Art, New York. Arthur H.
Hearn Fund, 1958 (58-26).

PRONUNCIATION GUIDE

Angelico, Fra—An JAY lee koh, Frah
Anguissola, Sofanisba—Ahn GWEES so la, So fah NISS bah

Balla, Giacomo—BAHL la, JAH koh moh
Barlach, Ernst, BAHR lahk, Airnst
Bellini, Giovanni—Bel LEE nee, Joh VAH nee
Bierstadt, Albert—Beer tstaht, Al bert
Boccioni, Umberto—Boh CHO nee, Oom BER toh
Bonheur, Rosa—Bahn uhr, Ros ah
Bonnard, Pierre—Bo NAHR, Pee EHR
Bosch, Hieronymus—BOSH, Heer AHN ni mus
Botticelli, Sandro—Bot ti CHEL lee, SAN droh
Boucher, François—Boo SHAY, Fran SWAH
Boudin, Eugene—Boo DINH, Uh ZHEN
Brancusi, Constantin—BRAHN koo see, KAHN stuhn teen
Braque, Georges—BRAHK, Zhorzh
Brueghel, Pieter—BROY gel, Peter
Brunelleschi, Filippo—Brew nell LESS kay, Fee LIP po

Canaletto—Kah nah LET toh
Caravaggio, Michelangelo—Kah rah VA joh, Mee kel AHN jay lo
Carriera, Rosalba—Car ree AYE rah, Rose AHL bah
Cassatt, Mary—Cah SAT
Cézanne, Paul—Say ZAHN
Chagall, Marc—Shah GAHL
Chardin, Jean-Baptiste—Shar DAN, Zhahn Bap TEEST
Cimabue—Tshee ma BOO aye
Copley, John Singleton—COP lee
Corot, Jean—Caw ROH, Zhahn
Courbet, Gustave—Koor BAY, Goos TAHV
Cranach, Lucas—KRAN uck

Dali, Salvador—DAH lee, SAHL van dore
Daumier, Honoré—Dohm YAY, Oh noh RAY
David, Jacques-Louis—Dah VEED, Zhahk Loo EE
de Chirico, Giorgio—de KEY ree co, JOHR jyo
Degas, Edgar—Duh GAH, ed GAHR
de Hooch, Pieter—dee HOKE, Peter
de Kooning, Willem—duh KOE ning, VILL em
Delacroix, Eugène—Duh lah KWAH, Uh ZHEN
De La Tour, Georges—Duh lah TOOR, Zhorzh
Demuth, Charles—Duh MOOTH
Derain, André—Duh RAN, ON dray
Diebenkorn, Richard—DEE ben korn
Donatello—Dah na TELL lo
Duccio—DO tshee yo
Duchamp, Marcel—Doo SHAHM, Mahr SELL
Dufy, Raoul—Dew FEE, Rah OOL
Dürer, Albrecht—DUHR er, AL brekt

Eakins, Thomas—A kinz
El Greco—El GREH coh
Escher, M. C.—ESH uhr

Feininger, Lyonel—FINE in gurr
Fouquet, Jean—Foo KAY, Zhahn
Fragonard, Jean-Honoré—Frah goh NAHR, Zhahn Oh noh RAY
Frankenthaler, Helen—Frank en TALL er

Gauguin, Paul—Goh GINH
Gentileschi, Artemisia—Djen tee LESS kay, Ar tay ME zee a
Géricault, Théodore—ZHAY re koh, TAY oh dor
Ghiberti, Lorenzo—Ghee BAIR tee, low RENT soh
Ghirlandaio, Domenico—Geer lahn DAH yoh, Doh MAY nee koh
Giacometti, Alberto—Jah ko MET tee, Ahl BAIR toh
Giorgione, Giorgio—Johr JOY nay, Johr joh
Giotto di Bondone—JOHT toh, dee Bohn DOH nay
Gorky, Arshile—GOR kee, ARSH shul
Goya, Francisco—Gaw Yuh, Fran SIS coe
Gris, Juan—GREES, Wahn
Gropius, Walter—GRO pih us, Wall tur
Grunëwald, Mathis—GREWN vahlt, MAH tis

Hals, Frans—HALLS, Frahnss
Hofmann, Hans—HOHF mahn, Hahns
Hogarth, William—HOE garth
Hokusai—Hohk SY
Holbein, Hans—HOHL bine

Ingres, Jean—IHN gr, Zhahn
Inness, George—IN us

Jawlensky, Alexei von—Yah VLENS key, Alex yee fon

Kandinsky, Wassily—Kan DIN skee, Va see l'yee
Kirchner, Ernst Ludwig—KEERKH ner, Airnst LOOT vik
Klee, Paul—Clay
Kokoschka, Oskar—Koh KOSH kah
Kollwitz, Käthe—KAHL wits, Kate uh

Laurencin, Marie—Loh rahn sinh
Le Corbusier—Luh Core boo zee ay
Léger, Fernand—Lay ZHAY, Fair NON
Le Nain, Antoine and Louis—Luh NINH, Ahn TWAHN, Loo EE
Leonardo da Vinci—Lay oh NAR doh da VIN chee
Leyster, Judith—LIE ster
Lichtenstein, Roy—LICK ten steen
Lipchitz, Jacques—LIP sheets, Zhahk
Lippi, Fra Filippo—LEEP pee, Frah Fill LEEP poh
Lorrain, Claude—Luh RAN, Klohd

Macke, August—MACK uh
Maes, Nicolaes—MASS
Magritte, René—Muh GREET, Ruh NAE
Maillol, Aristide—MY yoh
Manet, Edouard—Man AY, Ay doo ARH
Mantegna, Andrea—Man tay nya, Ahn DRAY ah

Marin, John—MARE uhn
Marini, Marino—Mah REE nee, Mah REE noh
Marisol—Mah ree SOHL
Masaccio—Mah SAH chyo
Matisse, Henri—Mah TEES, On REE
Medici-MED uh chee
Merian, Maria Sibylla—MARE e uhn, MAH REE ah Suh
    BEE La
Metsys, Quentin—MET sis, Kwen ten
Michelangelo Buonarroti—My kel AHN jay loe, Bwoh nah
    ROE tee
Mies van der Rohe, Ludwig—MEES vahn dair ROH-eh,
    Loot vik
Millet, Jean-François—Mil LAY, Zhahn Fran SWAH
Miró, Joan—Mee ROH, Ho AHN
Modigliani, Amedeo—Mo DEE lee ah nee, Ah meh DAY
    oh
Mondrian, Piet—MOHN dree ahn, PEET
Monet, Claude—MO nay, Klohd
Morisot, Berthe—Moh ree ZOH, BAIRT
Munch, Edvard—MOONK, ED var
Muybridge, Eadweard—MY brij, ED wurd

Nolde, Emil—NOHL duh, AY muhl

Oldenburg, Claes—OLE den berk, Clays
Orozco, José Clemente—Oh ROHS coe, Ho SAY Kleh
    MEN tay

Parmigianino—Par me dji ah KNEE no
Pechstein, Max—PEX stine
Peto, John Frederick—PEE toh
Picasso, Pablo—Pea CAH so, Pahb lo
Pissarro, Camille—Pee SAH roh, Ka MEE
Poussin, Nicolas—Poo SINH, Nee koh lahs

Raphael—RAHF ay el
Rauschenberg, Robert—ROW shen berg
Redon, Odilon—Ruh DAWN, Oh dee YON
Rembrandt van Rijn—REM brant van RYNE
Renoir, Pierre-Auguste—Ren WAHR, Pee EHR O
    GOOST
Rivera, Diego—Ree VAY rah, Dee AY goh

Rodin, François-Auguste—Roh DAN, Frahn swah Oh
    GOOST
Rouault, Georges—Roo Oh, Zhorzh
Rousseau, Henri—Roo SO, On REE
Rubens, Peter Paul—ROO benz
Ruysch, Rachel—RO iss, RAH shell

Saarinen, Eero—SAHR uh nen, EER oh
Sassetta—SAHS SAY tah
Schmidt-Rottluff, Karl—Shmeedt ROHT loof, Kahrl
Scholder, Fritz—SHOWL duhr
Seurat, Georges—Suh RAH, Zhorzh
Shahn, Ben—Shawn
Signac, Paul—SEEN yahk
Siqueiros, David—See key AIR ohz
Sisley, Alfred—SEES lee
Stieglitz, Alfred—STEEG lits

Tamayo, Rufino—Tah MAH yoh, Roo Fee noh
Thiebaud, Wayne—TEE bo
Tintoretto, Jacopo—Teen toh RET toh, Jah KOH poh
Titian—TISH yan
Toulouse-Lautrec, Henri de—Too LOOZ Lah TREK, On
    REE duh

Uccello, Paolo—Oo TCHEHL loh, POH loh
Utrillo, Maurice—Oo TREE oh

van der Weyden, Rogier—van duh VIE den
van Dyck—van DIKE
van Eyck, Jan—van IKE, Yahn
van Gogh, Vincent—van GO
Vasari—Va SAHR ee
Vaserely, Victor—Vah zuh RAY Lee
Velázquez, Diego—Vay LAS kes, Dee AYE goh
Vermeer, Jan—ver MAIR, Yahn
Veronese, Paolo—Ver oh NEES, POH loh
Verrocchio, Andrea del—Ver ROK kyoh
Vigée-Lebrun, Elisabeth—VEE zhaye lub run, Ale ee za
    bet
Vlaminck, Maurice de—Vlah MANK
Vuillard Édouard—VWEE yahr, Ay Doo ARH

Warhol, Andy—WOHR hohl
Watteau, Antoine—Wah TOH, Ahn TWAN

SYMBOLS IN ARTWORKS

The following lists provide codes for reading a few of the many symbols of figures and objects that are frequently seen in Western artworks. A rich cultural, social, and religious history is the derivation for their use. Answers are not always available as to how the objects, saints, and gods acquired their own symbols and attributes, but using these lists and adding other symbols as you find them in reference material can greatly assist and enhance your understanding and enjoyment of visual images.

GODS/GODDESSES

	IDENTIFICATION, MEANING
Apollo, Sun god; patron of archery, music and poetry	Handsome youth; crown of laurel leaves; with lyre
Bacchus, god of wine; fertility, passion	Nude youth; crown of grapes and vine leaves
Cupid, love	Child with bow, arrows and quiver; sometimes blindfolded
Diana, Moon goddess; chastity	Noble woman with stag and hounds; seen as huntress; wearing crescent moon
Hercules, courage and strength	Bearded muscular man with club; wearing lion skin
Juno, Chief goddess; guardian of women, marriage and childbirth	Stately woman with peacock
Jupiter/Zeus, ruler of men and gods	Noble figure with eagle or thunderbolt
Mars, god of war; aggressive, unpopular	Young, muscular; with spear, sword, and armor
Mercury, messenger of gods; reason and eloquence	Graceful athlete; winged sandals; magic wand and hat
Minerva, goddess of war and wisdom	Female with helmet, shield, and spear; with owl
Neptune, ruler of the sea	Old man with three-pronged spear
Saturn, time	Carries scythe and crutch
Venus, goddess of love	Beautiful young woman with Cupid or three graces
Vulcan, god of fire	Crippled blacksmith

SAINTS

Agnes, virgin martyr	Lamb
Andrew, patron saint of Greece and Scotland, Apostle	X-shaped cross
Anne, mother of Mary	Wearing green cloak over red robe
Augustine, founding father of the church	Flaming heart
Catherine, patroness of education	Wheel
Cecilia, patroness of music	Organ
Christopher, patron of travelers	Carrying child across river on shoulder
Francis, patron of animals	Stigmata and girdle with three knots
George, patron saint of England	On white horse, dressed in armor, slaying dragon
Hubert, patron of hunters	Stag's head with crucifix
James, patron of Spain, Apostle	Scallop shell; pilgrim's hat, cloak, and staff
John the Baptist, messenger of Christ	Cross made from reeds
Joseph, husband of Virgin Mary	Carpenter's tools
Jude, patron of lost causes, Apostle	Lance or club
Luke, patron saint of painters	Winged ox
Margaret, patroness of women in childbirth	Dragon which tried to devour her
Mark, patron saint of Venice	Winged lion
Martin, founded first monasteries in France	Seen with beggar; wearing a cloak
Mary Magdalene, repentant sinner who anointed Christ's feet	Vase of ointment
Matthew, writer of first Gospel	With winged figure, probably dictating
Michael, conqueror of the devil	Wears armor, slays dragon
Nicholas, patron of children, sailors, and travelers	Three golden purses or balls; anchor

GODS/GODDESSES	*IDENTIFICATION, MEANING*
Paul, one of founders of Church	Scroll, book, sword; often seen thrown from horse
Peter, leader of 12 Apostles	Upturned cross (he was crucified upside down); keys
Stephen, first Christian martyr	Stones (he was stoned to death)
Thomas, patron of builders and architects (Doubting Thomas)	Girdle, spear, set square and ruler

OBJECT

Apple	Fruit of Tree of Knowledge in Garden of Eden; fall of man and redemption
Anchor	Hope (Christianity)
Bear	Gluttony
Bird held by baby Jesus	Human soul
Boar	Lust
Bridle	Temperance
Bubbles	Brevity of life
Butterfly	Resurrected human soul (Christianity)
Cherries	Fruit of paradise, symbolizing heaven, reward for virtue (Christianity)
Clock	Time passing; temperance
Crane	Vigilance
Crow	Hope
Dandelion	Grief (Christianity)
Dog	Portraits: fidelity; envy, sense of smell, melancholy
Dove	Holy Ghost (Christianity); attribute of Venus, love and peace in mythology
Egg	Rebirth, creation
Goat	Lust
Grape	Blood of Christ and eucharistic wine (Christian art)
Hedgehog	Gluttony; sense of touch
Ivy	Eternal life
Lighted candle	Shortness of life
Lily	Purity and Virgin Mary
Olive branch	Peace
Palm branch	Held by martyrs (Christianity); victory, fame
Peach with one leaf attached	Truth
Peacock	Immortality (Christianity); pride
Playing cards	Idleness
Pomegranate	Resurrection, authority of Church, chastity (Christianity)
Rabbit	Lust
Skull	Death
Violet	Humility
Walled garden	Immaculate conception (Christianity)

Questions and Activities

1. Use a long piece of paper and make a chronological time-line of important periods of art, leading artists/artworks, characteristics of the period/style, and concurrent events in science, math, literature, music, drama, politics, and literature.

2. Study your art history time-line and reflect on how art was affected by or how it effected the events of its time.

3. Research and make a time-line of the traditional arts of one of the following: China, Japan, India, Africa, and the Indian arts of the Americas.

4. How did World War II affect art in the United States? Research and report on the major influences on art and the artists that were leaders at this time.

5. Research and report on world cultures and how their visual images were influenced by their religious beliefs. How are some of the changes reflected in religious architecture? Give your reasons.

6. From your time-line, select two periods and report on who supported the artists and how their sponsorship is reflected in artworks. Illustrate your report with slides of artworks to indicate these differences.

7. Select two or three symbols from the list on p. 151 and look in art books to help you locate these same symbols in contemporary artworks. Try to determine if any contemporary artists use the same symbols and what meanings artists may give to them today.

8. Make xerox copies of two or three artworks in reference books that contain one or more of the symbols on p. 151. Compare how they are used with regard to time period, purpose, style, and variation of meaning.

Bibliography

Introduction

1. *Quality Art Education, Goals for Schools: An Interpretation* (Reston, Va.: National Art Education Association, 1986).
2. *The Journal of Aesthetic Education* 21(1987): 151–59.
3. Elliot W. Eisner, *The Role of Discipline-Based Art Education in America's Schools* (Los Angeles: Getty Center for Education in the Arts), 16–21.
4. Ralph A. Smith, *Excellence in Art Education: Ideas and Initiatives, Updated Version* (Reston, Va.: National Art Education Association, 1987), 19.

Chapter 1

1. John A. Michael, *A Handbook for Art Instructors and Students Based upon Concepts and Behaviors* (New York: Vantage Press, 1970), 223.
2. David Hockney, *Paper Pools* (New York: Harry Abrams, 1980), 21–22.
3. David Smith, *David Smith,* ed. Cleve Gray (London: Thames and Hudson Publishers, 1968), 39.
4. Ellen H. Johnson, ed., *American Artists on Art from 1940 to 1980* (New York: Harper and Row, 1982), 90.
5. Ibid., 162.
6. Ibid., 161.
7. Ibid., 152–56.
8. Dore Ashton and Jack Flam, *Robert Motherwell* (New York: Ashville Press, 1982), 12.
9. *Dear Theo, The Autobiography of Vincent van Gogh,* ed. Irving Stone (Garden City, N.Y.: Doubleday, 1946).
10. *Joseph Raphael,* video (Sacramento: California State University, University Library Media Center, 1982).

11. W. J. Strachan and Bernard Jacobson, *Henry Moore Animals* (New York: Aurum Press, 1983), 13.
12. Cindy Nemser, *Art Talk* (New York: Charles Scribner's Sons, 1975), 179.
13. Diana MacKown, *Dawns + Dusks* (New York: Charles Scribner's Sons, 1976), 168.
14. Ben Shahn, *The Shape of Content* (Cambridge, Mass.: Harvard University Press, 1985), 113–14.
15. MacKown, *Dawns + Dusks,* 14.
16. Ellen Harkins Wheat, *Jacob Lawrence, American Painter* (Seattle: University of Washington Press, 1982), 41.
17. Jack Cowart and Juan Hamilton, *Georgia O'Keeffe: Art and Letters* (Washington: National Gallery of Art, 1987), 4.
18. Ibid., 202.
19. Kathleen Tompson, "Teachers as Artists," *Art Education,* November 1986, 48.
20. Frederick Spratt, *Discipline-Based Art Education: What Forms Will It Take?* (Los Angeles: Getty Center for Education in the Arts, 1987), 22–23.
21. Marjorie Wilson and Brent Wilson, *Teaching Children to Draw: A Guide for Teachers and Parents* (Englewood Cliffs, N.J.: Prentice-Hall, 1982), 77.

Additional Readings

Arthur, John. *Realists at Work.* New York: Watson/Guptill Publications, 1983.
Kandinsky, Wassily. *Concerning the Spiritual in Art.* New York: Dover Publications, 1977.
Rose, Barbara. *American Painting: The Twentieth Century.* New York: Rizzoli, 1980.

Chapters 2, 3, and 4

Battin, Margaret P.; Fisher, John; Moore, Ronald; and Silvers, Anita, *Puzzles About Art, An Aesthetics Casebook.* New York: St. Martins Press, 1989.
Clark, Kenneth. *What Is A Masterpiece?* New York: Thames and Hudson, 1979.
Finn, David. *How to Visit a Museum.* New York: Harry N. Abrams, 1985.
Goldstein, Ernest, et al. *Understanding and Creating Art.* Books 1 and 2. Dallas, Texas: Garrard, 1986.
Hughes, Robert. *The Shock of the New.* New York: Alfred A. Knopf, 1981.
Krathohl, David R., Bloom, Benjamin S., and Masia, Bertram B., "A Condensed Version of the Cognitive Domain of the Taxonomy of Educational Objectives," (Appendix B., p. 186–193). *Taxonomy of Educational Objectives: The Classification of Educational Goals, Handbook II: Affective Domain.* New York: David McKay Company, Inc., 1964.
Lanier, Vincent. *The Arts We See: A Simplified Introduction to the Visual Arts.* New York: Teachers College Press, 1982.
Malino, Frederick, *Understanding Paintings: The Elements of Composition.* Englewood Cliffs, N.J.: Prentice-Hall, 1980.
Malins, Frederick, *Understanding Paintings: The Elements of Composition.* Englewood Cliffs, N.J.: Prentice-Hall, Inc., 1980.
Maquet, Jacques. *The Aesthetic Experience: An Anthropologist Looks at the Visual Arts.* New Haven: Yale University Press, 1986.

Mittler, Gene A. *Art in Focus.* Mission Hills, Calif.: Glencoe, 1989.

Nash, Ann Bachtel. "Teaching Aesthetic Perception in the Elementary School." *Art Education,* Sept. 1985, 6–11.

Osborne, Harold. *The Art of Appreciation.* The Appreciation of the Arts Series. New York: Oxford University Press, 1970.

Parsons, Michael J. *How We Understand Art: A Cognitive Developmental Account of Aesthetic Experience.* New York: Cambridge University Press, 1987.

Phipps, Richard, and Richard Wink. *Invitation to the Gallery: An Introduction to Art.* Dubuque, Iowa: William C. Brown, 1987.

Ragans, Rosalind. *ArtTalk.* Mission Hills, Calif.: Glencoe, 1988.

Rosenberg, Harold. *Art and Other Serious Matters.* Chicago: University of Chicago Press, 1985.

Roskill, Mark, *The Interpretation of Pictures.* Amhearst, MA: The University of Massachusetts Press, 1989.

Sporre, Dennis J. *Perceiving the Arts: An Introduction to the Humanities.* Englewood Cliffs, N.J.: Prentice-Hall, 1985.

Waterfall, Milde, and Sarah Grusin, "Where's the Me in Museum," *Going to Museums with Children.* Arlington, VA: Vandamere Press, 1989.

Weitz, Morris. "The Role of Theory in Aesthetics." In *Aesthetics and Criticism in Art Education,* edited by Ralph A. Smith. Chicago: Rand McNally & Co., 1966.

Winner, Ellen. *Invented Worlds: The Psychology of the Arts.* Cambridge, Mass.: Harvard University Press, 1982.

Woodford, Susan. *Looking at Pictures: Cambridge Introduction to the History of Art.* Cambridge, Mass.: Cambridge University Press, 1983.

Zucker, Paul, *Styles in Paintings, a Comparative Study.* New York: Dove Publications, Inc., 1963.

Chapter 5

1. Claire Golding and Al Hurwitz, "Drawing: Its Purpose and Power," *School Arts,* Sept. 1985, 14.

2. Gary L. Gerhart, "Motivational Techniques in the Elementary Art Class," *NAEA Advisory,* Fall 1987.

3. Tom Anderson, "Talking About Art with Children from Theory to Practice," *Art Education,* Jan. 1986.

4. Howard Gardner, "Interview by Ron Brandt," *Educational Leadership,* Dec. 1987/Jan. 1988, 30–34.

5. Desmond Morris, *The Illustrated Naked Ape* (New York: Crown Publishers, 1967), 93–96.

6. Constance K. Kami and Norma I. Radin, "A Framework for a Preschool Curriculum Based on Some Piagetian Concepts," *The Journal of Creative Behavior* 1(1967):314–24.

7. Rob Barnes, *Teaching Art To Young Children, 4–9* (Boston: Allen & Unwin, 1987).

8. Guy Hubbard, *Art In Action,* Grade 1 (Austin, Texas: Holt, Rinehart and Winston, 1987), 62–63.

9. Laura Chapman, *Discover Art,* Grade 2 (Worcester, Mass: Davis Publications, 1985), 86–87.

Chapter 6

Baker, Samm S., and Natalie Baker. *Introduction to Art: A Guide to the Understanding and Enjoyment of Great Masterpieces.* New York: Harry N. Abrams

Brommer, Gerald F. *Discovering Art History.* 2d ed. Worcester, Mass.: Davis Publications, 1988.

Canaday, John. *What Is Art? An Introduction to Painting, Sculpture and Architecture.* New York: Alfred A. Knopf, 1980.

Clark, Kenneth. *What Is A Masterpiece?* New York: Thames and Hudson, 1979.

Cooper, J. C., *An Illustrated Encyclopedia of Traditional Symbols.* New York: Thames and Hudson Inc., 1988.

Feldman, Edmund Burke. *Thinking About Art.* Englewood Cliffs, N.J.: Prentice-Hall, 1985.

Feldman, Edmund Burke. *Varieties of Visual Experience.* 3d ed. Englewood Cliffs, N.J.: Prentice-Hall, 1987.

Fichner-Rathus, Lois. *Understanding Art.* Englewood Cliffs, N.J.: Prentice-Hall, 1986.

Gombrich, E. H. *The Story of Art.* New York: E. P. Dutton, 1972.

Heller, Nancy G. *Women Artists, An Illustrated History.* New York: Abbeville Press, 1987.

Herberholz, Barbara. *Art in Action Enrichment Programs, Levels I and II.* Austin, Texas: Holt, Rinehart and Winston, 1987.

Hobbs, Jack A. *Art in Context.* 3d ed. New York: Harcourt Brace Jovanovich, 1985.

Janson, H. W. *History of Art for Young People.* New York: Harry N. Abrams, 1987.

Janson, H. W., and Dora Jane Janson. *The Story of Painting from Cave Painting to Modern Times.* New York: Harry N. Abrams, 1977.

Lamm, Robert C., and Neal Cross. *The Humanities in Western Culture.* Vols. 1 and 2. Dubuque, Iowa: Wm. C. Brown, 1988.

Lipman, Jean, and Armstrong, Tom, *American Folk Painters of Three Centuries.* Arch Cape Press, N.Y., in association with the Whitney Museum of American Art, 1980.

McCarter, William, and Rita Gilbert. *Living with Art.* New York: Alfred A. Knopf, 1985.

Ocvirk, Otto G., et al. *Art Fundamentals: Theory and Practice.* Dubuque, Iowa: Wm. C. Brown, 1985.

Phipps, Richard, and Richard Wink. *Invitation to the Gallery: An Introduction to Art.* Dubuque, Iowa: Wm. C. Brown, 1987.

Preble, Duane, and Sarah Preble. *Artforms.* 4th ed. New York: Harper & Row, 1989.

Random House Library of Painting and Sculpture. Vols. 1–4. New York: Random House, 1981.

Richardson, John A. *Art: The Way It Is.* 3d ed. Englewood Cliffs, N.J.: Prentice-Hall, 1986.

Vasari, Giorgio, *The Great Masters.* N.Y.: Park Lane, 1986.

Weismann, Donald L. *The Visual Arts as Human Experience.* Englewood Cliffs, N.J.: Prentice-Hall, 1970.

Recommended Readings

Lanier, Vincent. *The Visual Arts and the Elementary Child.* New York: Teachers College Press, 1983.

Wilson, Marjorie, and Brent Wilson. *Teaching Children to Draw: A Guide for Teachers and Parents.* Englewood Cliffs, N.J.: Prentice-Hall, 1982.

Resources for Art Education

Student Textbooks for Elementary Classrooms

Art in Action, Guy Hubbard; Textbooks, Grades 1–8; Holt, Rinehart and Winston, 1627 Woodland Ave., Austin, TX 78741

Discover Art, Laura Chapman; Textbooks, Grades 1–6; Davis Publications, Worcester, MA 01608

Packaged Art Programs for Elementary Classrooms

Alarion Press, P.O. Box 1882, Boulder, CO 80306

Art Image, Grades 1–6, Monique Briere, Art Image Publications, P.O. Box 568, Champlain, NY 12919

Art in Action Enrichment Program, Levels I and II, Barbara Herberholz, Austin, TX: Holt, Rinehart and Winston, 1987

Art Smart, Susan Rodriguez, Prentice-Hall Englewood Cliffs, N.J.

Art Works, an Integrated Approach to Art Education, Holt, Rinehart and Winston, 1627 Woodland Ave., Austin, TX 78741

Clear: The Skills of Art, Levels I and II, Kay Alexander. Crystal Productions, Box 2159, Glenview, IL 60025, 1988

Creative Expressions: An Art Curriculum, Lee Hanson, Menlo Park, CA: Dale Seymour Publications, 1986

Spectra Program, Learning to Look and Create, Kay Alexander, Dale Seymour Publications, 1100 Hamilton Court, Menlo Park, CA:

1988; and *Take Five: Guided Analysis of 40 Artworks,* Crystal Productions, Box 2159, Glenview, IL 60025, 1989

Teaching Art 1–3, Laura Chapman, Austin, TX: Henrick-Long Publishing Co., 1989

Through Their Eyes, Primary Level—A Sequentially Developed Art Program for Grades 1–6, Brooks, et al., Austin, TX: W. S. Benson and Co., 1989

Reproductions of Artworks

Abrams Art Reproductions, Haddad's Fine Arts, P.O. Box 3016C, Anaheim, CA 92804

Art Education, Inc., 2 E. Erie St., Blauvelt, NY 10913

Art in Action Enrichment Programs I & II, Austin, TX, Holt, Rinehart and Winston

Austin Reproductions, Inc., 815 Grundy Ave., Holbrook, NY 11741 (sculpture replicas)

Fine Art Distributers/Haystack Publishers, 80 Kettle Creek Rd., Weston, CT 06883

Imaginus, RR4, Box 4021 B, Pennell Way, Brunswick, Maine 04011

Modern Learning Press, Rosemont, N.J. 08556

New York Graphic Society, Ltd., P.O. Box 1469, Greenwich, CT 06482

Shorewood Reproductions, 27 Glen Rd., Sandy Hook, CT 06482

Starry Night Distributors, Inc., 19 North St., Rutland, VT 05701

Universal Color Slide Co., 1221 Main St., Suite 203, Weymouth, MA 02190

University Prints, 21 East St., Winchester, MA 01890

Museum Reproductions (catalogs available)

Asian Art Museum of San Francisco, Golden Gate Park, San Francisco, CA 94118

Metropolitan Museum of Art, Special Services Office, Middle Village, NY 11381

Museum of Fine Arts, Boston, P.O. Box 74, Back Bay Annex, Boston, MA 02117

Museum of Modern Art, 11 West 53rd St., New York, NY 10019–5401

National Gallery of Art, Publications Service, Washington, D.C. 20565

Filmstrips

Alarion Press, Inc., P.O. Box 1882, Boulder, CO 80306

Crizmac Art and Cultural Education Materials, 1641 N. Bentley, Tucson, AZ 85716

Crystal Productions, P.O. Box 2159, Glenview, IL 60025

Dale Seymour, P.O. Box 10888, Palo Alto, CA 94303

Watercolor, See for Yourself, Firstart, 1143 Snyder Ave., Philadelphia, PA 19148

Wilton Progams, Reading and O'Reilly, Box 541, Wilton, CT 06897

Videos

Budek, Department AE11, 73 Pelham St., Newport, RI 02840

Great American Artist series (available in art supply catalogs)

Museum without Walls, video series (available in art supply catalogs)

Queue Education Video (Home Vision Videos—Portraits of Artists, Museum Tours and Collections, Major Exhibitions) 562 Boston Ave., Bridgeport, CN 06610

Roland Collection, 3120 Pawtaucket Rd., Northbrook, IL 60062

Magazines

Art and Man, Scholastic Inc., 902 Sylvan Ave., Box 2001, Englewood Cliffs, NJ 07632

Art Education, National Art Education Association, 1916 Association Dr., Reston, VA 22091

Arts and Activities, 591 Camino de la Reina, Suite #200, San Diego, CA 92108

School Arts, 50 Portland St., Worcester, MA 01608

Art Supply Catalogs

Beckley Cardy, One East First St., Duluth, MN 55802 (800–227–1178)

Dick Blick, Dept. A., Box 1267, Galesburg, IL 61401

Nasco, 901 Janesville Ave., Fort Atkinson, WI 53538; also 1524 Princeton Ave., Modesto, CA 95352 (800–558–9595)

Sax Arts and Crafts, P.O. Box 51710, New Berlin, WI 53151 (800–558–6696)

R. B. Walter, P.O. Box 920626, Norcross, GA 30092

Children's Books on Artists and Artworks

Art and Man (Magazine), Nat. Gallery of Art/Scholastic Publications, Scholastic Inc., P.O. Box 644, Lyndhurst, NJ 07071–9985

Bitossim, Sergio, *Vincent Van Gogh* (Why They Became Famous series), Silver Burdett Press

Bjork, Christina and Anderson, *Linnea in Monet's Garden*, R & S Books, Farrar, Straus and Giroux, NY

Borten, Helen, *A Picture Has a Special Look*, Abelard-Schuman

Borten, Helen, *Do You See What I See?* Abelard-Schuman

Brenner, Leah, *An Artist Grows Up in Mexico*, Scenes from the Boyhood of Diego Rivera, Albuquerque, NM: University of New Mexico Press

Brown, Laurene and Marc, *Visiting the Art Musuem*, New York: E. P. Dutton

Caselli, Giovanni, *The Everyday Life of a German Printer*, Peter Bedrick Books, 125 East 23 St., New York, NY 10010

Connor, Patrick, *Looking at Art: People at Home*, a Margaret K. McElderry Book. New York: Atheneum

Connor, Patrick, *Looking at Art: People at Work*, a Margaret K. McElderry Book. New York: Atheneum

Cumming, Robert, *Just Imagine, Ideas in Painting*, New York: Charles Scribner's Sons

Cumming, Robert, *Just Look, A Book About Paintings*, New York: Charles Scribner's Sons

D'Alelio, Jane, *I Know that Building: Discovering Architecture with Activities and Games*, Preservation Press, 1785 Massachusetts Ave., NW, Washington, D.C. 20036

Demi, *Liang and the Magic Paintbrush*, Henry Holt and Co.

Dickinson, Mike, *Smudge*. New York: Abbeville Press

Epstein, Vivian S., *History of Women Artists for Children*, VSE Publishers, 212 South Dexter, Denver, CO 80222

Fox, Dan and Claude Marks, *Go in and Out the Window*, New York: Metropolitan Museum of Art

Garrard Publishers, 1607 N. Market St., P.O. Box A, Champaign, IL; 61820 series: *Let's Get Lost in a Painting* (Homer, Hicks, Stella, Wood, Leutze, etc.) by E. Goldstein, and others

Glubok, Shirley, *The Art of . . . (series): Colonial America, Old West, China, Japan, etc.*, Macmillan Publishing Co., 866 Third Ave., New York, NY 10022

Grant, Joan, *The Blue Faience Hippopotamus*. LaJolla, CA: A Star and Elephant Book, The Green Tiger Press

Herman, David, *The Simon and Schuster Young Reader's Guide to Dates and Events*. New York: A Wanderer Book, Simon and Schuster, Inc.

Holme, Bryan, *Creatures of Paradise: Pictures to Grow Up With*, Oxford University Press, NY

Janson, H. W. and A. F. Janson, *History of Art for Young People*, New York: Harry N. Abrams book for American Book Co.

Janson, H. W. and D. J., *The Story of Painting From Cave Painting to Modern Times*, New York: Harry N. Abrams, Inc.

Koch, Kenneth and Kate Farrell, *Talking to the Sun*, New York: The Metropolitan Museum of Art, Holt, Rinehart and Winston

Korab, Balthazar, *Archabet: An Architectural Alphabet*, Preservation Press, 1785 Massachusetts Ave., NW, Washington, D.C. 20036

Lepscky, Ibi, *Leonardo da Vinci*, illustrated by Paolo Cardoni, Barron's Educational Series, Inc., 133 Crossways Park Dr., Woodbury, NY 11797

Lepscky, Ibi, *Pablo Picasso*, Barron's Educational Series, Inc., 113 Crossways Park Dr., Woodbury, NY 11797

Lerner Publishers, *Kings & Queens in Art, Circuses and Fairs in Art, Self-Portrait in Art*, etc. (series of 17 titles), Minneapolis, MN: Lerner Publications Co.

Lerner, Sharon, *Square is a Shape*, Minneapolis, MN: Lerner Publications Co.

Lerner, Sharon, *Straight Is a Line*, Minneapolis, MN: Lerner Publications Co.

Macaulay, David, *Cathedral, The Story of Its Construction; Castles* etc. Boston: Houghton-Mifflin

Mayers, Florence C., *ABC, Museum of Modern Art*, New York

Mayers, Florence C., *ABC, Museum of Fine Arts*, Boston

Miralles, Jose M., *Famous Artists & Composers*, London: Frederick Warne Publishers, Ltd.

Montreal Museum of Fine Arts, *Miro for Children*, 3400 Avenue du Musee, Canada H3G1K3

Munro, Roxie, *Architects Make Zigzags; Looking at Architecture from A to Z*, Preservation Press, 1785 Masssachusetts Ave., NW, Washington, D.C. 20036

Munthe, Nelly, *Meet Matisse*, Little, Brown & Co., 34 Beacon St., Boston, MA 02106

Newlands, Anne, *Meet Edgar Degas*, National Gallery of Canada, Kids Can Press, Toronto

Oneal, Zibby, *Grandma Moses, a Painter of Rural America* (Women of Our Time Series), Puffin Books, Viking Penguin Inc., 40 W. 23rd St., N.Y. 10010

O'Neill, Mary, *Hailstones and Halibut Bones,* New York: Doubleday

Peppin, Anthea, *The National Gallery Children's Book,* Publications Dept., National Gallery, London

Provensen, A. and M., *Leonardo da Vinci* (pop-up book), New York: Viking Press

Raboff, Ernest, *Art for Children (series): Leonardo, Chagall, Van Gogh, Klee, Picasso, Toulouse-Lautrec, Remington,* etc., A Gemini Smith Book, published by Doubleday & Co., Garden City, New York (more coming soon—*Dorothea Lange, Chagall, O'Keeffe, Matisse*)

Sills, Leslie, Inspirations: *Stories About Women Artists,* Niles, Il., Albert Whitman and Co.

Silver Burdett Co., *The Children's Art Series (Leonardo, The Grand Island of Jatte)*

Venezia, Mike, *Picasso,* Chicago: Children's Press

Venezia, Mike, *Rembrandt,* Chicago: Children's Press

Venezia, Mike, *Van Gogh,* Chicago: Children's Press

Ventura, Piero, *Great Painters,* New York: G. P. Putnam's Sons

Wilson, Forrest, *What It Feels Like to Be a Building,* Preservation Press, 1785 Massachusetts Ave., NW, Washington, D.C. 20036

Wolf, Aline D., *Mommy, It's a Renoir!,* Parent Child Press, P.O. Box 767, Altoona, PA 16603

Art Games

Artdeck, 52 paintings by 13 artists; second deck contains information on artists. Played in manner similar to gin rummy. Students learn by viewing images on cards. Available from Sax, Dale Seymour, and others.

Artpack, 30 postcard reproductions from Museum of Fine Arts, Boston, along with five folders of activities and information on portraits, landscapes, seascapes, everyday scenes, still lifes, and modern art. Available from Museum of Fine Arts, Boston, and Sax.

Art Rummy, 32 different cards in full color from Metropolitan Museum of Art (Egyptian, Greek, Japanese, etc., each with brief description). Students learn about art while collecting from opponent's hand. Available from Sax Arts and Crafts, National Gallery, Metropolitan Museum of Art, and others.

Black History Playing Cards, 52 portraits of distinguished Black Americans in four important fields including art, U.S. Games Systems, Inc., 179 Ludlow St., Stanford, CT. 06902

Meld Games and Art Learning Resources, 464 Walnut St., Kutztown, PA 19530.

The Art Game, and jigsaw puzzles, 18" × 24" of famous artworks, available from Starry Night Distributors, 19 North St., Rutland, VT 05701.

Ukiyoe Playing Cards, set of 2 decks featuring 54 different Japanese woodblock designs showing women in scenes of everyday life; also faces and scenes of men and women from the Kabuki. Museum of Fine Arts, Boston.

Index

Wm. C. Brown Publishers